REASON IN LAW

Reason in Law

9TH EDITION

LIEF H. CARTER

and

THOMAS F. BURKE

Foreword by
Sanford Levinson

THE UNIVERSITY OF CHICAGO PRESS

Chicago and London

Lief H. Carter is professor emeritus of political science at Colorado College. In addition to the previous eight editions of *Reason in Law*, he is the author of several books, including *Administrative Law and Politics*. Thomas F. Burke is professor of political science at Wellesley College and a visiting scholar at the University of California, Berkeley. He is the author or coauthor of three books, including, most recently, *How Policy Shapes Politics*.

The University of Chicago Press, Chicago 60637
The University of Chicago Press, Ltd., London
© 2016 by The University of Chicago
All rights reserved. Published 2016.
Printed in the United States of America

25 24 23 22 21 20 19 18   2 3 4 5

ISBN-13: 978-0-226-32804-1   (cloth)
ISBN-13: 978-0-226-32818-8   (paper)
ISBN-13: 978-0-226-32821-8   (e-book)

DOI: 10.7208/chicago/9780226328218.001.0001

LIBRARY OF CONGRESS CATALOGING-IN-PUBLICATION DATA

Carter, Lief H., author.
    Reason in law / Lief H. Carter and Thomas F. Burke ; foreword by Sanford Levinson. — 9th edition.
        pages cm
    Includes index.
    ISBN 978-0-226-32804-1 (cloth : alk. paper) — ISBN 978-0-226-32818-8 (pbk. : alk. paper) — ISBN 978-0-226-32821-8 (ebook) 1. Law—United States—Methodology. 2. Law—United States—Interpretation and construction. 3. Law—Political aspects—United States. I. Burke, Thomas Frederick, author. II. Title.
    KF380.C325 2016
    340'.11—dc23

                                                            2015018042

Earlier editions of this book were published by Pearson Education, Inc. Any questions concerning permissions should be directed to Permissions Department, The University of Chicago Press, Chicago, IL.

⊛ This paper meets the requirements of ANSI/NISO Z39.48-1992 (Permanence of Paper).

TO NANCY, ALWAYS
—*Lief Carter*

TO MY FATHER, FRED BURKE,
A MAN OF UNCOMMON KINDNESS,
GENEROSITY, AND SPIRIT
—*Tom Burke*

I was much troubled in spirit, in my first years upon the bench, to find how trackless was the ocean on which I had embarked. I sought for certainty. I was oppressed and disheartened when I found that the quest for it was futile. I was trying to reach land, the solid land of fixed and settled rules, the paradise of a justice that would declare itself by tokens plainer and more commanding than its pale and glimmering reflections in my own mind and conscience. . . . As the years have gone by, and as I have reflected more and more upon the nature of the judicial process, I have become reconciled to the uncertainty, because I have grown to see it as inevitable. I have grown to see that the process in its highest reaches is not discovery, but creation; and that the doubts and misgivings, the hopes and fears, are part of the travail of mind, the pangs of death and the pangs of birth, in which principles that have served their day expire, and new principles are born.

What is it that I do when I decide a case? To what sources of information do I appeal for guidance? In what proportions do I permit them to contribute to the result? In what proportions ought they to contribute? If a precedent is applicable, when do I refuse to follow it? If no precedent is applicable, how do I reach the rule that will make a precedent for the future? If I am seeking logical consistency, the symmetry of the legal structure, how far shall I seek it? At what point shall the quest be halted by some discrepant custom, by some consideration of the social welfare, by my own or the common standards of justice and morals? Into that strange compound which is brewed daily in the caldron of the courts, all these ingredients enter in varying proportions. I am not concerned to inquire whether judges ought to be allowed to brew such a compound at all. I take judge-made law as one of the existing realities of life. There, before us, is the brew. Not a judge on the bench but has had a hand in the making.

—JUDGE BENJAMIN N. CARDOZO, *The Nature of the Judicial Process*

CONTENTS

FOREWORD

I am pleased to write a few words about what is truly an outstanding book, *Reason in Law*. Although I am not a rigorous Darwinian, it nonetheless is worth noting that the very fact that you hold in your hand the ninth edition is a testament to its ability to survive—indeed, to flourish—in a very competitive world. Most books suffer the sad fate immortalized in David Hume's lament (which turned out to be false) that his books "fell stillborn from the press." It is no small matter for a book to establish itself as a classic, which *Reason in Law* is, and to live unto the next generation.

Central to any explanation for its survival is that both Lief Carter and his more recent collaborator, Thomas Burke, have an ability to write with admirable clarity about complex issues in legal analysis. As a professor of law, I can vouch for the fact that they introduce central topics in an extraordinarily reader-friendly way. Whether one is interested in classic common law reasoning, statutory interpretation, or my own specialty, constitutional interpretation, there is much to savor in this slim book.

The authors clearly admire law as a means of dispute resolution that serves to preserve social peace and order. But, of course, commands issued by an all-powerful Hobbesian sovereign could serve this role. As suggested by the American author Ring Lardner, "'Shut up,' he explained" is an ever-present possibility when responding to someone dissatisfied with the way he or she is being treated. Every parent has taken refuge in such a posture, and every child no doubt has felt frustrated by the perceived failure to be taken seriously. One might suggest that much of the conflict between police and the subjects of policing is the perception by the latter that they are given insufficient reason to submit to police commands, coupled with the perception by the former that their authority is constantly being threatened. Carter and Burke know that "shut up" is indeed inadequate. Winners may be delighted simply to be told, "You can do what you'd like," but losers want to know *why* they have lost. Receiving an adequate answer is essential to believing that one is being treated with the proper concern and respect that political philosophers John Rawls and Ronald Dworkin have identified as the essence of a defensible political order.

Reason in Law is based on the assumption that *someone* actually reads judicial decisions, and that the quality of reasoning will assuage the feelings even of those who disagree with the outcomes. *Who* reads judicial opinions is, of course, an interesting question in itself. Carter and Burke appear to agree with political scientists like Gerald Rosenberg that members of the general public rarely read judicial decisions; the public's responses are far more likely to depend on the bottom-line result—and how that result is portrayed in the popular press—than on the chain of legal reasoning supporting it. For better, and undoubtedly, for worse, one can be confident that very few Americans actually read various judicial decisions on such hot-button issues as the constitutionality of "Obamacare" or how to construe the Religious Freedom Restoration Act with regard to the duty of the state to exempt from the ordinary operation of the law those who claim inconsistent religious commitments. The authors admit that this is true as well with regard to the Terri Schiavo case, which is so carefully discussed in appendix B, culminating in the opinion by the obscure Judge Greer that is praised by the authors as a model of legal reasoning and, in their terms, legal "game playing" at its best. What one can be certain of, though, is that the lawyers involved in specific cases will surely read the opinions, and that it is particularly important that the losers in such cases feel at least somewhat less discontented after reading the Court's explanation of why they lost. Indeed, one function of lawyers in such instances is to assuage their client's anger by noting the strengths of the opinion. (Of course, this is a special difficulty for any lawyer who, by overestimating the strength of the case, leaves the client totally unprepared for loss.)

The central question posed by Carter and Burke is whether it is utopian to believe that judges can resolve disputes by using legal reasoning that gains the respect of all members of a community. Do we have sufficient faith in those who inhabit judicial office to respect a decision that goes against us even when we are deeply committed to the losing side? This is an *empirical* question. One can easily imagine communities in which such faith in law and legal officials exists. But, of course, it is as easy to imagine communities rent by a variety of cleavages, in which one trusts neither the law nor those who purport to "interpret" it. This may well describe the contemporary United States with regard to a host of issues that are the subject of litigation. Consider in this context the suspension in 2005 by

Harvard professor Laurence Tribe, surely one of the most distinguished constitutional lawyers of our time, of a proposed three-volume third edition of his classic treatise *American Constitutional Law*, the first volume of which had come out in 2000. What accounted for his throwing in the towel? According to a letter from Tribe to his friend and former colleague Supreme Court Justice Stephen Breyer, "I've suspended work on a revision because, in area after area, we find ourselves at a fork in the road—a point at which it's fair to say things could go in any of several directions—and because conflict over basic constitutional premises is today at a fever pitch." This means that it is basically foolhardy to attempt to ascertain answers to a variety of important questions, given that all purported answers "are passionately contested, with little common ground from which to build agreement."[1] Carter and Burke make much of the analogy between law and games. I have my own reservations inasmuch as we all know what "It's only a game" means; that is, a game is an entirely closed world with no genuine consequences beyond itself, save for the pleasure or dismay of fans of a team or a particular player. That is not true, of course, of law. But, even if one accepts the analogy in full, might not Professor Tribe's observation of the present state of constitutional law remind one of a baseball fan faced with the different rules of the American and National leagues concerning designated hitters and the changes that generates in the nature of the "classic" game? Are the two leagues playing "different games" or simply two quite radically dissimilar versions of what is, at the end of the day, the "same game," as proved by the continuation of the World Series and the willingness to play by the different rules depending on the home team?

Judicial reliance on previously decided cases, as Carter and Burke clearly acknowledge, presents a special problem for "reason in law." The paradox of precedent is that what might be called "pure precedent-based argument" is strongest precisely when the precedent is least persuasive or "reasonable." If one agrees with a precedent, then one isn't really "following precedent"; one is doing what one's own reason suggests is the right thing to do. A "strong" precedentalist will follow the prior decision even when it appears unreasonable or simply wrong. Whether this constitutes reason in law is, of course, an important question! "The deference that is due to the determination of former judgments," wrote Jeremy Bentham, "is due not to their wisdom, but to their authority." And one should certainly take note of one of the most famous passages in Oliver Wendell Holmes Jr.'s

---

1. Letter from Tribe to the Honorable Stephen G. Breyer, April 29, 2005, reprinted at *SCOTUSblog*.

"The Path of the Law," perhaps the most important speech on law in American history. Speaking to the students and faculty of Boston University Law
School in 1897, Holmes thundered: "It is revolting to have no better reason
for a rule of law than that so it was laid down in the time of Henry IV. It is
still more revolting if the grounds upon which it was laid down have vanished long since, and the rule simply persists from blind imitation of the
past." One suspects that Carter and Burke would agree. They are scarcely
uncritical devotees of what might be termed almost mindless stare decisis,
such as that exhibited by the Supreme Court in the baseball cases that Carter and Burke draw on in their own discussion. At the very least, it should
be clear that legal opinions call for critical analysis, and not for thoughtless acceptance. And what some admirers call "the genius of the common
law" includes, especially in the United States, the willingness of innovative
judges to know when even well-established decisions should be overruled,
often because of changes in the surrounding society that have made them
hard to defend in any terms other than almost literally thoughtless adherence to the status quo.

Critical analysis is encouraged by one very strong feature of the American legal system that is illustrated throughout this book: American judges,
to a degree unusual among the world's legal systems, are institutionally
encouraged to write dissenting opinions. This is no small matter. The European Court of Justice, for example, issues only one opinion, in the name
of "the Court," as was the case in Germany prior to 1971 and is the case
today in other countries, such as Greece and Ireland. The presumed reason
is that the possibility of a dissent, which can sometimes be quite harshly
written and accuse the majority of exhibiting "unreason in law," works to
undercut the faith of the citizenry—and especially the losers—that they
have been treated with the dignity they wish. There is more than one dissent in the pages of the *United States Reports*, for example, that basically
accuses the majority of being closer to Ring Lardner's character than to
what is required of what we might label a "Carter-Burke model judge."
Readers might ask themselves if the critical stance that is so much a feature
of this book would be possible if Carter and Burke offered only unanimous
opinions or suppressed the fact that there were vigorous—and often utterly
convincing—dissents.

There is one last point worth mentioning. If I have a disagreement with
the authors, it is in the extent to which "law" is identified as the work product of judges. In the American constitutional system, it is not only judges
who are invited to become constitutional interpreters. Presidents and
members of Congress must wrestle with their own oaths of office, which

require fidelity to the Constitution—and not simply to "the Constitution as interpreted by the majority of the Supreme Court." This casts into sharp relief the importance of President Andrew Jackson's statement in his famous 1832 veto of a bill renewing the charter of the Bank of the United States, whose constitutionality had been affirmed in John Marshall's classic opinion in *McCulloch v. Maryland* (1819). Jackson disagreed: "The authority of the Supreme Court must not, therefore, be permitted to control the Congress or the Executive when acting in their legislative capacities, but *to have only such influence as the force of their reasoning may deserve*" (emphasis added). And in a "republican" political order like the United States, which emphasizes the importance of participation by all citizens in civil governance, individuals themselves must develop confidence in their own capacity to critically analyze public officials' assertions about constitutional meaning.

Appendix B quotes a number of politicians and interest-group advocates issuing truly cringe-producing statements; Judge Greer's statement is indeed a relief for most readers. But is it really the case—perhaps it is!—that *only* judges will be able to play the game of constitutional fidelity truly well while everyone else succumbs to one or another temptation to cheat in order to make sure that the "right" team wins? Very few readers of this book will become judges, but almost all will become citizens. Its fundamental importance is therefore not vocational job training, but rather enabling each and every one of you to become a more effective citizen by deciding which standards of reasoning a court (or any other constitutional interpreter) must meet and what follows if one is not persuaded.

Sanford Levinson
W. St. John Garwood and W. St. John
Garwood, Jr. Centennial Chair in Law,
University of Texas Law School, and
Professor, Department of Government,
University of Texas at Austin

PREFACE TO THE NINTH EDITION

Men occasionally stumble over the truth, but most of them pick
themselves up and hurry off as if nothing happened.

—WINSTON CHURCHILL

From: Lief Carter
Sent: Tuesday, January 14, 2015
To: Tom Burke
Subject: Preface

Tom, I think we can make our hard deadline tomorrow with our new
publisher—all praise to the gods for the boon of John Tryneski, Rodney
Powell, Katherine Faydash, and the superb University of Chicago Press
staff—*if* we can just knock off this preface now. Any ideas on what you
would like to see in it?

From: Tom Burke
Sent: Tuesday, January 14, 2015
To: Lief Carter
Subject: Preface

Lief, you've been doing prefaces for this book since I was in the ninth grade.
I'm sure you will do fine. Just remember to keep your unhappiness at some
recent Supreme Court decisions in check. This has never been a book for
the legal professionals and scholars who are trying to "make a case." We're
here to give our readers the tools to make up their own minds about whether
a decision is well-reasoned. We promote the value of impartiality throughout the book, and we show how easy it is to achieve it. We have to practice
what we preach, or we'll be guilty of the charges of partisan bias that you
want to lay on some Supreme Court justices. We don't want to resemble
the corrupt umpires and referees we rightly condemn for deciding who will

win the game before they see it played. Besides, most appellate judges do a perfectly decent job most of the time; the Supreme Court is just, well, different.

From: Lief Carter
Sent: Tuesday, January 14, 2015
To: Tom Burke
Subject: Preface

Of course you're right. It's just that the Court gets a lot of press, and it does have the unique power of the final say. I keep thinking about that quote now posted in the United States Holocaust Memorial Museum, the one that starts out, "First they came for the Socialists, and I did not speak out— / Because I was not a Socialist." Paul Freund once wrote something to the effect that the only virtue more noble than a bias against bias is a bias against bias against bias. Well, I agree with him. When we criticize a judicial decision, we do so in terms of the craft of good reasoning rather than our personal political beliefs. Anyway, my personal political beliefs probably change some every day. But this book is swiftly moving to become your baby more than mine, so you change this material—as you have done so ably and so often throughout this edition—however you want, and I will cheer you on.

This book does not speak primarily to scholars of law and politics or to any other specialized subset of readers. It frames for everyone ideas that go to the heart of civic engagement and competence. By describing the basics of the legal process, and by augmenting and critiquing some of the classics of legal reasoning, we hope to articulate some ideas that scholars and practitioners find both theoretically fresh and practically useful. Indeed, the scholars and sitting judges who have read this book in some of its eight earlier editions have told us that it is stimulating and helpful. But our main aim is to make sense of a reality that we, laypeople and professionals alike, face throughout our lives: those who rule us, from parents to political rulers to umpires, referees and judges of all kinds, may act arbitrarily and hurtfully and corruptly when they operate outside "the rule of law."

The rule of law, one of the great advances of human civilization, enables a degree of trust among strangers without which the complex relationships of modern life fall apart. The rule of law is today's version of the center that must hold in W. B. Yeats's great poem "The Second Coming," describing the chaos in Europe after World War I, when the center fell apart and the falcon could no longer "hear the falconer." Legal reasoning, the performance art by which judges compose persuasive justifications for decisions they make, helps significantly to maintain social trust and thus to hold community together. And in case we are getting a bit too abstract and airy-fairy here, the great Stephen Colbert can bring us back to Earth. On his program of October 7, 2014, Colbert spoke with Leon Wieseltier, the former literary editor of the *New Republic*. Their banter included the following:

WIESELTIER: I believe in educated guts. The important thing is to have reasons for our beliefs and that we articulate those reasons and that we can defend them.

COLBERT: . . . Here's a reason for my beliefs. They feel good. It feels good to think that when I die I will go to heaven. That feels good, and it feels good to think that I am right. . . . It's truthy. It's unassailable because my truth is based upon what I want to be true rather than anything the facts could possibly support. Your truth requires work. My truth simply requires merely feeling. . . .

WIESELTIER: . . . I congratulate you for living entirely in a world of your own.

This is our point in a nutshell. People who take the easy way out, who let their feelings do their thinking for them, people who do not base their actions on the facts about, and the experiences of, the world that we can share and debate, ultimately live alone. When they seek to rule, they can do so only through the force of their office, not consensus. This is the reality we see in the parts of the world now ruled by religious and ideological fundamentalists. It is the world Thomas Hobbes famously described in his 1651 work *Leviathan*:

In such condition there is no place for industry, because the fruit thereof is uncertain, and consequently, no culture of the earth, no navigation, nor the use of commodities that may be imported by sea, no commodious building, no instruments of moving and removing such things as require much force, no knowledge of the face of the earth, no account of time, no arts, no letters, no society, and which is worst of all, continual fear and danger of violent death, and the life of man, solitary, poor, nasty, brutish, and short.

Alas, as Winston Churchill shrewdly observed, men in power do not routinely reason their way to their decisions and justify them. Much of the time they "feel" their way to decisions that bring only waste, loss, and death. We take President George W. Bush's 2003 invasion and subsequent occupation of Iraq as a prime example of this all-too-familiar pattern in human affairs. In the chapters that follow we describe a framework for thinking about the world that helps avoid such follies. This edition incorporates recent works by psychologists, particularly Jonathan Haidt and Daniel Kahneman, who flesh out David Hume's classic observation in *A Treatise of Human Nature*: "Reason is, and ought only to be, the slave of the passions." Inspired by these thinkers, we explore in this edition more fully just what human reason is and isn't, and explain how a passion for the craft of judging well can generate justice. In short, this book argues that reason in law, which is really a model of good reasoning about anything in our personal and civic lives, matters—a lot.

CHAPTER 1

What Legal Reasoning Is and Why It Matters

I have grown to see that the [legal] process in its highest reaches
is not discovery, but creation.

—BENJAMIN N. CARDOZO

They ain't nuthin' until I calls 'em.

—UMPIRE BILL KLEM (ATTRIBUTED)

An Overview of Law and Politics

In late June 2013, millions of Americans eagerly awaited the Supreme
Court's decision about whether the U.S. Constitution recognized the marriage of Edith Windsor to Thea Spyer, a same-sex couple who had been
partners for forty-two years. Edith and Thea had been married in Canada
in 2007, and their marriage was considered legal in the state of New York,
where they lived. But under a U.S. federal law, the Defense of Marriage Act,
the federal government refused to treat Edith and Thea as legally married.
This had powerful consequences: when Thea died in 2009, she left behind
a large estate, and because Edith was not recognized as Thea's spouse, she
had to pay more than $300,000 in inheritance taxes. This was just one of
the hundreds of ways in which the Defense of Marriage Act disadvantaged
same-sex couples, even those like Thea and Edith who were recognized as
legally married by the state in which they resided. Edith's lawyer, however,
argued that she shouldn't have to pay the tax because the Defense of Marriage Act was unconstitutional. The lawyer argued that the law violated the
Fifth Amendment of the U.S. Constitution, which guarantees fundamental
liberties, including, the lawyer argued, the right to marry whomever one
chooses. If the justices of the Supreme Court agreed with Edith, it would
affect not just her massive tax bill but also the rights of men and women

across the nation. Of course, for religious conservatives fighting for the "traditional marriage," the decision was equally consequential. Whatever the Court ruled, it would deeply disappoint many Americans.

A little more than a decade earlier, in 2001, a British court considered a more obscure but also very divisive matter: what to do about conjoined twin girls, Jodie and Mary. The two were joined at the pelvis, though each had her own organs and limbs. Doctors believed that both girls would eventually die if they were not separated. Separating them, however, would kill Mary, the weaker twin. The twins' parents, devout Roman Catholics, believed that it "was not God's will" that one child die to enable the other to live because "[e]veryone has the right to life."[1] The hospital in which the twins were treated, however, believed that failing to separate the twins would violate Jodie's right to life. Despite the parents' wishes, the hospital sought legal authorization to perform the separation, arguing that the operation would count under British law as saving Jodie's life, not as murdering Mary. The judges in the case faced an awful dilemma. If they sided with the hospital, they would be overriding the rights of the parents and the arguments of religious leaders, who argued that the hospital was trying to seek authorization for the murder of Mary. If they sided with the parents, though, they might be putting Jodie's life in jeopardy.

More than twenty years before the case of the conjoined twins, and back in the United States, a case of murder raised another complex legal issue. On August 9, 1977, a patron of a bar, Happy Jack's Saloon, saw a confrontation in which Darrell Soldano was being threatened. The patron, hoping the police could quell the fight, ran to the nearby Circle Inn, told the bartender about the threat, and asked that the bartender call 911. The bartender refused, even refusing to let the patron make the call himself. Back at Happy Jack's, the confrontation escalated and Darrell Soldano was shot dead. A lawsuit sought damages on behalf of Soldano's young son, not from the shooter but from the Circle Inn, blaming the bartender who had refused to call 911. The lawsuit contended that if the call had been made, the police could have stopped the fight and Soldano would not have been shot. The restaurant, however, argued that its bartender had no duty under the law to call 911. As in the other cases, the judges in this lawsuit had to declare one side a winner and the other a loser: the son left without a father, or the Circle Inn restaurant, which considered itself blameless for Soldano's death.

Every year courts decide millions of such disputes. Most, like the Happy

---

1. *In Re A (Children) (Conjoined Twins: Surgical Separation)*, [2001] 2 WLR 480.

Jack's case, don't receive much media attention; a few, like the same sex-marriage case, become worldwide news. But however famous or obscure, for the participants—the son of a murdered father, a restaurant owner worried about a huge liability bill, parents of children in a medical crisis, gay men and lesbian women hoping to be married—such lawsuits are of enormous consequence. These people's futures, sometimes even their lives, lie in the hands of judges. How should the judges decide their fates?

Laypeople unfamiliar with the legal process tend to assume that some simple legal rule—a statute or a constitutional clause or a judicial precedent—can settle the matter. But digging beneath the surface of these three cases, the rules turn out to be ambiguous. The Fifth Amendment to the Constitution, one of the rules in the same-sex marriage case, merely states: "No person shall . . . be deprived of life, liberty, or property, without due process of law." What does this have to do with same-sex marriage? There were a couple of previously decided cases interpreting this phrase to prohibit the government from discriminating against minority groups, but how far did that principle extend? In the case of the conjoined twins the rules were equally murky. Some of the judges cited *Airedale v. Bland,*[2] a case in which a hospital was authorized to stop life-sustaining support measures for a young man, Tony Bland, who was in a persistent vegetative state. But was Mary, the weaker twin, really in the same position as Bland? And wasn't a surgical separation a more violent mode of causing death than simply withholding treatment? In the case of Happy Jack's the previously decided cases were also no sure guide. There were cases in which courts had held individuals culpable for refusing to help others, like the Circle Inn's bartender who refused to make a 911 phone call. In all the previous cases, however, there was some kind of "special relationship" between the victim and the defendant. Was there really a special relationship between the Circle Inn's bartender and a stranger asking for help? Or was the existence of a special relationship in the previous cases really so important? In each case the rules were ambiguous, and judges could easily interpret them to the benefit of either side. Indeed, this is one of the reasons all three of these cases were so sharply contested—the law was unclear, so the parties needed the judges to resolve their dispute.

If rules by themselves couldn't resolve these lawsuits, perhaps the judges could consider instead the moral values at stake in each dispute. From this perspective courts should serve as a kind of moral forum in which judges articulate society's most deeply held values and interpret the rules so as

2. *Airedale NHS Trust v. Bland,* [1993] 2 WLR 316.

to advance those values. But in each of the cases there were several such values, and the competing values pushed the judges in different directions. Gay men and lesbian women claimed the values of freedom and equality, but cultural conservatives pointed to the value of the traditional family and hundreds of years of moral and legal prohibitions on homosexual conduct. Jodie and Mary's parents invoked their rights to make decisions for their children without interference from others, and they argued for the sanctity of the life of Mary; the hospital cited the right to life of Jodie. The lawsuit against the unhelpful bartender rested on a duty to help one's fellow human being; the restaurant owner could equally cite the value of freedom to do as one chooses, including the freedom not to help. How should judges choose among these competing, deeply held principles?

Making things even more difficult for the judges were the factual disputes in the cases. How could the doctors know for sure that Jodie and Mary couldn't survive together, or that Jodie would live if separated? How could anyone know if calling 911 would have prevented the escalation of the fight that killed Darrell Soldano? And there were also broader factual questions that went beyond the particularities of each case. When parents and doctors disagree about complicated medical treatments for children, are parents sophisticated enough about the science involved to make informed choices? Would expanding the duty to help others really make society more safe—or would it simply lead to more lawsuits against blameless bystanders wherever trouble erupted? Would the recognition of same-sex marriage really affect the well-being and robustness of the traditional family, as cultural conservatives claimed? What evidence should judges rely on in assessing this question?

This book describes how judges, despite the ambiguities and dilemmas that lurk in every corner of life and law, can use good legal reasoning to resolve difficult disputes. Laypeople, the people for whom we have written this book, may think that legal reasoning is so complex and technical that only those with professional training can possibly understand it. We believe, however, that laypeople with no such background are fully able to become sophisticated evaluators of legal opinions—judges of judging—and in the process, smarter and more engaged citizens. Indeed, we believe good citizenship requires some understanding of how legal reasoning works, because law, far from a dusty, dry, technical topic, is fundamental to politics. Legal reasoning serves simultaneously as the velvet glove covering the fist of governmental power and as the sincerest expression of a community's ideals of justice. To understand legal reasoning is to understand the rule of law itself.

Chapter 6 and appendix B explore more fully the relationship between law and politics, but we begin with three observations about the many ways in which they are intertwined.

The Law Is All around Us

When President Obama in a May 2013 speech defended his policy of using drones to kill people his administration had determined to be enemies of the United States, critics argued strenuously that the policy violated international law.[3] Because no world court had the power to resolve the matter and enforce its judgment, that legal issue remained just another political shouting match. Law becomes "the rule of law" only when courts have the power to resolve legal claims or when people, knowing that powerful courts can step in to settle matters for them, "bargain in the shadow of the law."[4]

The political system of the United States, unlike the international system, incorporates a powerful and independent judiciary. Our nation thereby claims to honor the rule of law. Alexis de Tocqueville wrote long ago that "there is hardly a political question in the United States that does not sooner or later turn into a judicial one."[5] The daily flow of news reports regularly reaffirms Tocqueville's observation:

- Civil rights groups and the Obama administration in 2014 challenged a Texas law that required voters to have a government-issued photo identification in order to cast a ballot. The group argued that because many minority voters lack such identification, the law would disproportionately block them from voting. A federal district court judge agreed with the challenge, concluding that Republican governor Rick Perry and the Republican legislature enacted the law to suppress the "overwhelmingly Democratic votes of African-Americans

---

3. Max Fisher, "Obama's Case for Drones," *Washington Post*, May 23, 2013. The group Amnesty International in 2013 issued a report condemning the U.S. drone program as unlawful and possibly involving international war crimes. Amnesty International, *Will I Be Next? U.S. Drone Strikes in Pakistan* (London: Amnesty International, 2013). A "white paper" produced by the Department of Justice and leaked in 2012 provides the Obama administration's argument for the legality of drone strikes even against U.S. citizens. U.S. Department of Justice, "Lawfulness of a Lethal Operation Directed against a U.S. Citizen Who Is a Senior Operational Leader of Al-Qa'ida or an Associated Force."

4. See Robert H. Mnookin and Lewis Kornhauser, "Bargaining in the Shadow of the Law: The Case of Divorce," *Yale Law Journal* 88 (1979): 950–997.

5. Alexis de Tocqueville, *Democracy in America*, ed. J. M. Mayer, trans. George Lawrence (New York: Harper and Row, 1969), 270.

and Latinos," thus bolstering their party's political prospects.[6] The judge ruled that the law violated both the Voting Rights Act and the Twenty-Fourth Amendment to the Constitution, which bars a "poll tax," a fee assessed for the privilege of voting; the judge concluded that the fees associated with the photo identification cards required by the law amounted to a poll tax. A federal appeals court, however, allowed Texas to proceed with the photo identification requirement for the 2014 election, and the U.S. Supreme Court refused to hear an appeal of that decision.[7]

- In 2012 the struggle over President Obama's major health-care reform law, the Patient Protection and Affordable Care Act (Obamacare), reached the Supreme Court, where Obamacare opponents argued that the law's requirement that individuals buy health insurance went beyond the powers granted to Congress by the Constitution. On June 28, 2012, the Court by a 5–4 vote upheld the constitutionality of Obamacare, ruling that the penalty assessed against those who would fail to buy health insurance could be considered a tax, and thus within Congress's taxing powers.[8]

- The South Carolina Supreme Court on November 12, 2014, declared that the state was not providing a "minimally adequate" education to all students as required by the state's constitution. The Court noted that in most of the school districts covered by the lawsuit, test scores revealed that more than half of students were failing to perform at even a minimum level for their grade. The Court by a 3–2 vote directed the state to address the problem. Dissenting from the decision, Judge Kittredge argued that the Court was stepping beyond its bounds and becoming a "super-legislature." He pointed out that words of the state constitution merely required the state legislature to create a "system of free public schools" and did not stipulate that the education received achieve any particular standard of quality.[9]

- An inmate awaiting execution on Texas's death row, Charles Hood, learned years after his initial conviction that the prosecuting attorney in his case and the judge who sentenced him to death were having a sexual affair at the time of his trial. Each was married to another at

6. *Veasey v. Perry*, Civil Action No. 2:13-CV-193 (S.D. Tex. 2014).

7. Adam Liptak, "Supreme Court Allows Texas to Use Strict Voter ID Law in Coming Election," *New York Times*, October 18, 2014.

8. *National Federation of Independent Business v. Sebelius*, 567 U.S. ___ (2012).

9. *Abbeville County School District v. South Carolina*, 767 S.E. 2d 157 (S.C. Sup. Ct. 2014).

the time and had vigorously denied the affair. Hood argued that the romance raised legitimate doubts about the impartiality of the judge, and so violated his right to a fair trial under the Constitution. A Texas appeals court, however, denied his claim.[10]

The Rule of Law Keeps the Peace

Many people, no doubt, react to such politically charged cases by comparing the legal result against their own political beliefs. Liberals and civil rights advocates critical of the Texas voter identification law excoriated the U.S. Supreme Court for allowing the law to stand; Republicans in Texas praised the result. Liberals cheered the Supreme Court's decision upholding Obamacare; conservatives decried it. But if you stop and think about it, judging a legal result simply in terms of one's own sense of right and wrong won't do. The whole point of the rule of law is to set standards of governance that transcend individual beliefs. If all we bring to law and politics is a determination that our values should prevail, we are no better than religious and political fundamentalists who insist that *their* moral scheme justifies destroying other incompatible moral systems. The claim of moral righteousness and superiority has driven many of our species' worst atrocities, such as the Holocaust, the genocide of American Indians, and the killing of millions of "enemies of the state" by various communist regimes.

So the rule of law substitutes legal reasoning for moral righteousness. In the sample of cases in the previous section, the legal reasoning question is not whether we like the result but whether the judge has given reasons we find trustworthy. If this distinction seems too abstract, think of an organized sport or game, one with umpires or referees. You may root passionately for one side, but when a referee's call goes against your team, you don't automatically condemn it. You consider whether you trust it, whether the facts on the field fit the call. It is indeed extraordinary that sports and games, contests among emotionally charged people whose self-

10. The Texas Court of Criminal Appeals ruled that Hood had failed to raise his argument by the deadline required under Texas law. Although a group of former prosecutors and thirty legal ethicists urged reversal of this decision and a new trial for Hood, the U.S. Supreme Court declined to hear his appeal. Prior cases in which a judge had accepted large campaign contributions from a litigant in a case before the judge had come to light, but never sex between judge and prosecutor. Dahlia Lithwick, "Courtly Love," *Newsweek*, May 3, 2010. Hood later won a new trial on other grounds, but he pled guilty to murder charges in exchange for a life sentence. Diane Jennings, "After Years of Insisting He Was Innocent of Murder, Death Row Inmate Charles Hood Pleads Guilty, Takes Life Sentence," *Dallas Morning News*, February 8, 2013.

respect and wealth may be on the line, remain for the most part civil and peaceful.[11]

The Critical Importance of Judicial Impartiality

Reflect a bit further on your experience of sports referees and you will soon realize that a critical call against the home team does not normally turn a peaceful home crowd into a rebellious mass of frothing maniacs (who would throw beverage bottles at the refs if glass containers were still allowed in the stands). Only blatantly erroneous calls and, worse, a *pattern* of wrong calls that suggests a bias against the home team cause fan rage. The impartiality of legal judges is as necessary for political peace as the impartiality of referees and umpires is to keeping peace in the stands.

Indeed, we find that in most human societies, trusted third parties routinely resolve disputes. Alec Stone Sweet and Martin Shapiro call this phenomenon "triadic dispute resolution":

> If a conflict arises between two persons and they cannot resolve it themselves, then in all cultures and societies it is logical for those two persons to call upon a third to assist in its resolution. That assistance falls along a spectrum that stretches from the mediator to the arbitrator to the judge. . . . The triad contains a basic tension. To the extent that the triadic figure appears to intervene in favor of one of the two disputants and against the other, the perception of the situation *will shift from the fairest to the most unfair of configurations: two against one.* Therefore the principal characteristics of all triadic conflict resolvers will be determined by the need to avoid the perception of two against one, for only then can they rely on their basic social logic.[12]

How can judges, the triadic conflict resolvers we are concerned with, overcome the "two against one" perception? In most nontrivial appeals cases, judges write opinions explaining and thereby justifying the results they reach.[13] This makes appellate judges different from baseball umpires, who make most of their calls automatically. It is the job of appellate judges

---

11. Lief Carter explains in detail the peacekeeping tendencies of "good games" in "Law and Politics as Play," *Chicago-Kent Law Review* 83 (2008): 1333–1386; and see appendix B.

12. Martin Shapiro and Alec Stone Sweet, *On Law, Politics, and Judicialization* (New York: Oxford University Press, 2002), 211 (emphasis added).

13. For an introduction to the legal procedures and terms by which cases reach the appellate level, see appendix A.

to write opinions that justify their decisions on impartial grounds, grounds that don't seem to take partisan sides. (The concept of impartiality is explored more fully in chapter 6.)

Because law gains its authority through impartiality, people often assume that law isn't "political." We, however, view law and legal reasoning as a special kind of politics. *Politics*, in our definition, refers to all the things people do in communities in order to minimize threats to their well-being. People sometimes cooperate with each other to resist perceived threats, but sometimes they fight. Political behavior sometimes tries to conserve what is and sometimes tries to change what is. Hence, like other forms of politics, law can either preserve communities or change them. By the end of this book, you will have encountered many examples of legal actions that resulted in both change and preservation.

If referees and umpires do triadic dispute resolution badly, public belief in the integrity of a game can suffer. If *judges* do triadic dispute resolution badly, the whole community can be affected. When people believe that judges cynically manipulate legal language to reach partisan and self-interested political ends, faith in fairness and equity ebbs, motives for social cooperation falter, and communal life becomes nastier and more brutish. The sense of injustice can cause explosive social damage. When in 2014, for example, a grand jury refused to indict Ferguson, Missouri, police officer Darren Wilson for shooting Michael Brown, an unarmed black man, communities throughout the United States were outraged by what they considered a racially biased verdict, and some protests against the decision became violent. The violence escalated a few weeks later when a grand jury in New York chose not to indict a police officer for choking to death Eric Garner, another unarmed black man. The reactions to the Ferguson and Garner cases were an echo of the major riots that erupted more than two decades before when a suburban Los Angeles jury acquitted police officers in the beating of Rodney King. Distrust in the impartiality of judging creates disrespect for legal institutions and ultimately the rule of law.

The problem of judicial impartiality seems particularly acute in the United States today because of growing controversy over the selection of judges. Other books examine judicial selection in more detail.[14] We must,

14. See, for example, Herbert J. Kritzer, *Justices on the Ballot: Continuity and Change in State Supreme Court Elections* (New York: Cambridge University Press, 2015); Herbert Melinda Gann Hall, *Attacking Judges: How Campaign Advertising Influences State Supreme Court Elections* (Palo Alto, CA: Stanford University Press, 2015); James L. Gibson, *Electing Judges: The Surprising Effects of Campaigning on Judicial Legitimacy* (Chicago: University of Chicago Press, 2012); Keith J. Bybee, *All Judges Are Political—Except When*

however, report that the systems of judicial selection in the United States are not designed to recruit judges on the basis of their ability to reason well and rule impartially. Nor does the United States systematically teach future judges about the basic social logic that avoids "two against one." Indeed, compared with the systems of judicial selection in many nations (or most organized sports leagues!), American selection processes almost seem designed to make this problem worse. Many state judges are elected, and campaigns for judicial office can be polarizing and partisan.[15] Other judges are appointed by politicians, for life in some cases, for partisan reasons.

No one would trust a home-plate umpire who calls pitches before they leave the pitcher's hand. Should the public trust those who become judges only because they have already taken sides on legal issues? Remember that this book has ruled out the simplest method of judging judges: cheering the ones who decide "for our side" and scorning those who don't. Instead, we must decide whether judges have used their power legitimately. We may believe that a referee missed an obvious foul under the basket, or a player straying offside, and still believe that the ref is trying his or her best to judge the game fairly, even when a particular bad call hurts our team. Similarly, even when judges make rulings with which we disagree, we must be able to trust that those judges decide impartially. At bottom, then, this book explores a classic political question: how can we be confident that someone we disagree with nevertheless acts with integrity? Our answer is that judges can convince others of their integrity when they reason persuasively. The rest of this book illustrates how judges, by reasoning well or badly, either succeed or fail at this task.

A Definition of Law

Law is a language, not simply a collection of rules. What distinguishes law from other ways of making sense of life? Lawyers and judges attempt to prevent and solve other people's problems, but so do physicians, priests, professors, and plumbers. The term *problem solving* therefore includes

They Are Not (Palo Alto, CA: Stanford University Press, 2010); Nancy Scherer, *Scoring Points* (Palo Alto, CA: Stanford University Press, 2005); Sheldon Goldman, *Picking Federal Judges* (New Haven, CT: Yale University Press, 1999).

15. Both Kritzer and Hall find evidence that systems for selecting state court judges are no more politicized than in the past, and that political conflict over the selection of judges does not seem to hurt the standing of courts with the public. See Kritzer, *Justices on the Ballot*, and Hall, *Attacking Judges*, as well as Gibson, *Electing Judges*. For an explanation of why this may be so, see Bybee, *All Judges Are Political*.

too much. Lawyers and judges work with certain kinds of problems that can lead to conflicts, even physical fights, among people. Contrary to the television's emphasis on courtroom battles, however, most lawyers try to stop conflicts before they start. They help people discover ways to reduce their taxes or write valid wills and contracts. They study complex insurance policies and bank loan agreements. They help people and organizations to govern their own affairs so as to minimize conflicts.

Yet some conflicts start anyway, perhaps because a lawyer did the planning and preventing poorly or because the client did not follow a lawyer's good advice. Many conflicts, such as an auto collision, a dispute with a neighbor over a property line, or the angry firing of an employee, begin without lawyers. Then people may call them in after the fact, not for an ounce of prevention but for the pounding of a cure.

Once such a battle starts, lawyers may find a solution in the rules of law, although when people get angry at each other, they may refuse the solution lawyers offer. If the lawyers don't find a solution or negotiate a compromise, then either one side gives up or the opponents go to court; they call in the judges to resolve their dispute.

You may now think that you have a solid definition of law: law is the process of preventing or resolving conflicts between people. Lawyers and judges do this; professors, plumbers, and physicians, though they do solve problems, do not routinely resolve conflicts. But parents prevent or resolve conflicts among their children daily. And parents, perhaps exasperated by family fights, may turn to a family counselor to deal with their own conflicts. Many ministers no doubt define one of their goals as reducing conflict. Lawyers, then, aren't the only people who try to resolve conflicts.

Law, like the priesthood and professional counseling, encounters an immense variety of problems. Law requires the ability to see specifics and to avoid premature generalizing and jumping to conclusions. But so do good counseling, good ministry, and good parenting. What distinguishes the conflict solving of lawyers and judges from the conflict solving of parents, counselors, or ministers?

Consider again the cases at the outset of this chapter, in which judges had to wrestle over the federal government's refusal to recognize same-sex marriages, whether to authorize the surgical separation of conjoined twins, and whether a restaurant should be held responsible for its bartender's refusal to call 911 to stop a fight at a neighboring bar. These are legal problems, not counseling or parental problems, because we define their nature and limits—though not necessarily their solution—in terms of rules that the state, the government, has made. The judges in the same-sex marriage case weren't asked to decide how best to resolve the struggle over rights for gay men and lesbian women; they based their decision on their understanding of what was required by the Fifth Amendment to the Constitution. The case of the conjoined twins was decided under British and European laws regarding murder and the right to life. The Happy Jack's case was decided according to California common law, which requires people to treat strangers with the care expected of a "reasonable and prudent person," the fictional legal character judges have invoked for centuries. The process of resolving human conflicts through law begins when people decide to take advantage of the fact that the government has, one way or another, made rules to prevent or resolve such conflicts. And by taking their disputes to court, litigants benefit from another distinctive aspect of legal problem solving: the court's resolution of the problem has the force of the government behind it. This makes a decision rendered by a judge or jury quite different from one made by a counselor or minister. Even in noncriminal cases, if those on the losing side fail to comply with a legal decision, a judge can use the government's authority to order compliance, if necessary by imprisoning the losers.

The law, then, is a language that lawyers and judges use when they try to prevent or resolve problems—human conflicts—using official rules made by the state as their starting point. To study reason in this process is to study how lawyers and judges justify the choices they inevitably make among various legal solutions. It is to study, for example, how in *McBoyle v. United States* the justices of the Supreme Court made sense of the National Motor Vehicle Theft Act, which prohibits transporting a stolen "motor vehicle" across state lines. (This case is discussed in appendix A on legal terminology, which we invite readers to consult.) In that case, McBoyle hired a man to steal an airplane in Illinois and fly it to Oklahoma. The hired thief was caught, and his confession led investigators back to Mr. McBoyle, who was tried and convicted of violating the National Motor Vehicle Theft Act. But McBoyle argued on appeal that the Act, which prohibits the theft of "any self-propelled vehicle not designed for running on rails," did not cover the airplane he stole. Does an airplane fall within that definition? In studying legal reasoning, we examine the methods by which judges and lawyers work through such a puzzle. We ask the same key questions they do: What does the law mean as applied to the problem before me? Which different and sometimes contradictory solutions to the problem does the law permit in this case?

Now stop and compare our definition of law and legal reasoning with your own intuitive conception of law, with the definition of the legal process you may have developed from television, movies, and other daily experiences. Do the two overlap? Probably not very much. The average person usually thinks of law as trials, and criminal trials at that. But trials are one of the less legal, or "law-filled," parts of the legal process. For example, the jurors in the trial of George Zimmerman, the man accused of murdering Trayvon Martin, the seventeen-year-old wearing a hoodie on a rainy Florida night, were asked to assess whether or not Zimmerman reasonably feared for his own safety when he shot Mr. Martin. The jurors were not asked to determine what the proper standard for self-defense should be; that was set by the judge's instructions, which were in turn an interpretation of Florida's "stand your ground" law. Instead, the jury was told to put all the facts in the case together to decide whether a "cautious and prudent person under the same circumstances" as Zimmerman would have believed it necessary to shoot Martin.[16] That involved some fine-grained historical research: Was Zimmerman returning to his car when Martin lunged at him? Did Martin or Zimmerman throw the first punch? Was Martin on top of Zimmerman when he was shot? We are confident enough that such historical problems do not require legal reasoning that we often turn the job of solving them over to groups of amateur historians, better known as jurors.

Of course, juries don't simply determine the facts of case; they also must apply law to the facts, and that requires them to think carefully about the legal standards given to them by the judge. In deciding whether Zimmerman acted reasonably, they had to decide whether the facts of the situation would justify a "cautious and prudent person" to fear Martin. This meant that the jury had to assess what it meant to be a "cautious and prudent person."

Facts and law, then, are intertwined. Yet the heart of the reasoning part of law, and the subject of this book, involves not deciphering the facts of a case but figuring out what to make of the facts once we "know" them. In the airplane theft case, for example, the historical problem was whether the defendant hired someone to steal a plane and fly it across state lines. The legal reasoning problem was whether the statute's definition of a "vehicle" included airplanes.

The illustrative case at the end of this chapter sets out the distinction between trial and appellate decisions. In that case, a trial court had decided

---

16. Mark Memmott, "READ: Instructions for the Jury in Trial of George Zimmerman," *The Two Way: Breaking News from NPR* (blog), July 12, 2013.

that a certain Mr. Prochnow was the father of his wife's baby. The facts—which included a suspicious liaison between the wife and another man, the physical separation of the husband and wife except for one encounter eight months before the birth of a full-term baby, and the incompatibility of the husband's blood type with that of the child—seemed to point conclusively in the other direction. Nevertheless, certain official rules of law, as interpreted by the appellate court, seemed to prevent the trial judge from holding that the husband was not the child's natural father. This case also provides our first full-length example of a court trying—and demonstrably failing—to do legal reasoning well.

A Definition of Legal Reasoning

It is a fundamental political expectation in the United States that those in power justify the way in which they use that power. We expect, both in private and in public life, that people whose decisions directly affect our lives will show how their decisions serve common, rather than purely selfish, ends. We expect teachers to articulate grading standards. We expect elected politicians to respond to the needs of voters. In all such cases, we reject the authoritarian notion that power justifies itself, that those with money or political office can do whatever they please. If we merely want a decision—any decision—to settle a case, we could simply appoint a dictator to pronounce one. In his foreword to this book, Sanford Levinson writes:

> As suggested by the American author Ring Lardner, "'Shut up,' he explained" is an ever-present possibility when responding to someone dissatisfied with the way he or she is being treated. Every parent has taken refuge in such a posture, and every child no doubt has felt frustrated by the perceived failure to be taken seriously.

Holding public officials responsible for justifying their power may seem obvious to us, but this practice is actually a fairly recent development in Western political philosophy. The alternatives—governing through greater physical strength and brute force, or through tradition and authoritarian right (as did kings when they proclaimed "divine right" to rule)—may have seemed acceptable when people believed that God willed everything. However, religious theories of government, still prevalent in many parts of the world, tend to produce so much warfare and bloodshed that liberal philosophers from John Locke forward have tried to substitute reason and justification for the force of armies and for the unchallengeable authority of kings, tyrants, and other "supreme leaders."[17]

The rule of law transforms the way power is exercised. Yet we must never forget that law itself is a form of power. Indeed, though law may seem civilized, even erudite, it is also violent, as the essays of Robert Cover remind us. "Legal interpretation," he wrote, "takes place in a field of pain and death." Law often justifies violence that has occurred or that is about to occur.[18] Judicial outcomes in lawsuits can literally kill and bankrupt people. Courts govern, and government, at its core, is the collective use of authority backed by threats of violence. Whether appellate judges meet or fail to meet our fundamental expectation about the use of judicial power depends on the quality of their legal reasoning. We hold legislators, governors, presidents, and many other politicians to account by forcing them to run for election, but we hold appellate judges accountable primarily by examining the honesty and quality of their opinions.[19]

Legal Reasoning Does Not Discover the "One Right Answer"

Western culture reinforces some misunderstandings of legal reasoning. Perhaps because, starting in the Renaissance, a stream of discoveries about the physical world has continuously bombarded Western civilization, we too often assume that legal reasoning is aimed at discovering the law's "right answer," the correct legal solution to a problem. The idea that we live under a government of laws, not people, seems based on the assumption that correct legal results exist, like undiscovered planets or subatomic particles, quite independent of man's knowledge.

Of course, if law actually worked that way, a book on legal reasoning would be absurd. To see whether a judge settled a contract dispute correctly, we would simply study the law of contract. In all cases, trained lawyers and legal scholars would, like priests in the olden days, have access

17. Lief Carter develops this theme further in his first chapter of *An Introduction to Constitutional Interpretation: Cases in Law and Religion* (White Plains, NY: Longman, 1991).

18. Robert Cover, "Violence and the Word," in *Narrative, Violence and the Law: The Essays of Robert Cover*, ed. Martha Minow, Michael Ryan, and Austin Sarat (Ann Arbor: University of Michigan, 1995), 203.

19. All federal judges who are appointed under Article III of the Constitution, the judicial article, serve for life. Impeachment and removal from office are rare. Many state appellate judges, however, must win an election either to gain or retain their seat on the bench.

to correct answers that laypeople—most readers of this book—could not hope to match. A layperson would either defer to the conclusion of the expert or else rebel.

Appellate judges do justify their power through the quality of the opinions they write. The quality of their opinions, however, depends on something other than proving that they found the one correct legal answer. After all, when the law is clear enough that people on opposite sides of a case can agree on what law commands, they usually don't spend the many thousands of dollars that contesting a case in an appellate court requires. Inept or apathetic litigants do, of course, bring "easy" cases, but resolving those does not require persuasive legal reasoning.[20] Legal reasoning describes what judges do to justify their decision when they *cannot* demonstrate or prove that they have reached the "right" answer. As Benjamin Cardozo pointed out the better part of a century ago (see the epigraph that opens this book), appellate judges usually *create* law. The uncertainties and imperfections in law force judges to choose what the law *ought* to mean, not merely to report on what it does mean.

The Four Elements of Legal Reasoning

To persuade us that the law ought to mean what the judge has decided, the well-reasoned judicial opinion will harmonize the following four basic building blocks present in every case:

1. The *case facts* established in the trial and preserved in the record of the evidence produced at the trial.
2. The facts, events, and other conditions that we observe in the world, quite apart from the case at hand, which we call *social background facts.*
3. What the *rules of law*, that is, the official legal texts created by the state, say about the case.
4. Widely shared moral *values* and social principles.

20. Federal judge Richard Posner contends that appeals courts with mandatory jurisdiction, meaning those that cannot pick the cases they hear (unlike the U.S. Supreme Court, which chooses its cases), mostly get such "easy" cases. Hopeless appeals are made for many reasons, among them: the appellant's lawyer may be inept, the appellant may have lost perspective on whether the case is winnable, the appellant may have little to lose by appealing, or the appellant may have strategic reasons for appealing that have nothing to do with winning the case. Posner, *Reflections on Judging* (Cambridge, MA: Harvard University Press, 2013), 106–107.

These four building blocks are the foundation of good legal reasoning. Judges need to take account of each of them in explaining their decisions. When judges reason well, their opinions "harmonize" or fit together these four elements. When they don't fit together the elements, their opinions become less persuasive.

Our criteria for good legal reasoning, no doubt, seem abstract and fuzzy at first. Our suggestion that legal reasoning is at heart a kind of artistic practice, a "harmonizing" of elements akin to the harmonies constructed by a music composer, is probably at odds with your understanding of law. We hope that by the time you finish this book you will see why accounting for each of the four elements is essential for a well-reasoned legal opinion, and why harmonizing them is so important (and often, so difficult). The following sections present illustrations of each of the four at work. You should practice identifying and distinguishing them.

Case Facts

Of the four building blocks, case facts are perhaps the easiest to understand. These are facts about the dispute between the parties in the case as developed during a trial. In a jury trial, the judge usually charges the jury that it must find certain things to be true in order to find for the plaintiff, or to find a defendant guilty; a jury verdict of guilt or liability necessarily finds those particular facts to be true. In trials in which a judge sits without a jury, the judge usually reads into the court record his or her findings of fact. In either situation, the only way an appellate court can overturn a trial court's factual conclusions is to hold that they have no substantial basis in the evidence and are therefore "clearly erroneous,"[21] a rare event.

At the center of the case of the conjoined babies Mary and Jodie were several case facts about their condition. Medical experts determined that the two would likely die if not separated and that Jodie (but not Mary) could live on her own. The judges in the case had to wrestle with the implications of these troubling facts. In the case of the Texas voter identification law, a trial determined that minority voters are more likely than white voters to lack government-issued photo identification. This key case fact became an essential building block of the trial judge's finding that the law violated the Voting Rights Act.

21. See Rule 52A, Federal Rules of Civil Procedure.

Social Background Facts

Social background facts are conclusions about the world independent of the specific case facts that the parties are disputing. In the Happy Jack's case, about the unhelpful bartender, the Court cited as key social background facts the rising crime problem and the significance of the telephone for stopping crimes. The opinion noted that the state had established the 911 telephone system as a public resource for citizens to call the police quickly and without paying a charge. Seen in the light of these social background facts, the case facts—that a bartender refused to let a stranger use a phone to call 911—suggested to the Court an "attitude of extreme individualism" at odds with the needs of society.[22]

More than thirty years later, in 2014, the Supreme Court rested an important criminal justice case on social background facts about another kind of phone, the smartphone. In *Riley v. United States*, after police arrested some suspects in a crime, they searched the suspects' smartphones and found evidence of further crimes. Did these searches, conducted without warrants, violate the Fourth Amendment's ban on "unreasonable searches and seizures"? The Court concluded they did, in part because of the powerful storage capacities of smartphones. Chief Justice John Roberts argued that because cell phones contain so much sensitive private data, "a cell phone search would typically expose to the government far *more* than the most exhaustive search of a house."[23]

Social background facts can include anything about how the world works. Often they are so obvious that parties do not argue over them or even remark on them. For example, in *Prochnow v. Prochnow*, the child support case presented at the end of this chapter, both sides acknowledged that babies do not arise spontaneously in the womb but only from a sperm's insemination of an ovum. Sometimes when the social background facts in a case are not so clear, judges and juries will rely on hunches about them, something Judge Learned Hand does openly in a case you will read in chapter 2, *Repouille v. United States.*

Rules of Law

Judges must take account of all the rules of law that are relevant to a case. Rules of law come from statutes or constitutions, but they can also come from precedents—previously decided cases. For example, in the Happy Jack's case, in which a bartender refused to call 911, the judges had to con-

---

22. *Soldano v. O'Daniels*, 141 Cal. App. 3d 443, 450 (1983).
23. *Riley v. California*, 573 U.S. ___ (2014), slip op., 20.

sider "the established rule that one who has not created a peril ordinarily does not have a duty to take affirmative action to assist an imperiled person." The Court's opinion acknowledges that many precedents are based on this rule, but explained why in the particular case the rule should not determine the outcome.[24]

Widely Shared Values

To be convincing, judges must also take account of social values. This is not an invitation for judges to recite their own values or to pick the values they deem most worthy. Instead, judges must try to persuade communities that they have considered the widely shared values that ordinary members of the community can see embedded in the dispute.

We have already witnessed the collision of two widely held values—religious liberty and human life—in the case of Jodie and Mary. Indeed, all the cases described in this chapter involve deep value conflicts over such principles as individual freedom, equality and integrity in voting, the rights and duties of parents, and the right to an education.

In a widely praised 2010 commencement address at Harvard University, retired Supreme Court justice David Souter said he had learned in his nineteen years on that bench that the Supreme Court's highest function may be to help society resolve the "conflict between the good and the good." Souter noted that in many cases, the legal rules don't tell judges which "good" to choose:

> A choice may have to be made, not because language is vague, but because the Constitution embodies the desire of the American people, like most people, to have things both ways. We want order and security, and we want liberty. And we want not only liberty but equality as well. These paired desires of ours can clash, and when they do a court is forced to choose between them, between one constitutional good and another. The court has to decide which of our approved desires has the better claim, right here, right now, and a court has to do more than read fairly when it makes this kind of choice.[25]

Judges can't maximize all goods, so they must acknowledge those they choose and explain their choices.

---

24. *Soldano v. O'Daniels*, 447.
25. Linda Greenhouse, "Justice Souter's Class," *New York Times*, June 3, 2010.

Several immensely important corollaries follow from our definition of legal reasoning. First, two judges may reach different decisions in the same case, yet each may reason equally well or badly. Like two excellent debaters, opposing opinions from two judges may still persuade us that each judge has fit together the four elements into a vision of justice that we trust.

Second, because of the wide range in people's experiences and beliefs, no single opinion will persuade everyone. Laypeople who read judicial opinions can and should react to them and decide whether the opinion actually persuades them. Reactions for and against judicial decisions about such volatile issues as gay rights, voting rights, education, and health care inevitably shape the further evolution of law.

Third, legal reasoning does *not* refer to the specific calculations that go on in a judge's head. In 1929, U.S. district judge Joseph Hutcheson confessed that the actual decision-making process revolved around the judicial "hunch."[26] Professor Warren Lehman in 1986 agreed: "What we call the capacity for judgment . . . is an intellectualized account of the capacity for decision making and action, whose nature is not known to us."[27] Legal reasoning justifies the decision but does not explain how the judge arrived at it. In theory, a devilishly partisan judge could decide cases solely to advance her political agenda, yet write masterful opinions that appear fair and impartial. A truly apathetic judge could flip a coin to make a decision, then write a brilliant opinion that convincingly justified it. We will never know with certainty why judges decide as they do, and it would be foolish to assume that a judge's opinion is some kind of record of the decision process.

Psychologically speaking, however, a judge's internal mental process and the quality of her public justification for the result may interact. The discipline of writing thoughtful opinions can, through a mental feedback loop, make a judge's reasoning itself more thoughtful and well considered. Some particularly intriguing research suggesting this possibility surfaced in 2014, when researchers in Spain posed difficult moral dilemmas—scenarios

---

26. Joseph C. Hutcheson Jr., "The Judgment Intuitive: The Function of the 'Hunch' in Judicial Decision," *South Texas Law Review* 39 (1998): 889–903. Hutcheson defined *hunch* as "that intuitive flash of understanding which makes the jump-spark connection between question and decision, and at the point where the path is darkest for the judicial feet, sheds its light along the way."

27. Warren Lehman, *How We Make Decisions* (Madison: Institute for Legal Studies of the University of Wisconsin Law School, 1986), 12. See also the reflections of Judge Richard Posner, *How Judges Think* (Cambridge, MA: Harvard University Press, 2008), and Carter, "Law and Politics as Play," 1342–1348.

pitting the pull of an emotional attachment against a rational utilitarian outcome—to bilingual subjects, either in their native language or in their second language. They found that subjects were consistently better able to reach well-reasoned outcomes when their minds were not "freighted" with all the subtle associations of words in their native tongues. If law, as we argue, is a distinct language for engaging the world, reason in law may work the same way, helping judges to avoid the subtle freightings of ordinary language that would lead them to conclusions based on emotion rather than logic.[28] It is no stretch, then, to believe that judges who write well-reasoned opinions are also likely to make good decisions.[29] Still, there is always a gap between the decision and the reasoning that explains it. A judge's opinion is a public justification of the choice she has made, not a moving brain scan of a mind at work.

Finally, the process by which judges seek to fit the four elements of legal reasoning together inevitably requires them to simplify and distort each element to some degree. Therefore, most opinions will fail to meet the requirements of formal logic. (The Supreme Court's rulings about establishment of religion—which allow churches and church schools many tax advantages, yet prohibit the government from providing certain forms of financial aid to church schools—are notoriously incoherent by purely logical standards.) So, too, opinions will simplify the moral and empirical issues in them. Simplification and alteration are facts of life. We always must reshape raw materials if we want to fit them together smoothly.

Thus we return to the point made previously: law does not provide a technique for generating "right answers." This book's analysis assumes that nothing, including science and technology, can ever be demonstrated to be universally, singularly, and objectively correct. For the same reasons, pitches in baseball become balls and strikes, tripping becomes a yellow-card foul in soccer, and elbowing becomes a foul in basketball for all practical purposes because the umpire or referee calls them that way—even when we, as spectators, may see things differently. Just so with judges and lawyers, who agree to follow certain procedures and to use a common vocabulary of legal reasoning but do not automatically agree on legal outcomes, or even on which techniques of legal reasoning to use and when to use them.

---

28. "Gained in Translation," *Economist*, May 17, 2014, 74.

29. We explore this possibility more fully in our discussion of the psychology of judging in "A Psychological Sidebar" in chapter 6.

Sources of Official Legal Texts

The range of legal problems and conflicts is infinite, but lawyers and judges will, one way or another, resolve disputes by referring to and reasoning about official legal texts created by the state, texts that these practitioners usually call "rules of law," or "legal rules." Lawyers and judges usually resort to four categories of these legal rules: statutes, common law, constitutional law, and administrative regulations.

The easiest category to understand is what we often call "laws"—the *statutes* passed by legislatures. Laypeople tend to think of statutes as the rules defining types of behavior that society wishes to condemn: crimes. However, legislatures enact statutes governing (and sometimes creating!) many problems unrelated to crime—civil rights, income tax rates, and Social Security benefit levels, for example. Statutory law, the subject of chapter 4, also includes the local ordinances passed by the elected bodies of cities and counties.

But there is a problem here. Legislatures do not enact statutes to cover everything. And when lawyers and judges face a problem not covered by a statute, they normally turn to that older set of legal texts called *common law*, the subject of chapter 3. In fact, the traditions and practices of common law shape how judges interpret statutes, so this book examines common law before moving to statutory interpretation.

Judges make law in a way completely different from legislators. Instead of meeting together to draft, argue about, and vote on proposals to change the law, judges decide individual cases—and in so doing create legal rules. Common law rules emerged through a process introduced in England before the "discovery" of the New World. The process began because the king of England chose to assert national authority by sending judges throughout the country to decide cases in the name of the Crown, but the king did not write rules to govern all judges' decisions. It was because the judges acted in the name of the central government, a shaky government by our standards, that their decisions became law common to the king's entire domain. Many common law rules originated in local custom or in the minds of the judges themselves.

Chapter 5 explores the third category of official legal texts, *constitutional law*. The Constitution of the United States and the fifty state constitutions set out the structure and powers of government. They also place legal limits on the way those who govern can use their power. While statutes and common law, where statutory law is silent, can govern anybody, constitutions govern the government.[30] The U.S. Constitution even governs presidents, although most constitutional cases involve an alleged conflict between a constitutional provision and a decision made by a public administrator who claims to act under statutory authority.

Administrative regulations—of the Internal Revenue Service, or the San Francisco Planning Department, or any of the thousands of national, state, and local administrative agencies—make up the fourth category of legal texts. Problems in administrative law can fascinate and perplex as much as any. Because this book's length and your time both have limits, we examine reasoning about administrative regulations only indirectly. Do not, however, let this deliberate neglect mislead you into thinking that the subject is unimportant. Administrative regulations shape our lives more and more.[31] The scope of this book, however, is mainly confined to historically more developed official legal texts: statutes, common law, and constitutional law.

The Choices That Legal Reasoning Confronts

While official legal texts are the starting point for legal reasoning, they are rarely the endpoint. If judges could resolve disputes simply by reciting the words of a legal text, disputes would not come to court in the first place. Anybody can read. People can usually find ways to dispute what words mean. The George W. Bush administration engaged in a long-running dispute over the meaning of the word *torture* as used in international treaties and federal law, at one point defining it so narrowly as to include only techniques that inflict pain that one would feel from "organ failure, impairment of bodily function or even death."[32] For better or worse, it takes judicial reasoning and judgment to say what legal texts actually mean in the context

30. If I, as a private citizen, don't like a speech of yours and forcibly remove you from your podium, I will probably violate a principle of common or statutory law. I will also violate the value favoring free exchange of ideas. But I will not violate the First Amendment of the U.S. Constitution. If, however, I did this while employed by a government agency, such as the FBI, my action could be a constitutional violation.

31. See Christine B. Harrington and Lief H. Carter, *Administrative Law and Politics*, 5th ed. (Washington, DC: CQ Press, 2015).

32. Deputy Assistant Attorney General John Yoo, Memorandum to White House Counsel Alberto Gonzales regarding Standards of Conduct for Interrogation under 18 U.S.C. §§ 2340–2340A, August 1, 2002. This memo, as well as other documents from the Bush administration regarding torture, is reprinted in Karen J. Greenberg, ed., *The Torture Debate in America* (New York: Cambridge University Press, 2006), 317. And see U.S. Senate Select Committee on Intelligence, "Committee Study of the Central Intelligence Agency's Detention and Interrogation Program," December 9, 2014.

of specific cases. In most cases, judges must reconcile the potential inconsistencies and contradictions among widespread values, the actual words
of legal rules and prior judicial opinions, and their own views of the case
facts and the social background facts in the cases before them. Judges must
make difficult choices, such as the following:

- Does the case before me call for continued adherence to the historical meaning of legal words? Must I do what the framers of statutory
  or constitutional language intended their language to accomplish?
  Isn't it impossible to know what other people in the past intended?
  When do social, political, and technological changes permit or require a different or revised interpretation of legal concepts?
- Should I always follow the literal meaning of words? In which circumstances can I ignore the literal meaning of words altogether?
- Does this case obligate me to follow a judicial precedent the wisdom
  of which I doubt? When am I free to ignore a relevant precedent? Just
  what makes a precedent relevant in the first place?

Throughout the following chapters, we shall see that choices such as
these—the choice of change or stability and of literal or flexible interpretation of words and precedents, for example—have no "right answer." Judges
inevitably have discretion to decide.

Judges also must make choices when a case pits widely shared moral
values against each other. Thus, the Constitution contains language protecting the freedom of the press. It also contains language ensuring the
fairness of criminal trials. But an unrestrained press can do much to prejudice the members of the jury who follow the news, and hence impair the
fairness of a trial.

In this instance, perhaps judges can do justice by reaching a fair compromise between values. A more difficult problem arises not when two values
collide but when two ideas of justice itself collide. One such collision pits
general justice against *particular* justice. Is it just for bus drivers and train
engineers always to pull away from the station exactly on time, even if it
means that a soldier on leave and racing down the platform to get home
for Christmas will miss his ride? Isn't it true in the long run, to paraphrase
Professor Zechariah Chafee, that fewer people will miss buses and trains if
they all know that buses and trains always leave on the dot, and that more
people will miss if they assume that they can dally and still find the vehicle
at the station? While it is often possible to engineer compromises among
competing values, it is often impossible to compromise between different

visions of justice itself. Unless they are corrupt or lazy, judges will *strive* to do justice, but whether they succeed often remains debatable.

Because legal decisions require choices from among competing values, judges and others who analyze legal problems cannot be "objective" in any simple sense. The problem of general versus particular justice is a good illustration. Neither one will mechanically dictate "the correct" result. A value, a preference, or a moral feeling is not a concept we can prove to be right or wrong. Those who adopt values that conflict with yours will call you biased, and you may feel the same way about those people's values. In the final chapter, we examine more fully the nature of bias and impartiality in law. If biases and values are psychological feelings or beliefs about right and wrong, then legal reasoning cannot eliminate them, but we will see that judges can act impartially nevertheless.

The value of giving sincere reasons to justify our choices that have serious consequences for the lives of others has been woven into our political culture and lore from the beginning. In the Declaration of Independence, Thomas Jefferson, claiming inherent equality between Americans and the British, concluded that "a decent respect to the opinions of mankind requires that they [the Americans, who were abruptly proclaiming their divorce from the British Crown] should declare the causes which impel them to the separation." In effectively explaining "the causes" that lead a judge to rule for one person and against another, the impartial judge will persuasively harmonize, or coherently fit together, the four elements described in this chapter. The examples of both impartial (good) and partial (bad) legal reasoning presented in chapters 2–5 prepare the way for the more complete development of this idea in chapter 6.

Impartiality is a critical component of good judging anywhere, in sports or politics or life itself, but it does not eliminate the tragic element in law. In Martha Nussbaum's *The Fragility of Goodness*, we learn that tragic situations exist whenever circumstances pull people in two inconsistent but equally good directions at once. Imagine yourself having to decide the case of the conjoined twins, and you will feel its inherently tragic nature. Immanuel Kant believed, as Nussbaum puts it, "that objective practical rules be in every situation consistent, forming a harmonious system like a system of true beliefs." Nussbaum (and most contemporary moral philosophers), however, rejects Kant's claim that an internally consistent structure of rules can eliminate the need to make tragic choices in life. Think of all the tragic consequences that even the routine award of child custody in a contested divorce case can have on the parent denied custody, and perhaps on the child. Impartiality requires judges to persuade us that they have reached, if not the better result, at least a good one. But if judges deny the tragic choices in a case by pretending there is an easy answer, they will not persuade us to trust their exercise of power over us. We will know better, because we know from Greek mythology and from our own experience that we often cannot do right without doing wrong. Legal reasoning matters because, done well, it helps communities acknowledge that something is necessarily and unavoidably lost whenever a judge has to choose between competing values, commitments, and principles that we all share. As Nussbaum writes, "If we were such that we could in a crisis dissociate ourselves from one commitment because it clashed with another, we would be less good."[33]

ILLUSTRATIVE CASE

Each chapter ends with an illustrative case that gives you a chance to apply what you have learned to an example of legal reasoning. After presenting each case, we pose questions that will help you identify the four legal reasoning elements in its majority and dissenting opinions. (Routine embedded citations and footnotes have been omitted without ellipses in all illustrative cases.)

Prochnow v. Prochnow
Supreme Court of Wisconsin
80 N.W.2d 278 (Wis. 1957)

A husband appeals from that part of a decree of divorce which adjudged him to be the father of his wife's child and ordered him to pay support money. The actual paternity is the only fact which is in dispute.

Joyce, plaintiff, and Robert, defendant, were married September 2, 1950, and have no children other than the one whose paternity is now in question. In February 1953, Robert began his military service. When he came home on furloughs, which he took frequently in 1953, he found his wife notably lacking in appreciation of his presence. Although he was home on furlough for eight days in October and ten in December, after August 1953, the parties had no sexual intercourse except for one time, to be mentioned later. In Robert's absence, Joyce had dates with a man known as Andy, with whom she danced in a tavern and went to a movie, behaving in a manner which the one witness

---

33. Martha Nussbaum, *The Fragility of Goodness: Luck and Ethics in Greek Tragedy and Philosophy* (New York: Cambridge University Press, 1986), 31 and 50.

who testified on the subject thought unduly affectionate. This witness also testified that Joyce told her that Robert was dull but that she and Andy had fun. She also said that a few days before Friday, March 12, 1954, Joyce told her she had to see her husband, who was then stationed in Texas, but must be back to her work in Milwaukee by Monday.

On March 12, 1954, Joyce flew to San Antonio and met Robert there. They spent the night of the 13th in a hotel where they had sex relations. The next day, before returning to Milwaukee, she told him that she did not love him and was going to divorce him. Her complaint, alleging cruel and inhuman treatment as her cause of action, was served on him April 8, 1954. On September 16, 1954, she amended the complaint to include an allegation that she was pregnant by Robert and demanded support money.

The child was born November 21, 1954. Robert's letters to Joyce are in evidence in which he refers to the child as his own. He returned to civilian life February 13, 1955, and on February 18, 1955, answered the amended complaint, among other things denying that he is the father of the child born to Joyce; and he counterclaimed for divorce alleging cruel and inhuman conduct on the part of the wife.

Before trial, two blood grouping tests were made of Mr. and Mrs. Prochnow and of the child. The first was not made by court order but was ratified by the courts and accepted in evidence as though so made. This test was conducted in Milwaukee on March 21, 1955. The second was had in Waukesha [on] September 29, 1955, under court order. The experts by whom or under whose supervision the tests were conducted testified that each test eliminated Robert as a possible parent of the child. An obstetrician, called by Robert, testified that it was possible for the parties' conduct on March 13, 1954, to produce the full-term child which Mrs. Prochnow bore the next November 21st. Mrs. Prochnow testified that between December 1953 and May 1954, both inclusive, she had no sexual intercourse with any man but her husband. . . .

BROWN, JUSTICE.

The trial judge found the fact to be that Robert is the father of Joyce's child. The question is not whether, on this evidence, we would have so found: we must determine whether that finding constituted reversible error.

Section 328.39 (1) (a), Stats., commands:

Whenever it is established in an action or proceeding that a child was born to a woman while she was the lawful wife of a specified man, any party asserting the illegitimacy of the child in such action or proceeding shall have the burden of proving beyond all reasonable doubt that the husband was not the father of the child. . . .

Ignoring for the moment the evidence of the blood tests and the effect claimed for them, the record shows intercourse between married people at a time appropriate to the conception of this baby. The husband's letters after the child's birth acknowledge it is his own. The wife denies intercourse with any other man during the entire period when she could have conceived this child. Unless we accept the illegitimacy of the baby as a fact while still to be proved, there is no evidence that then, or ever, did she have intercourse with anyone else. The wife's conduct with Andy on the few occasions when the witness saw them together can justly be called indiscreet for a married woman whose husband is absent, but falls far short of indicating adultery. Indeed, appellant did not assert that Andy is the real father but left that to the imagination of the court whose imagination, as it turned out, was not sufficiently lively to draw the inference. Cynics, *among whom on this occasion we must reluctantly number ourselves* [emphasis added], might reasonably conclude that Joyce, finding herself pregnant in February or early March, made a hasty excursion to her husband's bed and an equally abrupt withdrawal when her mission was accomplished. The subsequent birth of a full-term child a month sooner than it would usually be expected if caused by this copulation does nothing to dispel uncharitable doubts. But we must acknowledge that a trial judge, less inclined to suspect the worst, might with reason recall that at least as early as the preceding August, Joyce had lost her taste for her husband's embraces. Divorce offered her freedom from them, but magnanimously she might determine to try once more to save the marriage: hence her trip to Texas. But when the night spent in Robert's arms proved no more agreeable than such nights used to be[,] she made up her mind that they could live together no more, frankly told him so and took her departure. The medical testimony concerning the early arrival of the infant does no more than to recognize eight months of gestation as unusual. It admits the possibility that Robert begat the child that night in that San Antonio hotel. Thus, the mother swears the child is Robert's and she knew, in the Biblical sense, no other man. Robert, perforce, acknowledges that it may be his. Everything else depends on such reasonable inferences as one chooses to draw from the other admitted facts and circumstances. And such inferences are for the trier of the fact. Particularly, in view of Sec. 328.39 (1) (a), Stats., *supra*, we cannot agree with appellant that even with the blood tests left out of consideration, the record here proves beyond a reasonable doubt that Joyce's husband was not the father of her child.

Accordingly we turn to the tests. The expert witnesses agree that the tests excluded Mr. Prochnow from all possibility of this fatherhood. Appellant argues that this testimony is conclusive; that with the tests in evidence Joyce's testimony that she had no union except with her husband is insufficient to support a finding that her husband is the father. . . . But the Wisconsin statute authorizing blood tests in paternity cases pointedly refrains from directing courts to accept them as final even when they exclude the man sought to be held as father. In its material parts it reads:

> Sec. 325.23 *Blood tests in civil actions.* Whenever it shall be relevant in a
> civil action to determine the parentage or identity of any child, . . . the
> court . . . may direct any party to the action and the person involved in
> the controversy to submit to one or more blood tests, to be made by duly
> qualified physicians. Whenever such test is ordered and made the results
> thereof shall be receivable in evidence, but only in cases where definite
> exclusion is established. . . .

This statute does no more than to admit the test and its results in evidence— there to be given weight and credibility in competition with other evidence as the trier of the fact considers it deserves. No doubt in this enactment the legislature recognized that whatever infallibility is accorded to science, scientists and laboratory technicians by whom the tests must be conducted, interpreted, and reported retain the human fallibilities of other witnesses. It had been contended before this that a report on the analysis of blood is a physical fact which controls a finding of fact in opposition to lay testimony on the subject, and the contention was rejected. . . . When the trial judge admitted the Prochnow tests in evidence and weighed them against the testimony of Mrs. Prochnow he went as far in giving effect to them as our statute required him to do. Our opinions say too often that trial courts and juries are the judges of the credibility of witnesses and the weight to be given testimony which conflicts with the testimony of others for us to say that in this case the trial court does not have that function. . . .

The conclusion seems inescapable that the trial court's finding must stand when the blood-test statute does not make the result of the test conclusive but only directs its receipt in evidence there to be weighed, as other evidence is, by the court or jury. We hold, then, that the credibility of witnesses and the weight of all the evidence in this action was for the trial court, and error cannot be predicated upon the court's acceptance of Joyce's testimony as more convincing than that of the expert witnesses.

Judgment affirmed.

WINGERT, JUSTICE (DISSENTING). With all respect for the views of the majority, Mr. Chief Justice Fairchild, Mr. Justice Currie, and the writer must dissent.

In our opinion the appellant, Robert Prochnow, sustained the burden placed upon him by Sec. 328.39 (1) (a), Stats., of proving beyond all reasonable doubt that he was not the father of the child born to the plaintiff.

To meet the burden, appellant produced two classes of evidence, (1) testimony of facts and circumstances, other than blood tests, which create grave doubt that appellant is the father, and (2) the evidence of blood tests and their significance, hereinafter discussed. In our opinion the blood[-test] evidence should have been treated as conclusive in the circumstances of this case.

Among the numerous scientific achievements of recent decades is the development of a method by which it can be definitely established in many cases, with complete accuracy, that one of two persons cannot possibly be the parent of the other. The nature and significance of this discovery are summarized by the National Conference of Commissioners on Uniform State Laws, a highly responsible body, in the prefatory note to the Uniform Act on Blood Tests to Determine Paternity, as follows:

> In paternity proceedings, divorce actions and other types of cases in which the legitimacy of a child is in issue, the modern developments of science have made it possible to determine with certainty in a large number of cases that one charged with being the father of a child could not be. Scientific methods may determine that one is not the father of the child by the analysis of blood samples taken from the mother, the child, and the alleged father in many cases, but it cannot be shown that a man is the father of the child. If the negative fact is established it is evident that there is a great miscarriage of justice to permit juries to hold on the basis of oral testimony, passion, or sympathy, that the person charged is the father and is responsible for the support of the child and other incidents of paternity. . . . There is no need for a dispute among the experts, and true experts will not disagree. Every test will show the same results. . . .
>
> [T]his is one of the few cases in which judgment of court may be absolutely right by use of science. In this kind of a situation it seems intolerable for a court to permit an opposite result to be reached when

the judgment may scientifically be one of complete accuracy. For a court to permit the establishment of paternity in cases where it is scientifically impossible to arrive at that result would seem to be a great travesty on justice. (Uniform Laws Annotated, 9 Miscellaneous Acts, 1955 Pocket Part, p. 13.)

In the present case the evidence showed without dispute that the pertinent type of tests were made of the blood of the husband, the wife, and the child on two separate occasions by different qualified pathologists, at separate laboratories, and that such tests yielded identical results, as follows:

	3/17/55	9/29/55
	Blood types	
Robert Prochnow (Husband)	AB	AB
Joyce Prochnow (Wife)	O	O
David Prochnow (Child)	O	O

There is no evidence whatever that the persons who made these tests were not fully qualified experts in the field of blood testing, nor that the tests were not made properly, nor that the results were not correctly reported to the court. . . .

Two qualified experts in the field also testified that it is a physical impossibility for a man with type AB blood to be the father of a child with type O blood, and that therefore appellant is not and could not be that father of the child David. Both testified that there are no exceptions to the rule. One stated[,] "There is no difference of opinion regarding these factors amongst the authorities doing this particular work. None whatsoever." The evidence thus summarized was not discredited in any way and stands undisputed in the record. Indeed, there was no attempt to discredit it except by the wife's own self-serving statement that she had not had sexual relations with any other man during the period when the child might have been conceived. . . .

QUESTIONS ABOUT THE CASE

---

1. This case requires the Court to interpret several statutes. Which are they? The case also involves a procedural rule that differentiates the work of appellate courts from that of trial courts. What is that rule?

2. Which factual assertions about this dispute did the trial court accept as proved? Which factual assertions did it reject?

3. What are the social background facts at issue here? What choice did the appellate court have to make about social background facts in order to decide this case?[34]

4. Does not the majority's decision to reject the conclusive proof of the blood tests rest on some value choices? What values do you think are involved in this case? Does the Court articulate them? Does this decision depend on a religious conviction that God can always alter nature if God wishes? Or might the Court have believed that, in the interest of giving the child any father at all, it was best to assign paternity to Robert despite science?[35]

5. Why was the law ambiguous in this case?

6. Do you find that the majority or the dissenting opinion does a better job of legal reasoning? Why?

7. How does this opinion change the law? That is, if the dissent had prevailed in this case, how would the reading of the rules of law at issue in this case change?

34. Hint: don't discount the social background fact that medical practitioners make mistakes. In 1995, a Harvard School of Public Health research team studying two well-regarded Boston hospitals found 334 errors in drug delivery to patients over a six-month period. "Drug Errors Found to Be Common in Hospitals," *New York Times*, July 6, 1995.

35. A twenty-first-century Massachusetts case may offer a clue to the *Prochnow* court's thinking. The Massachusetts Supreme Judicial Court rejected a man's motion to be released from paying child support to his seven-year-old daughter after DNA tests revealed several years after her birth that the man was not in fact the father of the child. The court reasoned that "Cheryl's" interest in having the "legal rights and financial benefits of a parental relationship" outweighed the man's interests, particularly because he had delayed contesting a paternity agreement for several years. *In Re Paternity of Cheryl*, 746 N.E. 2d (Mass. 2001). Most state courts, faced with a wave of DNA-based lawsuits, have ruled similarly, fearing the consequences of leaving children "fatherless." Kathleen Burge, "SJC Says Fatherhood Goes Past DNA Test," *Boston Globe*, April 25, 2001.

CHAPTER 2

Change and Stability in Legal Reasoning

It is revolting to have no better reason for a rule of law than that so it was laid down in the time of Henry IV. It is still more revolting if the grounds upon which it was laid down have vanished long since, and the rule persists from blind imitation of the past.

—OLIVER WENDELL HOLMES JR.

The first chapter began to narrow this book's scope of inquiry. We do not put ourselves in the shoes of legislators, nor do we examine how elections or lobbying or presidential leadership produce new law. But though this book does not explore many important political issues, it inevitably steers us into thinking about politics, for three important reasons.

First, studying legal reasoning shows us that "the law" does not substitute for politics—it *is* a form of politics because judges exercise political power. Unless the parties agree that "the law" automatically resolves a case (and when this happens, they usually don't go to court in the first place), the judge will make and defend a choice. That is, judges will use their political power to change people's lives—to enrich or bankrupt them, to free or jail them, sometimes to send them to the death chamber. As explained in the first chapter, legal reasoning is the language we use for analyzing whether the judge has used this political power fairly and persuasively.

Second, once we learn from studying legal reasoning that the most impartial and fair judges inevitably make political choices when they decide cases, we learn that we must take other questions about legal politics very seriously. Whom we elect as president, for example, will affect the selection of people who sit on the federal courts, and that, in turn, will affect who wins and who loses in the judicial system. At a hearing on his nomination to the Supreme Court, Clarence Thomas once asserted that he would "strip down like a runner" and leave a life's worth of beliefs and political attitudes behind him when he ascended to the bench. If Thomas was simply promising that he would not allow his attitudes to *predetermine* his decisions, his statement was unremarkable. If instead Thomas's pledge was to become an attitudeless judge, his promise was not simply unrealistic but also nonsensical.[1]

A long line of political science research demonstrates that the world-views and experiences of judges affect the decisions they make.[2] Professors David Schkade and Cass Sunstein reported strikingly different outcomes in the U.S. Court of Appeals depending on whether the judges had been appointed by a Republican or a Democratic president.[3] Judges of the U.S. Court of Appeals are assigned randomly to hear cases in clusters of three-judge panels. Schkade and Sunstein found that women who sued for sex discrimination won 75 percent of the time when a panel of three Democrat-appointed judges decided their case but only 31 percent of the time when three Republican-appointed judges presided. Research findings such as these, we emphasize, do *not* reflect some monstrous failure by judges to achieve objective, and hence "correct," legal judgments. There is, remember, no single "right answer" to legal questions, so it is absurd to condemn a judge for making an "incorrect" decision merely because he or she disagrees with another judge about a case.[4]

That said, judges can be evaluated according to how persuasively they

1. David Broder, "A Justice with No Agenda," *Washington Post*, September 15, 1991. Martha Minow makes Justice Thomas's comments the starting point of her analysis in her chapter "Stripped Down Like a Runner or Enriched by Experience: Bias and Impartiality of Judges and Jurors," in G. Larry Mays and Peter R. Gregware, eds., *Courts and Justice: A Reader* (Prospect Heights, IL: Waveland Press, 1995), 366–382.

2. See, for example, Michael Bailey and Forrest Maltzman, "Does Legal Doctrine Matter? Unpacking Law and Policy Preference on the Supreme Court," *American Political Science Review* 102 (2008): 369–384; Jeffrey A. Segal and Harold J. Spaeth, *The Supreme Court and the Attitudinal Model Revisited* (New York: Cambridge University Press, 2002); *Majority Rule or Minority Will: Adherence to Precedent on the U.S. Supreme Court* (New York: Cambridge University Press, 1999); Forrest Maltzman, James F. Spriggs, and Paul J. Wahlbeck, *Crafting Law on the Supreme Court: The Collegial Game* (New York: Cambridge University Press, 2000); and Saul Brenner and Harold Spaeth, *Stare Indecisis* (New York: Cambridge University Press, 1995).

3. David Schkade and Cass R. Sunstein, "Judging by Where You Sit," *New York Times*, June 11, 2003. See Cass Sunstein, David Schkade, Lisa M. Ellman, and Andres Sawicki, *Are Judges Political? An Empirical Analysis of the Federal Judiciary* (Washington, DC: Brookings Institution, 2006).

4. For a wide-ranging treatment of why language and logic do not yield objectively "correct" interpretations of the world, see Stanley Fish's essays collected in *There's No Such Thing as Free Speech* (New York: Oxford University Press, 1994).

explain their decisions. If a judicial opinion uses the elements of legal reasoning nonsensically, then those who read the opinion may infer, rightly
or wrongly, that reason in law took a backseat and that personal factors,
perhaps a loyalty to a friend or worries about political pressures, prejudiced the decision. Judges don't find "the one and only" right answers to
legal questions, but in their opinions they do create good and bad answers,
and bad answers have consequences. Judges who use good legal reasoning
bolster a community's confidence in the legal system by demonstrating
that they have thought carefully about the factors that are relevant to a
decision. That—not attitudelessness—should be our standard for judging
judges. Invariably, then, judges bring their attitudes with them when they
ascend to the bench, and controversy over judicial appointments such as
Thomas's is to be expected.

Third, as our emphasis on good reasoning suggests, the legal process, for
all its political characteristics, is still a distinctive kind of politics. The practices, customs, and norms that go with being a U.S. congressperson or senator inevitably shape how that kind of politician thinks. Judges, because they
have been trained in the law and are constantly exposed to legal arguments,
think differently about politics than do legislators. Moreover, the audience
for legal opinions expects a different set of justifications for political action
than does the audience for legislative decisions. It is, for example, perfectly
acceptable for senators to explain that they made a particular decision because it benefited their home state or some interest group they support
(and, alas, that most likely supported them through a major donation to
their campaign); a judge who explained a decision in this way would be
considered corrupt and/or incompetent. In appendix B we examine more
thoroughly the differences between legislative and judicial politics through
our account of the story of Terri Schiavo, a woman in a persistent vegetative
state whose fate was fought over both in courts and in legislatures.

Legal words, like words used in any social practice—religion, sports,
dance—condition and limit what people who operate within that practice
can think and express. What counts as good evidence, or an appropriate
case to hear, or a recognizable social background fact, or a legitimate social value depends on the tradition of legal practices that make such things
thinkable in the first place. So readers grappling with issues of legal reasoning throughout this book are simultaneously studying the political language
by which the legal system creates and perpetuates its power.[5]

---

5. Stanley Fish's essay "The Law Wishes to Have a Formal Existence," in *There's No
Such Thing as Free Speech*, 141–179, describes this phenomenon particularly well. We're

The first section of this chapter explores why legal language does not generate "correct" answers to contested legal questions. The second section asserts that this uncertainty and ambiguity, on balance, is more benefit than cost. The third section examines the other side of the uncertainty coin, the general philosophical conditions in which judges should choose legal clarity and stability at the expense of other values. This chapter's concluding section reviews some general and inevitable characteristics of law that make it forever changing, never perfected.

Sources of Unpredictability in Law

The Disorderly Conduct of Words

Cases often go to courts (and particularly to appellate courts) because the law does not determine the outcome. Both sides believe they have a chance to win. The legal process is in these cases *unpredictable*. Law is unpredictable in part because legal rules are made with words, and words when applied in new contexts are inherently ambiguous. So we begin by examining the "disorderly conduct of words," as Professor Chafee put it.[6]

Consider the following:

- What is a *knee*? Baseball aficionados know that for a pitch to be a strike it must reach home plate somewhere between the batter's knees and his or her shoulders. But what exactly counts as part of the knee? The rules of Major League Baseball prove helpful here because they define the knee, for strike-zone purposes, as extending up from "the hollow beneath the kneecap." This may seem trivial, but it is not to baseball fans. The average number of runs scored in a game since 2000 have fallen by 20 percent. Why? Because new pitch-tracking technology revealed that home-plate umpires were consistently ignoring the rule and calling as balls pitches running well above "the hollow."[7]

---

grateful to Michael McCann for showing us why specifying this point is so essential to this book's larger argument. For a thorough description of how law helps constitute the hopes and expectations of laypersons outside the judicial system, see McCann's *Rights at Work* (Chicago: University of Chicago Press, 1994).

6. Zechariah Chafee, "The Disorderly Conduct of Words," *Columbia Law Review* 41 (1941): 381. Seemingly objective photographs, videos, and digital imagery are no less ambiguous as spoken or written words when used as evidence in law. See Jessica Silbey, "Judges as Film Critics: New Approaches to Filmic Evidence," *Michigan Journal of Law Reform* 37 (2004): 493–572.

7. David Leonhardt, "That Was a Strike? It Is Now," *New York Times*, October 24, 2014. Baseball followers may also want to ponder that Rule 1.01 of the official rules of Ma-

- What is a *vessel*? Federal admiralty law gives the federal courts jurisdiction over all cases involving vessels, and it defines *vessels* as "every description of watercraft or other artificial contrivance used, or capable of being used, as a means of transportation on water." One Fane Lozman lived in a houseboat, a home constructed on a barge that was occasionally towed from one marina to another. A dispute over moorage fees led a marina owner to sue Lozman in federal court. Lozman defended himself by arguing that his houseboat was not covered under federal law because it was not in fact a vessel. He reasoned that his houseboat was not "capable" of moving on water without a tugboat to power and steer it, but the marina contended that because the houseboat floated on water and could be moved, it fit within the definition. The dispute reached all the way to the U.S. Supreme Court, which sided 7–2 with Lozman. The majority held that interpreting the law to cover virtually everything that floats—which could include "a large fishing net, a door taken off its hinges, or Pinocchio (when inside the whale)"—went too far.[8] The case may seem trivial, but it was closely watched by owners of floating casinos, hotels, and restaurants, who deemed it critical to their business planning and insurance arrangements.[9]

- Who counts as *family*? New York City rent control laws prohibit a landlord, after the death of a tenant in the landlord's building, from evicting a "member of the deceased tenant's family who has been living with the family." That's important, because rent control can keep the price of a New York apartment well below the market rate. But New York's rent control laws do not define *family*. Presumably, the rules include people who are not themselves related by blood, for example, married couples and adopted children. But do the rules cover unmarried couples, either heterosexual or homosexual, who live together but whose relationship is not recognized by law? New York State's highest court held, in the case of a same-sex couple, that they did, defining a protected family member to include "a cohabiting nonrelative."[10]

---

jor League Baseball holds that "[b]aseball is a game between two teams of nine players each." Is the designated hitter, the tenth batter in the American League lineup, illegal?

8. *Lozman v. Riviera Beach*, 568 U.S. ___ (2013), slip op., 4.

9. Adam Liptak, "It May Float, but a Home Isn't a Boat, Justices Rule," *New York Times*, January 16, 2013.

10. *Braschi v. Stahl Associates Co.*, 74 N.Y.2d 201 (1989).

The disorderly conduct of words affects legal reasoning most immediately when a judge faces the task of interpreting a statute for the first
time. Therefore, we shall refine the problem of disorderly words in chapter 4, which examines judicial choices in statutory interpretation "in
the first instance." For now it suffices to say that, while words can have
important practical consequences and judges must pay close attention
to their meaning, words *never* "speak for themselves." Consider three
examples:

- The U.S. Constitution requires a president to be a "natural born Citizen" of the United States. Senator John McCain, the unsuccessful
  Republican presidential candidate in 2008, was born in 1936 to U.S.
  citizen parents on a military base in the Panama Canal Zone. The
  Canal Zone was a legally recognized U.S. territory, but Congress conferred U.S. citizenship on people born in the Canal Zone only a year
  after McCain was born. The Constitution's "natural born" provision
  bars Americans who were born outside the United States and subsequently became citizens from the presidency. Is McCain a "natural
  born Citizen"?[11]
- In *Massachusetts v. Environmental Protection Agency*, a case regarding
  greenhouse gases and climate change, the Supreme Court wrestled
  with whether carbon dioxide is an "air pollutant" and thus subject to
  regulation under the Clean Air Act. It is a social background fact that
  the emission of carbon dioxide causes climate change, yet we breathe
  it every day, and the plants that sustain us would not exist without it.
  So, is carbon dioxide an air pollutant?[12]
- We all have experienced the emotion of hatred at times, and so we assume that we know what counts as a "hate crime." Of course, hatred
  motivates many crimes that are not classified hate crimes—wives,
  for example, sometimes murder abusive husbands because of hatred.
  Thus, a hate crime is typically defined to include a categorical hatred
  of the class of people, like racial minorities or homosexuals, to which
  the victim belongs. But what about a 2007 case in which practiced
  muggers used the Internet to lure a gay man to a known trysting spot

11. Adam Liptak, "McCain's Eligibility Is Disputed by Professor," *New York Times*,
July 11, 2008.
12. The Supreme Court ruled that carbon dioxide is an "air pollutant" under the
Clean Air Act, although Justice Scalia dissented on this point, arguing that the Environmental Protection Agency reasonably concluded that carbon dioxide was not covered
by the statute. *Massachusetts v. EPA*, 549 U.S. 497 (2007).

only to rob him? They were charged with a hate crime, but the muggers swore that they bore no hatred of gay men; they simply found them to be particularly easy marks. Does targeting a particular group, by itself, make a crime a hate crime?[13]

The Unpredictability of Precedents

We have argued that precedents help narrow the range of legal choices judges face when they justify a decision. Indeed, precedents do just that, but they never provide complete certainty. Reasoning by example also perpetuates a degree of unpredictability in law. To see why, we proceed through six levels of analysis.

LEVEL ONE: REASONING BY EXAMPLE IN GENERAL

Reasoning by example, in its simplest form, means accepting one choice and rejecting another, because the past provides an example that the accepted choice somehow "worked." Robert, for example, wants to climb a tree but wonders whether its branches will hold. He chooses to attempt the climb because his older sister has just climbed the tree without mishap. Robert reasons by example. His reasoning hardly guarantees success: his older sister may be skinnier and lighter than he. If his reasoning ends in a broken branch and a long fall, Robert will regret his choice, but if he survives, he will have a much better example from which to reason in the future.

The most important characteristic of reasoning by example in any area of life is that no rules tell the decider *how* to choose which examples are similar and which are different. Is Robert's sister really so much lighter that she provides a bad example for him? Hard to know until Robert tries the climb himself. Let us see how this indeterminacy occurs in legal reasoning.

LEVEL TWO: EXAMPLES IN LAW

In law, decisions in prior cases provide examples for legal reasoning. A judge hearing a case about whether an airplane thief had violated the National Motor Vehicle Theft Act wouldn't simply read the statute; he or she would look at previous cases in which judges had interpreted that statute, such as the *McBoyle* case mentioned in chapter 1 (and reprinted in appendix A). Precedents like *McBoyle* provide examples of factual situations and

---

13. Clyde Haberman, "An Easy Target, but Does That Mean Hatred?" *New York Times,* June 26, 2007.

ways of reasoning about them that judges should consider and then interpret. A judge will look at what other judges have said about the meaning of a statute, a constitutional provision, or a common law rule when they applied it to similar facts and answered similar legal questions.

Precedents typically emerge out of appellate law, cases in which someone has appealed a trial court's decision. Why can't a trial court's decisions create precedents? As described in chapter 1, trials are mostly about facts and history, not law. Trials seek primarily to discover who is lying, whose memory has failed, and who can reliably speak to the truth of the matter. Of course, trial judges do make many legal decisions before, after, and during trials. For one thing, trial judges often decide whether a trial is even necessary—the judge may find that the legal rules in the case obviate the need for the fact-finding process of a trial. Trial judges also make legal decisions about the procedures by which trials take place and the legal standards that will be applied to the facts established in the trial.[14] The conscientious trial judge will explain to the parties orally and for the record why and how she resolves the key legal issues in their case. In some instances, the judge will give the parties a written opinion explaining her legal choices, and this may be published. But since at trial judges pay most attention to the historical part of the case, deciding what happened, they usually keep their explanations at the relatively informal oral level. As a result, other judges will not find these opinions reported anywhere; they cannot discover them even if they try. Hence even though they resolve legal issues, trial judges don't usually produce precedents. The masses of legal precedents that fill the shelves of law libraries (and, today, legal databases like LexisNexis and Westlaw) mostly emerge from the appellate process.

LEVEL THREE: THE THREE-STEP PROCESS
OF REASONING BY EXAMPLE

Powerful legal traditions impel judges to resolve cases by using solutions drawn from similar problems reached by judges in the past. How does the judge do this? Professor Edward Levi described it as a three-step process in which the judge (1) sees a factual similarity between the current case and one or more prior cases, (2) announces the rule of law on which the earlier case or cases rested, and (3) applies the rule to the current case.[15]

---

14. The fact-finding can be done by a jury or, in a "bench trial," by the judge.

15. Edward Levi, *An Introduction to Legal Reasoning* (Chicago: University of Chicago Press, 2013), 1–2.

LEVEL FOUR: HOW REASONING BY EXAMPLE
PERPETUATES UNPREDICTABILITY IN LAW

Notice that in the first step of reasoning by example judges choose which case or cases are similar to the current case. They have the obligation, made powerful by legal tradition, to "follow precedent," but they are not obliged to follow any particular precedent. Judges complete the first step *by deciding for themselves* which of the many precedents are similar to the facts of the case before them, and *by deciding for themselves* what they mean.

How does a judge decide which previous case or cases are most similar? The judge must determine which facts in the current case are most important to the outcome and link them to cases with facts that the judge thinks are similar. You can see how much power this gives judges, not only over their own cases but also over their interpretation of precedents. No judicial opinion can force a future judge to sift the facts of the case in any particular way. In writing an opinion, judges can influence a future user of the precedent they create by leaving out potentially important facts revealed in the trial transcript, but once judges report those facts, judges in later similar cases can use the facts as they choose. They can call a fact critical that a prior judge reported but deemed insignificant; they can make a legal molehill out of what a prior judge called a mountain. Thus, the present judge, the precedent user, retains the freedom to choose the example from which the legal conclusion follows.

Fact freedom is how we refer to the judicial freedom to choose the governing precedent by selectively sifting the facts of prior cases and weighing their relative significance. Fact freedom is a major source of uncertainty in law because it is impossible to predict with total accuracy how judges will use this freedom. Thus, we cannot say that "the law" applies known or given rules to diverse factual situations, because we don't know the applicable rules until after the judge uses fact freedom to choose the precedent.

LEVEL FIVE: ILLUSTRATIONS OF FACT FREEDOM IN ACTION

Consider the following example from the rather notorious history of the Mann Act. The Mann Act, passed by Congress in 1910, provides in part that "[a]ny person who shall knowingly transport or cause to be transported . . . in interstate or foreign commerce . . . any woman or girl for the purpose of prostitution or debauchery, or for any other immoral purpose . . . shall be deemed guilty of a felony." Think about these words for a minute: "any other immoral purpose" seems rather sweeping. Does this mean that if we take our wives to Colorado, where recreational marijuana use is legal, in order to get stoned we have violated the Mann Act? (As we write, recreational marijuana use is still illegal in the states in which we reside, Georgia and California.) What if we take them to Tennessee to rob a bank? Judges or lawyers asked to decide such a question would not simply stare at the words in the Mann Act; they would turn to leading precedents that interpret the law. That is precisely what judges did in 1944 when they decided whether to send Mr. and Mrs. Mortensen to prison.[16]

The Mortensens, owners and operators of a house of prostitution in Grand Island, Nebraska, went with two employees on a well-earned vacation to Yellowstone and Salt Lake City. The women did lay off their occupation completely for the duration of the trip, and they paid for much of the trip themselves. Upon their return, they resumed their calling. More than a year later, federal agents arrested the Mortensens and, on the basis of the vacation trip, charged them with violation of the Mann Act. The jury convicted the Mortensens, but their lawyer appealed, arguing that the trip was not for an "immoral purpose."

Unpredictability in law arises when the judge cannot automatically say that a given precedent is or isn't factually similar. To simplify matters here, assume that only one precedent exists, the decision of the U.S. Supreme Court in *Caminetti v. United States*, announced in 1917.[17] In *Caminetti*, two married men took two young women (aged nineteen and twenty) who were not their wives from Sacramento, California, to a cabin near Reno, Nevada, where they had sexual relations. The girls went voluntarily, and they were not prostitutes. By traveling to Reno, the men may have hoped to avoid prosecution in California as adulterers. On these facts, the Supreme Court in *Caminetti* upheld the conviction under the Mann Act.

Does *Caminetti* seal the Mortensens' fate? Does this precedent require the courts to find Mr. and Mrs. Mortensen guilty under the Mann Act? To answer these questions, the judge must decide whether this case is factually similar to *Mortensen*. Is it?

In one sense, of course it is. In each case, the defendants transported women across state lines, after which sex out of wedlock occurred—in the case of the Mortensens, after they returned home. But in another sense, it isn't. Without going to Reno, the girlfriends in *Caminetti* might not have had sex with the defendants. But if the Mortensens had not sponsored the vacation, the women would have continued their work. The Mortensens' transportation *reduced* the frequency of prostitution. The two boyfriends

16. *Mortensen v. United States*, 322 U.S. 369 (1944).
17. *Caminetti v. United States*, 242 U.S. 470 (1917). *Caminetti*'s facts and holding cover noncommercial as well as commercial sexual immorality.

in *Caminetti* maintained or increased "illicit" sex. Should this difference matter? The judge is free to select one or the other interpretation of the facts in order to answer this question. Either decision will create a new legal precedent. It is precisely this freedom to decide either way that increases unpredictability in law.

A full century after Congress passed the Mann Act, it enacted the Patient Protection and Affordable Care Act, known as Obamacare. As described in chapter 1, the U.S. Supreme Court in 2012 ruled that the provision of Obamacare penalizing individuals who failed to buy health insurance was within Congress's power because the penalty counted as a kind of tax. In the same opinion, though, a 5–4 majority of the Court ruled that Obamacare's "individual mandate" was not within Congress's power to regulate commerce "among the several states." This conclusion, though it did not affect the Court's decision on the constitutionality of Obamacare, nicely illustrates the fact freedom of judges. Obamacare supporters argued that the individual mandate fell within the interstate commerce clause because it was crucial to lowering the cost of health care and health insurance nationwide. If individuals could avoid buying health insurance, they reasoned, it would affect the national health-care system because those same individuals would have no way to pay their bills if they were hospitalized, thereby forcing everyone else in the system to subsidize them. Supporters pointed to precedents in which the Court upheld Congress's power to, among other things, regulate the growing of grain in a private garden and the growing of marijuana for private use.[18] If those humble activities fell within Congress's power "to regulate commerce . . . among the several States," why not the individual mandate? But the Supreme Court majority used its fact freedom to distinguish those precedents. All previous cases, they argued, regulated *activities*. The individual mandate was different, the majority insisted, because it regulated *inactivity*—not buying health insurance. If Congress had the power to regulate inaction, they argued, then its power was almost limitless. Could Congress require everyone, Chief Justice Roberts asked in oral argument, to buy a cell phone in order to be able to call in emergency information quickly and save lives? Justice Scalia contended that under the same logic, Congress could require everyone to buy nutritious foods like broccoli.[19] Justice Ginsburg, though, found the inaction-action distinction an unconvincing use of fact freedom. Everyone eventually needs health

18. *Wickard v. Filburn*, 317 U.S. 111 (1942), and *Gonzales v. Raich*, 545 U.S. 1 (2005), respectively.

19. Adam Liptak, "Key Justices Questions Are Tough on the Health Law Mandate," *New York Times*, March 28, 2012.

care, she argued, so a failure to buy insurance was a form of action, a choice to self-insure. Besides, *Wickard*, the wheat-growing precedent, could just as easily be characterized as a case about inactivity, the grower's failure to purchase his wheat in the marketplace. After all, the main reason the Court ruled that the farmer's activity, growing wheat for personal use during the Great Depression, affected interstate commerce was that it would lead him *not* to buy wheat in an interstate marketplace—the purpose of the law was to increase the market demand for wheat, propping up wheat prices so that growers would not go bankrupt.[20]

LEVEL SIX: REASONING BY EXAMPLE
FACILITATES LEGAL CHANGE

Why does judicial fact freedom make law change constantly? Legal rules change every time they are applied because no two cases ever have exactly the same elements. (If you doubt the infinite variability of the world, just consider this example: Pills to treat real or imagined health problems need to be visibly distinguishable enough so that people, particularly the old and infirm, do not confuse one pill with a different pill and double dose or miss a dose. The number of ordinary pills that the eyes and brains of mentally normal people could in theory distinguish as they assemble their daily medications is at least 2.4 trillion![21]) Although judges treat cases as if they were legally the same whenever they apply the rule of one case to another, deciding the new case in terms of the rule adds to the list of cases a new and unique factual situation. Ruling in the Mortensens' favor, as the Supreme Court did in 1944, gave judges new ways of looking at the Mann Act. With the facts of the Mortensens' case, judges after 1944 could, if they wished, read the Mann Act more narrowly than they did in *Caminetti*. *Mortensen* thus potentially changed the meaning of the Mann Act, thereby changing the law.

But as the situation turned out, the change did not endure. In 1946, the Court upheld under the Mann Act the arrest and conviction of certain Mormons, members of a branch known as Fundamentalists, who took "second-

20. *NFIB v. Sebelius*, 567 U.S. ___ (2012) (Ginsburg, J., concurring), slip op., 25.

21. A very low estimate of the number of colors that the human brain can distinguish (think of the number of visibly different paint swatches you see on display in a paint store) is 100,000, although research shows that the number is much larger. Assume pill makers can design any pill to come either in one of those colors or divided into any two of those colors. Then assume that these pills can come in six different shapes (e.g., round, square, etc.), ten different sizes (the combined outer dimensions of length and width), and four degrees of thickness. Under these artificially small limits, the number of recognizable pills is 2.4 trillion.

ary" wives across state lines. No prostitution at all was involved here, but the evidence did suggest that some of the women did not travel voluntarily. Fact freedom worked its way again.[22] The Court extended *Caminetti* and by implication interpreted *Mortensen* as an isolated example of interstate travel that did not fall under the Mann Act. The content of the Mann Act, then, has changed with each new decision and each new set of facts, just as the "action versus inaction" factual distinction chosen as critical by the five justices in the Obamacare case changed the law governing Congress's commerce power. Only time—and the choices of future judges using their own fact freedom—will tell how dramatic that change will be.

Is law always as confusing and unclear as these examples make it seem? In one sense, certainly not. To the practicing lawyer, most legal questions the client asks have clear and predictable answers. But in such cases—and here we return to the definition of legal conflicts in chapter 1—the problems probably do not get to court at all. Uncertainty helps convert a human problem into a legal conflict. We focus on uncertainty in law because that is where reason in law takes over.

In another sense, however, law never entirely frees itself from uncertainty. Lawyers always cope with uncertainties about the facts of cases. Even when they think the law is clear, the introduction of new factual evidence or the unexpected testimony of a witness at trial may raise new and uncertain legal issues that the lawyers didn't consider before the trial. Lawyers know they can never fully predict the outcome of a client's case, even though much of the law is clear most of the time.

Is Unpredictability in Law Desirable?

Is it desirable that legal rules do not always produce clear and unambiguous answers to legal conflicts? Should the legal system strive to reach the point at which legal rules solve problems in the way, for example, that the formula for finding the square root of numbers provides automatic answers to all square root problems?

Despite the human animal's natural discomfort in the presence of uncertainty, some unpredictability in law is desirable. Indeed, if a rule had to provide an automatic and completely predictable outcome before courts could resolve conflicts, society would become intolerably repressive, if not altogether impossible. There are two reasons for this.[23]

---

22. *Cleveland v. United States*, 329 U.S. 14 (1946).
23. Levi, *Introduction to Legal Reasoning*, 1–6.

First, since no two cases ever raise entirely identical facts, society must have some way of convincing litigants that treating different cases *as if they were the same* is fair. But if the legal system resolved all conflicts automatically, people would have little incentive to *participate* in the process that resolves their disputes. If a loser knew in advance she would surely lose, she would not waste time and money on litigation. He would not have the opportunity to try to persuade the judge that his case, always factually unique, *ought* to be treated by a different rule. Citizens who lose will perceive a system that allows them to make their best case as fairer than a system that tells them they lose while they sit by helplessly.

Only in unpredictable circumstances will each side have an incentive to present its best case. When the law is ambiguous, each side thinks it might win. This produces an even more important consequence for society as a whole, not just for the losers. The needs of society change over time. The words of common law, precedents, statutes, and constitutions must take on new meanings. Ambiguity encourages litigants to constantly bombard judges with new ideas. The ambiguity inherent in reasoning by example gives the attorney the opportunity to persuade the judge that the law *ought* to say one thing rather than another. Lawyers thus keep pushing judges to make their interpretation of "the law" fit new circumstances and changes in social values.

We do not encourage legislators and judges to applaud legal uncertainty, much less to maximize it by deliberately crafting vague statutes and ambiguous opinions. Rather, we argue that uncertainty in law is unavoidable. This uncertainty is, however, more of a blessing than a curse. The participation that uncertainty in law encourages gives the legal process and society itself the vital capacity to change its formal rules as human needs and values change.

Vertical and Horizontal Stare Decisis: A Stabilizing and Clarifying Element in Law

This discussion of unpredictability in law should not give the impression that law is never clear. The law is usually clear enough to discourage parties from fighting over the meaning of the law in court. If society is to work, most law must be clear much of the time. We must be able to make wills and contracts, to insure ourselves against disasters, and to plan hundreds of other decisions with the confidence that courts will back our decisions if the people we trust with our freedom and our property fail us.

There is indeed a force pushing toward stability within reasoning by example itself: once judges determine that a given precedent is factually similar enough to determine the outcome in the case before them, then in normal circumstances they follow the precedent. This is the doctrine of *stare decisis*, meaning "to let the prior decision remain" or "stand still."

Stare decisis operates in two dimensions. In the first, or *vertical*, dimension, it acts as a marching order in the chain of judicial command. Courts in both the state and federal systems are organized in a hierarchy within their jurisdictions. Thus, the supreme court of each state, as well as the U.S. Supreme Court, sits atop an "organization chart" of courts. The rulings of the highest court in any jurisdiction legally control the rulings of all courts beneath it. Stare decisis stabilizes law vertically because no court should ignore a higher authoritative decision on a legal point. As long as the U.S. Supreme Court holds that airplanes are not "vehicles" within the National Motor Vehicle Theft Act, all courts beneath it must legally honor that ruling in any future airplane theft case that may arise under the Act.

There is, however, a more interesting, *horizontal* dimension to stare decisis. Horizontal stare decisis is the binding force of a precedent *on the court that created that precedent* over time. What should a court do if it makes a decision that, a few years or decades later, judges come to believe made "bad" law or law that is outdated because of changes in social background facts or social values? Horizontal stare decisis describes the circumstances in which judges should continue to follow and apply their court's own decisions even when they believe that those decisions were misguided or are outdated.

The U.S. Supreme Court's decision in June 1992 to continue to follow *Roe v. Wade*—and to reaffirm that the Constitution implicitly grants a female a right to choose whether to continue a pregnancy prior to the viability of that pregnancy—amounted to a debate on this very question. The *New York Times* quoted on its front page the essence of the Court's horizontal stare decisis reasoning. The three justices whose votes determined the outcome, O'Connor, Souter, and Breyer, wrote an opinion extolling the importance of keeping law clear and stable. "Liberty finds no refuge in a jurisprudence of doubt," the opinion began. The opinion argued that Americans had relied on the ruling in *Roe* in making their life plans: "An entire generation has come of age free to assume *Roe*'s concept of liberty in defining the capacity of women to act in society, and to make reproductive decisions." The opinion also argued that upholding precedent would preserve the Court's image: "A decision to overturn . . . would address error, if error there was, at the cost of both profound and unnecessary damage to the Court's legitimacy, and to the Nation's commitment to the rule of law."[24]

Eleven years later, the same three justices encountered another prominent—and problematic—precedent, this one involving laws criminalizing sodomy. In *Lawrence v. Texas*, the Court considered the case of two men convicted under Texas's "Homosexual Conduct" law. The men argued that the law violated their liberties under the due process clause of the Fourteenth Amendment—an argument the Supreme Court had rejected in a very similar 1986 case, *Bowers v. Hardwick*. Writing for the majority, which included Justice Souter,[25] Justice Kennedy concluded that "*Bowers* was not correct when it was decided, and it is not correct today." And though "[t]he doctrine of *stare decisis* is essential to the respect accorded to the judgments of the Court and to the stability of the law," it is not "an inexorable command."[26] Unlike *Roe*, Kennedy argued, no one was relying on *Bowers*, so overruling it would do more good than harm.

Justice Scalia found the distinction unconvincing. He argued that the Court and many other institutions had relied on *Bowers* in criminalizing private sexual behavior. The overruling of *Bowers*, Scalia predicted, would create "a massive disruption in the current social order."[27]

Scalia's dissent raises the central issue in stare decisis: under which conditions should judges ignore or follow what they consider to be bad precedents? Professor Thomas S. Currier has examined the values justifying the principle of horizontal stare decisis. He suggests five values that should lead judges toward continuing to follow such precedents:

---

24. "The Supreme Court; Three Who Spoke as One," *New York Times*, June 30, 1992; and *Planned Parenthood v. Casey*, 505 U.S. 833 (1992). The Court's decision in *Planned Parenthood* has been interpreted to allow much more regulation of abortion than was possible under *Roe v. Wade*, 410 U.S. 113 (1973). See also *Dickerson v. United States*, 530 U.S. 428 (2000), in which the Supreme Court voted to retain its controversial "*Miranda* rule" requiring advising a criminal of his or her rights before obtaining any incriminating evidence for use in trial. Chief Justice Rehnquist, who had expressed skepticism about the rule, wrote, "Whether or not we would agree with *Miranda*'s reasoning and its resulting rule, were we addressing the issue in the first instance, the principles of stare decisis weigh heavily against overruling it now."

25. Justice O'Connor, who had voted in 1992 to uphold *Roe* despite her misgivings, also voted to strike down the law in *Lawrence* but on separate equal protection grounds.

26. *Lawrence v. Texas*, 539 U.S. 577 (2003), citing *Payne v. Tennessee*, 501 U.S. 828 (1991).

27. *Lawrence v. Texas*, 539 U.S. 591.

1. *Stability.* It is clearly socially desirable that social relations should have a reasonable degree of continuity and cohesion, held together by a framework of reasonably stable institutional arrangements. Continuity and cohesion in the judicial application of rules [are] important to the stability of these institutional arrangements, and society places great value on the stability of some of them. Social institutions in which stability is recognized as particularly important include the operation of government, the family, ownership of land, commercial arrangements, and judicially created relations. . . .

2. *Protection of Reliance* . . . . [T]he value here is the protection of persons who have ordered their affairs in reliance upon contemporaneously announced law. It is obviously desirable that official declarations of the principles and attitudes upon which official administration of the law will be based should be capable of being taken as determinate and reliable indications of the course that such administration will in fact take in the future. . . . This value might be regarded as a personalized variation on the value of stability; but it is broader in that it is recognized even where no social institution is involved, and stability as such is unimportant.

3. *Efficiency in the Administration of Justice.* If every case coming before the courts had to be decided as an original proposition, without reference to precedent, the judicial workload would obviously be intolerable. Judges must be able to ease this burden by seeking guidance from what other judges have done in similar cases.

4. *Equality.* By this is meant the equal treatment of persons similarly situated. It is a fundamental ethical requirement that like cases should receive like treatment, that there should be no discrimination between one litigant and another except by reference to some relevant differentiating factor. This appears to be the same value that requires rationality in judicial decision-making, which in turn necessitates that the law applied by a court be consistently stated from case to case. The same value is recognized in the idea that what should govern judicial decisions are rules, or at least standards. The value of equality, in any event, appears to be at the heart of our received notions of justice.

5. *The Image of Justice.* This phrase does not mean that any judicial decision ought to be made on the basis of its likely impact upon the court's public relations, in the Madison Avenue sense, but merely that it is important not only that the court provide equal treatment

to persons similarly situated, but that, insofar as possible, the court should appear to do so. Adherence to precedent generally tends not only to assure equality in the administration of justice, but also to project to the public the impression that courts do administer justice equally.[28]

The following chapters will describe more precisely the circumstances in which Currier's reasons for horizontal stare decisis should and should not compel a judge to follow rather than depart from a precedent. Here you should simply note that, in part because of stare decisis, most law is clear enough to prevent litigation most of the time. Lawyers can advise us on how to make valid wills and binding contracts, trusting that the arrangements they help us make will be upheld by courts. And if someone steals our car and takes it to another state, federal officials, under the authority of the National Motor Vehicle Theft Act, can try to track down the car and the criminal. Without a system of precedents, it would be harder for us to predict judicial decisions and therefore more difficult for us to plan to avoid legal conflicts.[29]

These forces in law pushing toward predictability and stability should not, however, obscure this chapter's main conclusion. Cases routinely arise in which the best possible legal reasoning *cannot* provide a "right" answer. New mixes of facts and legal rules pop up every day. The basic principle of the rule of law obligates judges to justify the result they reach in each new case in such a way that we trust their impartiality. Only good legal reasoning can build and maintain that trust.

28. Thomas S. Currier, "Time and Change in Judge-Made Law: Prospective Overruling," *Virginia Law Review* 51, no. 201 (1965): 235–238.

29. Judges who refuse to follow the precedents of their superior courts face the embarrassment of having their decisions reversed by a higher court, but judges face no such sanction when they refuse to follow their own court's precedent, and so scholars have wondered why judges often do so. There are at least two possibilities. First, following precedent makes the job of deciding cases easier. As Benjamin Cardozo put it in his 1921 work *The Nature of the Judicial Process*, the "labor of judges would be increased almost to the breaking point if every past decision could be reopened in every case, and one could not lay one's own course of bricks on the secure foundation of the courses laid by others who had gone before him." Quoted in *District of Columbia v. Heller*, 554 U.S. 570 (2008) (Stevens, J., dissenting). Second, judges may follow precedent because they have a sense of institutional loyalty and respect for colleagues on the court who created it. These two factors, further, may reinforce each other. For a thorough analysis of the role of precedents in law, see Michael Gerhardt, *The Power of Precedent* (New York: Oxford University Press, 2008). For analyses of why precedent does not seem to be so powerful for justices on the Supreme Court, see the books cited in note 2 of this chapter.

ILLUSTRATIVE CASES

In the federal judicial system, it is common for the intermediate appellate courts to hear cases in panels of three judges, with the outcome determined by majority vote. Here are two opinions, both interpreting the Nationality Act of 1940 and both written by Judge Learned Hand, sitting on two separate panels. The first is a precedent for the second. Notice that they were decided just a month apart. You should read the second case, *Repouille*, to see how Judge Hand uses his fact freedom to distinguish it from the first case, *Francioso*. Did Judge Hand use fact freedom foolishly in *Repouille*?

United States v. Francioso
U.S. Court of Appeals for the Second Circuit
164 F.2d 163 (2nd Cir. 1947)

L. HAND, CIRCUIT JUDGE.

This is an appeal from an order admitting the appellee, Francioso, to citizenship. At the hearing the "naturalization examiner" objected to his admission upon the ground that he had married his niece and had been living incestuously with her during the five years before he filed his petition. Upon the following facts the judge held that Francioso had been "a person of good moral character" and naturalized him. Francioso was born in Italy in 1905, immigrated into the United States in 1923, and declared his intention of becoming a citizen in 1924. His wife was born in Italy in 1906, immigrated in 1911, and has remained here since then. They were married in Connecticut on February 13, 1925, and have four children, born in 1926, 1927, 1930, and 1933. Francioso was the uncle of his wife, and knew when he married her that the marriage was unlawful in Connecticut and that the magistrate would have not married them, had they not suppressed their relationship. They have always lived together in apparent concord, and at some time which the record leaves indefinite, a priest of the Catholic Church—of which both spouses are communicants—"solemnized" the marriage with the consent of his bishop.

In United States ex rel. *Iorio v. Day*, in speaking of crimes involving "moral turpitude" we held that the standard was, not what we personally might set, but "the commonly accepted mores": i.e., the generally accepted moral conventions current at the time, so far as we could ascertain them. The majority opinion in United States ex rel. *Berlandi v. Reimer* perhaps looked a little askance at that decision; but it did not overrule it, and we think that the same test applies to the statutory standard of "good moral character" in the naturalization statute. Would the moral feelings, now prevalent generally in this country, be outraged because Francioso continued to live with his wife and four children between 1938 and 1943? Anything he had done before that time does not count; for the statute does not search further back into the past.

In 1938 Francioso's children were five, eight, eleven and twelve years old, and his wife was 31; he was morally and legally responsible for their nurture and at least morally responsible for hers. Cato himself would not have demanded that he should turn all five adrift. True, he might have left the home and supported them out of his earnings; but to do so would deprive his children of the protection, guidance and solace of a father. We can think of no course open to him which would not have been regarded as more immoral than that which he followed, unless it be that he should live at home, but as a celibate. There may be purists who would insist that this alone was consistent with "good moral conduct"; but we do not believe that the conscience of the ordinary man demands that degree of ascesis; and we have for warrant the fact that the Church—least of all complaisant with sexual lapses—saw fit to sanction the continuance of this union. Indeed, such a marriage would have been lawful in New York until 1893, as it was at common law. To be sure its legality does not determine its morality; but it helps to do so, for the fact that disapproval of such marriages was so long in taking the form of law, shows that it is condemned in no such sense as marriages forbidden by "God's law." It stands between those and the marriage of first cousins which is ordinarily, though not universally, regarded as permissible.

It is especially relevant, we think, that the relationship of these spouses did not involve those factors which particularly make such marriages abhorrent. It was not as though they had earlier had those close and continuous family contacts which are usual between uncle and niece. Francioso had lived in Italy until he was eighteen years of age; his wife immigrated when she was a child of four; they could have had no acquaintance until he came here in August, 1923, only eighteen months before they married. It is to the highest degree improbable that in that short time there should have arisen between them the familial intimacy common between uncle and niece, which is properly thought to be inimical to marriage. . . .

Order affirmed.

Repouille v. United States
165 F.2d 152 (2nd Cir. 1947)

L. HAND, CIRCUIT JUDGE.

The District Attorney, on behalf of the Immigration and Naturalization Service, has appealed from an order, naturalizing the appellee, Repouille. The ground of the objection in the district court and here is that he did not show himself to have been a person of "good moral character" for the five years which preceded the filing of his petition. The facts are as follows. The petition was filed on September 22, 1944, and on October 12, 1939, he had deliberately put to death his son, a boy of thirteen, by means of chloroform. His reason for this tragic deed was that the child had "suffered from birth from a brain injury which destined him to be an idiot and a physical monstrosity malformed in all four limbs. The child was blind, mute, and deformed. He had to be fed; the movements of his bladder and bowels were involuntary, and his entire life was spent in a small crib." Repouille had four other children at the time towards whom he has always been a dutiful and responsible parent; it may be assumed that his act was to help him in their nurture, which was being compromised by the burden imposed upon him in the care of the fifth. The family was altogether dependent upon his industry for its support. He was indicted for manslaughter in the first degree; but the jury brought in a verdict of manslaughter in the second degree with a recommendation of the "utmost clemency"; and the judge sentenced him to not less than five years nor more than ten, execution to be stayed, and the defendant to be placed on probation, from which he was discharged in December 1945. Concededly, except for this act he conducted himself as a person of "good moral character" during the five years before he filed his petition. Indeed, if he had waited before filing his petition from September 22, to October 14, 1944, he would have had a clear record for the necessary period, and would have been admitted without question.

Very recently we had to pass upon the phrase "good moral character" in the Nationality Act; and we said that it set as a test, not those standards which we might ourselves approve, but whether "the moral feelings, now prevalent generally in this country" would "be outraged" by the conduct in question: that is, whether it conformed to "the generally accepted moral conventions current at the time."[a] In the absence of some national inquisition, like a Gallup poll, that is indeed a difficult test to apply; often questions will arise to which the answer is not ascertainable, and where the petitioner must fail only because he has the affirmative. Indeed, in the case at bar itself

the answer is not wholly certain; for we all know that there are great numbers of people of the most unimpeachable virtue, who think it morally justifiable to put an end to a life so inexorably destined to be a burden on others,
and—so far as any possible interest of its own is concerned—condemned to
a brutish existence, lower indeed than all but the lowest forms of sentient
life. Nor is it inevitably an answer to say that it must be immoral to do this,
until the law provides security against the abuses which would inevitably
follow, unless the practice were regulated. Many people—probably most
people—do not make it a final ethical test of conduct that it shall not violate
law; few of us exact of ourselves or of others the unflinching obedience of
a Socrates. There being no lawful means of accomplishing an end, which
they believe to be righteous in itself, there have always been conscientious
persons who feel no scruple in acting in defiance of a law which is repugnant to their personal convictions, and who even regard as martyrs those
who suffer by doing so. In our own history it is only necessary to recall the
Abolitionists. It is reasonably clear that the jury which tried Repouille did not
feel any moral repulsion at his crime. Although it was inescapably murder
in the first degree, not only did they bring in a verdict that was flatly in the
face of the facts and utterly absurd—for manslaughter in the second degree
presupposes that the killing has not been deliberate—but they coupled even
that with a recommendation which showed that in the substance they wished
to exculpate the offender. Moreover, it is also plain, from the sentence which
he imposed, that the judge could not have seriously disagreed with their
recommendation.

One might be tempted to seize upon all this as a reliable measure of current morals; and no doubt it should have its place in the scale; but we should
hesitate to accept it as decisive, when, for example, we compare it with the
fate of a similar offender in Massachusetts, who, although he was not executed, was imprisoned for life. Left at large as we are, without means of
verifying our conclusion, and without authority to substitute our individual
beliefs, the outcome must needs be tentative; and not much is gained by
discussion. We can say no more than that, quite independently of what may
be the current moral feeling as to legally administered euthanasia, we feel
reasonably secure in holding that only a minority of virtuous persons would
deem the practise morally justifiable, while it remains in private hands, even
when the provocation is as overwhelming as it was in this instance.

However, we wish to make it plain that a new petition would not be open
to this objection; and that the pitiable event, now long passed, will not prevent
Repouille from taking his place among us as a citizen. The assertion in his

brief that he did not "intend" the petition to be filed until 1945, unhappily is irrelevant; the statute makes crucial the actual date of filing.

Order reversed; petition dismissed without prejudice to the filing of a second petition.

---

a*United States v. Francioso*, 164 F.2d 163 (2nd Cir., 1947). [Note in original.]

QUESTIONS ABOUT THE CASE

1. Which legal questions does Judge Hand ask about Mr. Francioso's behavior? How does Judge Hand answer them?
2. Which facts about the *Repouille* case make *Francioso* factually similar enough to serve as a precedent?
3. The problem in both cases is how a court should determine whether an applicant for naturalization has the required good moral character. In *Francioso*, Judge Hand uses a method that permits him to conclude that Mr. Francioso should become a citizen. How does he do so?
4. Does Judge Hand use the same method in *Repouille*? If so, which facts distinguish the two cases so that even though Francioso won, Repouille lost?
5. Why is Judge Hand's concluding clause allowing Repouille to file a second petition significant? If in fact Repouille can still become a U.S. citizen, does Hand's use of fact freedom in his case matter? Is this a case of "no harm, no foul"?

CHAPTER 3

Common Law

The life of the law has not been logic; it has been experience. The felt necessities of the time, the prevalent moral
and political theories, intuitions of public policy, avowed or
unconscious, even the prejudices which judges share with
their fellow-men, have had a good deal more to do than the
syllogism in determining the rules by which men should be
governed.

—OLIVER WENDELL HOLMES JR.

Readers who have had the good fortune to spend leisure time in New
York City probably know the serene relief from the city's bustle that
parks like Central Park in Manhattan and Prospect Park in Brooklyn provide. In 2007 Alexis Handwerker, a social worker, was relaxing in one such
park under an elm tree when one of its branches suddenly snapped off and
fell thirty feet, trapping and smothering Ms. Handwerker under its leaves.
"I don't want to die!" she screamed in panic to bystanders who tried des-
perately to free her. She survived her serious injuries, sued New York City,
and recovered $4 million.

Lawsuits against New York for injuries caused by falling tree limbs average about one a year and are routinely settled for large amounts. In recent years budget cuts have seriously reduced the funds the city spends
on tree care, and city workers are no longer trained to spot rotten or otherwise weakened trees. Indeed, the elm tree in question was so aged and
rotten that observers reported its trunk had turned "gooey." In 2009 a
falling limb permanently maimed a Google engineer and another seven
months later killed a restaurant worker. How do courts decide whether
a defendant like New York is liable for injuries like these, and if so, for

how much? The answer begins with the *common law*, the subject of this chapter.[1]

Common law at first may seem a bizarre creature. You have already seen judges interpreting *statutory* law in the Mann Act, Nationality Act, and *Prochnow* cases. And you are probably somewhat familiar with *constitutional* law, like the case with which this book began, *United States v. Windsor*, in which the Supreme Court wrestled with whether the Defense of Marriage Act violated the Fifth Amendment of the Constitution. We examine statutory and constitutional law in greater depth in chapters 4 and 5. Common law is different from these other forms of law because in common law cases the judges have no text to interpret, no statute or constitutional provision that guides their decision. Instead, they look only to cases other judges decided in the past and the doctrines that have emerged from those cases. But if judges in common law cases reason solely from earlier precedents, what were *those* precedents based on? The surprising answer is that they, too, were based on precedents, in fact on chains of precedents that stretch back into the practice of law in England well before Columbus's arrival in America.[2]

Origins of Common Law

To understand the beginnings of the common law, start by thinking of a major sport. How did it get started? Here we take what is probably the most popular game on the planet, football, or soccer, as it is usually called in the United States. Does the fun of kicking around an inflated animal bladder—or the head of an enemy—come to mind? Ancient texts suggest that people were kicking leather balls into small nets in China as early as 3000 BC, although historians trace the origins of soccer to games played variously by the Greeks, Romans, and Japanese in the second and third

1. William Glaberson and Lisa Foderaro, "Neglected, Rotting Trees Turn Deadly," *New York Times*, May 14, 2012.

2. Plucknett's "concise" history of the common law is more than seven hundred pages long. Theodore F. T. Plucknett, *A Concise History of the Common Law*, 5th ed. (Boston: Little, Brown, 1956). For real concision, try Frederick G. Kempin, *Historical Introduction to Anglo-American Law in a Nutshell*, 2nd ed. (St. Paul, MN: West Publishing, 1973). To contrast common law systems with the deductive or "code-based" systems of law in Europe and South America, see John Henry Merryman and Rogelio Perez-Perdomo, *The Civil Law Tradition: An Introduction to the Legal Systems of Europe and Latin America*, 3rd ed. (Palo Alto, CA: Stanford University Press, 2007).

centuries BC.[3] Soccer began as a vicious sport in which, legend has it, a human head was sometimes used—and as one commentator puts it, you "can imagine the sportive instinct that demanded a head for play, or the natural outlet of impulsive action against a fallen foe."[4] The game was played before unruly crowds who regularly joined in when fights broke out. In medieval times soccer apparently became a bit more orderly, but it was still "a wild and brutal game played according to oral rules which allowed a high level of tolerated physical violence." Because of the violence it produced, soccer was banned by English lawmakers more than thirty times between the fourteenth and the seventeenth centuries, though the bans never stuck.[5]

Soccer's origin as serious mayhem suggests the next question: what factors over time converted soccer from a melee into the dramatically less violent game that preteen children happily and peacefully play today in junior soccer leagues around the country? It is not hard to imagine something like the following history: Early players found that when the game deteriorated into violence, it became both more painful and less fun to play. The players began to see that when they agreed with one another not to punch or bite, if not kick and trip, the game was more fun. After a while the older generation of players, in passing on to the younger generation the lore of their game, transmitted what over time become the "rules of the game."[6]

The point of this exercise in imagination should be obvious. The common law of England evolved in a roughly analogous way as the game of soccer, and at roughly the same time. The story begins in 1066 with William the Conqueror, who got his name by assembling thousands of troops, crossing the English Channel, and conquering England in battle. In order to watch over the administration of his new possession, William sent his personal advisers around the country administering ad hoc justice in the

3. Jaime Orejan, *Football Soccer: History and Tactics* (London: McFarland Publishers, 2011), 10–13.

4. John D. Brock, "Elementary Team Play in Soccer," *Journal of Health and Physical Education* 1, no. 7 (1930): 34–35.

5. Benny Josef Peiser, "Football Violence: An Interdisciplinary Perspective," in *Science and Soccer*, ed. Thomas Reilly (London: E. & F. N. Spon, 1996): 328–329.

6. Only in the nineteenth century did English players get together to formalize these rules. The process took many years of struggle, in part over whether players should be allowed to kick and trip one another or carry the ball. After a series of stormy meetings, a committee of undergraduates from six English schools in 1863 produced "The Cambridge Rules," which split off rugby, in which "hacking" and carrying the ball would be allowed, from soccer, in which it would not. Eric Dunning, Dominic Malcolm, and Ivan Waddington, *Sports Histories: Figurational Studies in the Development of Modern Sports* (London: Routledge, 2004), 48–49.

king's name—settling land disputes, collecting the king's rents, and keeping the peace by punishing acts of robbery and murder, though not with punching and biting. Additionally, William appointed the "Great Council" to handle more serious transgressions, what we would today call *crimes*.

Nonetheless, local courts, not the king's judges, still did much of the adjudicating during William's reign. It was not until a century later that Henry II began the actual takeover of the lower local courts. Initially, the king required litigants to get permission to bring a case in local court for any dispute involving title to his land. A litigant would have to obtain from London a *writ of right* and then produce it in the local court. Shortly thereafter, the king's council began to bypass the local courts altogether on matters of land title. Certain council members heard these cases at first, but as they became more and more specialized and experienced, they split off from the council to form the king's Court of Common Pleas. Similarly, the council members assigned to criminal matters developed into the Court of King's Bench. The Court of Exchequer, which handled rent and tax collections, evolved in similar fashion.

Thus the king began supplanting local courts with his own. But whose law would the king's judges apply? In most of Europe, the kings' judges simply adopted the old Roman codes. In England, however, partly because it was easy and partly because it possessed considerable local political appeal, the king's judges adopted the practice of the preconquest local courts. This practice of the lower courts consisted of adopting the local customs of the place and time and applying to daily events what people felt was fair. We might call this the *custom of following custom*, just as early soccer players honored the customs of good play established by players before them.

The custom of following custom, however, created difficulties. In a sparsely populated area—a primitive area by today's standards of commerce and transportation—customs about crimes, land use, debts, and so forth varied considerably from shire to shire, village to village, and manor to manor. But the king's judges could hardly decide each case on the basis of whatever local custom or belief had happened to evolve among those living where the dispute arose. To judge that way would amount to judging on shifting and inconsistent grounds. Judging would occur not in the name of the king but in the name of the location where the dispute arose. Following local custom would undercut the king's long-range political objective to rule fully over his lands.

Thus, in an attempt to rule consistently in the king's name, the royal courts slowly adopted some customs and rejected others. Because justice in England rested on the custom of customs, the customs that the royal courts adopted and attempted to apply uniformly became the customs *common* to the king's entire realm. Indeed, though the judges no doubt felt that what they decided was right because it had its roots in some customs, it would be wiser to say that they created not common custom but common law—law common throughout England.

Though the law in England became "common," it remained complex. Procedure—the correct way to handle a lawsuit—rapidly became rigid, and the legal players who could not master all the strict technicalities involved lost their cases. To remember the technicalities, they needed to write them down. Out of necessity, some judges and other observers of the English common law began the tradition, very much expanded today, of writing down in what came to be called "commentaries" the essential facts and conclusions of court decisions. These collected records naturally became a convenient guide for helping judges decide later cases.

These early common law judges did not, however, create the practices of reasoning by example and stare decisis as we now know them. Indeed, until the American Revolution, men actively rejected the notion that judges actually made law as they decided cases. Men believed rather in natural law—if not God's law, then at least nature's own. To them, the proper judicial decision rested on "true" law. The decision that rested elsewhere was in a sense unlawful. Prior to and throughout most of the nineteenth century, lawyers and judges thought of common law as a collected body of "correct" legal doctrine, not as the process of growth and change that reasoning by example—to say nothing of the inevitable changes and compromises required in democratic political systems—makes inevitable. Moreover, the commentaries were "unofficial, incomplete, and thus unreliable. Only a radical change in viewpoint, the recognition that law comes from politicians and not from God or nature, coupled with accurate court reporting, permitted reasoning by example and stare decisis to flourish."[7]

In referring, then, to the common law as judge-made law, we mean that, for a variety of historical reasons, judges created without legislative help a

---

7. Kempin, *Historical Introduction*, 85, suggests that as late as 1825 in the United States and 1865 in England, stare decisis rested on very shaky ground. Anthropologists are quite comfortable with the conclusion that rules of law, in contrast to imperfectly articulated customs and interpersonal understandings, play a relatively insignificant role in many, if not most, of the world's justice systems. See Stanley Diamond, "The Rule of Law vs. the Order of Custom," *Social Research* 51 (1984): 387–418. For a particularly concise review of how slowly and fitfully common law judges came to appreciate that they inevitably make law as they decide each case, see Roger Cotterrell, *The Politics of Jurisprudence* (London: Butterworth and Co., 1989), chap. 2.

large body of legal rules and principles in the course of deciding cases. As long as judges continue to apply these rules and principles, they will continue to remake them with each application. The fact that judges for most of this history thought that they simply restated divine or natural law matters relatively little to us today. What matters is that the United States has inherited a political system in which, despite legislative supremacy, judges constantly and inevitably make law. How they do so—how they reason, in other words—thus becomes an important question in the study of politics and government. The central question in this book is not *whether* courts should make law but *what* law they make, and *how*.

Reasoning by Example in Common Law

Much of the everyday law around us falls into the category of common law. When, for example, you sign a contract—an everyday event these days given that software companies require a signed release every time you download their programs—your agreement is governed by common law principles. Although modern statutes have supplanted much common law, particularly in the important area of commercial transactions, these statutes for the most part preserve basic definitions, principles, and values articulated first in common law.

One of the most important fields of common law is tort. Tort law wrestles with questions such as these: What defines and limits a person's liability to compensate those whom he injures? What counts as a hurt serious enough to merit compensation? Letting a tree rot and then fall on someone? Breaking someone else's leg? Embarrassing someone? When does law impose liability on me if I threaten someone with a blow (assault)? If I strike the blow (battery)? What if I do so in self-defense? Am I liable if I publicly insult another (libel and slander)? What if I can show that my insult is factually accurate? These may sound like questions of criminal law, but they are not, for the law of torts does not expose the lawbreaker to punishment by the state. Instead, tort law gives people the right to sue to collect compensation from those who have injured them. Tort law is constantly in the news, in lawsuits over the harms caused by prescription drugs, cigarettes, asbestos, even high-fructose sodas and fatty foods at fast-food restaurants. And as always, tort law is evolving in response to, as Justice Holmes put it in the epigraph to this chapter, the "felt necessities of the time" and the "prevalent moral and political theories" of the day.

In this section, indeed in the bulk of the chapter, we illustrate common law in action with problems of tort law, mostly of negligence. We do not discuss tort law in its entirety, for it would take a book triple the size of this one to review all the subtleties and uncertainties in this branch of law. We shall instead focus in some detail on an important and perennial question in the law of tort: at what point do the rights and privileges of owning property stop, and at what point does our legal obligation not to hurt others who have encroached on our property begin?

We start with some old cases that may seem fairly irrelevant today. In the nineteenth and early twentieth centuries, the legal question in tort disputes often took the following form: to what extent may we hurt other people without incurring a legal liability to compensate those we hurt *because we hurt them on our own land*? By the end of this chapter, you will see that the common law process has transformed that question about property into this one: where do the rights and privileges of being private and free stop and our legal obligation to help others begin? For example, does a therapist have a duty to warn potential targets of a patient who is threatening violence? Or, as in the case of the unhelpful bartender discussed in chapter 1 and featured again at the end of this chapter, does a restaurant employee have an obligation to let a stranger claiming an emergency use the restaurant's business phone? No doubt fifty years from now the question will have transformed yet again. Common law is a process of continual incremental adjustment, a story that by its nature can have no final chapter.

Let us begin with a review of some basic rules of common law that seemed to govern in the middle of the nineteenth century. First, the common law of negligence required one to act in a way a reasonable and prudent person would act and to refrain from acting in a way a reasonable and prudent person would refrain from acting. Lawyers would say that a *standard of care* existed. Second, the law defined the classes of persons to whom a *duty* to act carefully was owed. Third, the law imposed liability upon those who carelessly violated the *reasonable man* standard. (Whether a person in fact acts negligently in a specific case is one of those legal history questions that trial courts, with or without juries, often decide.) Fourth, someone to whom a duty is owed must actually have suffered an injury as a result of the hurt. Trial courts also usually made this factual decision. Thus, the critical legal questions in negligence cases involved the definition of the reasonable man standard of care and duty.

Similarly, the law of battery commands us not to strike another deliberately unless a reasonable person would do so, as in self-defense. If we strike another unreasonably, then we become liable as long as we owe a duty to the injured person not to strike.

As you may already suspect, the requirement of a duty before liability attaches can make a great difference. One of the common law principles of the nineteenth century quite plainly said that people do not owe a duty to avoid injuring, carelessly or deliberately, people who *trespass* (encroach without express or implied permission) on their property.

We shall examine three common law cases to illustrate some of the main features of reasoning in common law. These cases suggest the following basic features of the common law process:

- General principles, including the rules of negligence and battery just described, do not neatly resolve legal problems.
- Precedents do not neatly resolve legal problems, either.
- In reasoning from precedents, judges do make choices and exercise fact freedom; it is this exercise that best describes how and why they decide as they do.
- Social background facts often influence case outcomes more powerfully than the facts in the litigation itself.
- The beliefs and values of individual judges do influence law.
- The precise meaning of common law rules—here of trespass and of duty—changes as judges decide each new case.
- Over time, as fundamental values change, the common law shifts in ways that reflect those changes.
- Judges have shifted their conception of their role from a belief that they are required to apply divine or natural law toward a more pragmatic recognition of the inevitability of judicial lawmaking and its consequences.
- Judges have also shifted the way they explain their decisions, moving from mechanical jurisprudence to "realism," a style that acknowledges the role of social background facts and changing values (the "felt necessities" and "prevalent moral and political theories" that Justice Holmes described) in their judgments. They have, in short, become more philosophically pragmatic.

Here are the three cases.

The Cherry Tree

It is summer in rural New York. The year is 1865. The heat of midday has passed. Sarah Hoffman, an unmarried woman living with her brother, a country doctor, sets out at her brother's request to pick ripe cherries for dinner.

A cherry tree stands on her brother's land, about two feet from the fence separating his land from that of his neighbor, Abner Armstrong. Sarah's previous pickings have left few cherries on Hoffman's side of the fence. Hence, nimbly enough for her age, Sarah climbs the fence and from her perch upon it begins to take cherries from the untouched branches overhanging Abner's yard.

Angered by this intrusion, Abner runs from his house and orders her to stop picking his cherries. She persists. Enraged, he grabs her wrist and strong-arms her down from the fence. Ligaments in her wrist tear. She cries from the pain and humiliation. She sues at common law for battery. The trial jury awards her $1,000 in damages.

Abner appealed. He claimed that *he*, not Sarah or her brother, owned the cherries overhanging his land. Because he owned the cherries, he had every right to protect them, just as he could prevent Sarah from pulling onions in his garden with a long-handled picker from her perch. In other words, Sarah was not a person to whom Abner owed a duty. By her trespassing and her interference with Abner's property, Sarah exposed herself to Abner's battery committed in defense of his property.

Abner's lawyer cited many legal sources in support of his argument. He began with the maxim *cujus est solum, ejus est usque ad coelum et ad inferos*, sometimes translated as "he who has the soil has it even to the sky and the lowest depths." He then referred the appellate judge to the great English commentator Blackstone, quoting: "Upwards, therefore, no man may erect any building, or the like to overhang another's land." He also cited *Kent's Commentaries, Bouvier's Institutes, Crabbe's Text on Real Property*, and seven cases in support of his position. One of these, an English case titled *Waterman v. Soper*, held "that if A plants a tree upon the extremest limits of his land and the tree growing extends its roots into the land of B next adjoining," then A and B jointly own the tree.[8]

Sarah's lawyer responded that, in law, title to the tree depends on who owns title to the land from which the tree's trunk emerges from the ground. Sarah did not trespass; therefore, Abner owed her the duty not to batter her. In support of this argument, her lawyer cited several commentaries, Hilliard's treatise on real property, and four cases. Sarah's lawyer relied especially on a case, *Lyman v. Hale*, decided in Connecticut in 1836.[9] In *Lyman*, the defendant picked and refused to return pears from branches

8. *Waterman v. Soper*, 1 Ld. Raym. 737 (opinion undated). Some sources cite this case as *Waterman v. Toper*.

9. *Lyman v. Hale*, 11 Conn. 177 (1836).

overhanging his yard from a tree the plaintiff had planted four feet from the line. The *Lyman* opinion explicitly rejected the reasoning of the English precedent, *Waterman*. Despite the antiquated language, *Lyman* is a remarkably sensible rather than "legalistic" opinion. The Court held that *Waterman*'s "roots" principle is unsound because of the practical difficulties in applying it:

> How, it may be asked, is the principle to be reduced to practice? And here, it should be remembered, that nothing depends on the question whether the branches do or do not overhang the lands of the adjoining proprietor. All is made to depend solely on the enquiry, whether any portion of the roots extend into his land. It is this fact alone, which creates the [joint ownership]. And how is the fact to be ascertained?
>
> Again; if such [joint ownership] exist, it is diffused over the whole tree. Each owns a certain proportion of the whole. In what proportion do the respective parties hold? And how are these proportions to be determined? How is it to be ascertained what part of its nourishment the tree derives from the soil of the adjoining proprietor? If one joint owner appropriates . . . all the products, on what principle is the account to be settled between the parties?
>
> Again; suppose the line between adjoining proprietors to run through a forest or grove. Is a new rule of property to be introduced, in regard to those trees growing so near the line as to extend some portions of their roots across it? How is a man to know whether he is the exclusive owner of trees, growing, indeed, on his own land, but near the line; and whether he can safely cut them, without subjecting himself to an action?
>
> And again; on the principle claimed, a man may be the exclusive owner of a tree, one year, and the next, a [joint owner] with another; and the proportion in which he owns may be varying from year to year, as the tree progresses in its growth.
>
> It is not seen how these consequences are to be obviated, if the principle contended for be once admitted. We think they are such as to furnish the most conclusive objections against the adoption of the principle. We are not prepared to adopt it, unless compelled to do so, by the controuling [sic] force of authority. The cases relied upon for its support have been examined. We do not think them decisive.[10]

---

10. *Lyman v. Hale*, 183–184.

In effect, the *Lyman* opinion says that property titles must be clear to help us plan our affairs, to help us know whether we can or can't cut down a tree for winter firewood, for example. Given the inescapable social background facts about trees, the roots rule introduces inevitable uncertainty. We must therefore reject it.

The appellate court in New York found *Lyman* most persuasive and followed it. Sarah won.[11]

Abner appealed again, to the state's highest court of appeals. In 1872 (court delays, as Charles Dickens's great novel *Bleak House* teaches, are not a uniquely modern phenomenon), Abner lost again. The attorneys presented the same arguments. Perhaps surprisingly, however, the highest court did not mention *Lyman*. Instead, it seemed to say that *Waterman* does correctly state the law, but Abner's lawyer forgot to prove that the cherry tree's roots actually extended across the property line:

> We have not been referred to any case showing that where no part of a tree stood on the land of a party, and it did not receive any nourishment therefrom, that he had any right therein, and it is laid down in Bouvier's Institutes . . . that if the branches of a tree only overshadow the adjoining land and the roots do not enter into it, the tree wholly belongs to the estate where the roots grow.[12]

Therefore Abner lost once again.

This simple case, occupying only a few pages in the reports of the two New York appellate courts, richly illustrates many features of common law. First, note that none of the judges either in *Hoffman* or in *Lyman* questioned their authority to decide these cases without reference to statutes. The laws, both of assault and battery and of the more fundamental problem of ownership, come from the common law heritage of cases, commentaries, and treatises. The judges automatically assumed the power to make law governing a very common human conflict—overlapping claims to physical space on this planet. Surely a legislature could legislate on the subject, but judges blithely do so themselves in the face of legislative silence.

In this connection, recall that legislatures pass statutes addressing general problems. How likely is it that a legislature would ever pass a statute regulating tree ownership on or near property lines? Isn't it better that our

11. *Hoffman v. Armstrong*, 46 Barb. 337 (1866).
12. *Hoffman v. Armstrong*, 48 N.Y. 201 (1872), 203–204.

government contains a mechanism, the courts, that must create some law on this subject once the problem turns out to be a real one?

Second, the general common law definitions of battery and of property ownership do not resolve this case. Neither do specific precedents. Instead, both sides cite conflicting principles and inconsistent precedents and urge from them contradictory conclusions. The judge must find some justification or reason for choosing, but nothing in either side's argument, at least in this case, compels the judge to choose one way rather than another. Judges possess the freedom to say that either *Lyman* or *Waterman* expresses the right law for resolving this problem.

Consider specifically the matter of the Connecticut precedent, *Lyman*. Judges possess the freedom to go one way, as when the first appellate court in effect said, "We find the facts of *Lyman* much like those in Abner's conflict with Sarah. We also find *Lyman*'s reasoning persuasive; therefore, we apply the rule of *Lyman* to this case and rule for Sarah." But judges also possess the freedom to go another way, as did the second court when it in effect said, "Connecticut precedents do not govern New York. Older common law precedents and principles from England conflict with Connecticut's law. We choose the older tradition. Abner would win if only he could show that the roots really grew on his property."

The New York courts in *Hoffman* had other options. The second court could have easily assumed, because of the social background fact that roots underground normally grow about the same distances as do branches above ground, that the roots did cross the line and that their nourishment probably supported the cherries Sarah tried to pick. Or the Court could have taken judicial notice of the social background fact that any reasonably sized tree grows roots in all directions more than two feet from its base. But it didn't.

Judges must decide which facts in the case before them matter and what those facts mean. They must simultaneously decide what the facts in often inconsistent precedents mean as well. The two appellate courts reached the same conclusion but by emphasizing different facts. The first court found that roots shouldn't matter. Even though legal authorities sometimes mention them, the Court believed the location of roots should have no legal significance. To give root location legal significance suddenly makes our knowledge of what we own more uncertain. Before we can cut down a tree, we must risk illegally trespassing on our neighbor's land and dig a series of holes in our neighbor's yard looking for roots. And what if the neighbor has flowers growing in a bed near the tree that he or she doesn't want dug up? The root rule leaves us out on a limb.

Third, to understand how these two courts choose differently to reach the same result, examine the difference in their basic approach to the problem. The first appellate court seems eager to assume the responsibility to shape law, to acknowledge relevant background facts, and hence to make laws that promote human cooperation in daily affairs. The second court approaches the problem much more cautiously. It seems to say: "We admit the precedents conflict. Fortunately, we do not really need to choose between them. As long as Abner failed to prove that the roots grow on his side of the fence, he loses either way. Therefore, we choose the path that disturbs common law the least. The lower appellate court explicitly chose to reject *Waterman*, but we don't have to do that, so we won't."

This judicial caution is very common, but it is not particularly wise. Without realizing it, the highest New York court (whose opinion therefore overrides the precedential value of the practically much wiser opinion of the court below) has made new law. Now we have New York precedent endorsing *Waterman*. Future courts will have to wrestle with the problem of overruling it or blindly following it and producing all the practical problems against which *Lyman* wisely warned.

The reason these two sets of judges ruled differently, therefore, rests precisely on the fact that they are different people with different values and beliefs about what judges ought to do. Their values help determine the law they create.

Fourth, at a deeper level, the difference reflects much more than a difference in judicial philosophies. These two approaches illustrate two contrasting common law styles. The final higher court opinion in *Hoffman* views common law as fixed, stable, and true. It wants to avoid upsetting *Bouvier's Institutes* and Blackstone's maxims if it possibly can. The Court thinks these are the common law. In contrast, the lower court's *Lyman* approach, while predating *Hoffman* by nearly forty years, observes the spirit rather than the letter of common law. It views common law as a tradition in which judges seek to adapt law so that it improves our capacity to live together peacefully and to plan our affairs more effectively. It retains the capacity to change with changing conditions. This more modern style comes closer to helping law foster social cooperation—our legal system's most fundamental goal.

Finally, the case of the cherry tree illustrates a fundamental difference between common law and statutory interpretation. In statutory interpretation, as we explain in chapter 4, judges must think carefully about the purposes behind the laws they interpret. Once a court determines a statute's purpose, namely the range of problems in society that a statute presumably seeks to tackle, it has no need to second-guess the wisdom of that purpose.

In common law, however, the judge who reasons from a precedent does not care about what the prior judge thought or about the purpose of the announced rule of law. In common law, the judge is always free to decide on his own what the law *ought* to say. The prior judge's intent or purpose does not dictate how his opinion will bind as precedent. Put another way, the legislature's classification of what does and does not belong in its legal category, a classification created by the words of the statute, does bind the judge. In common law, the judge deciding the case creates the classification. The judge sets his or her own goals.

This goal setting occurred in both the first and second *Hoffman* opinions. The first court wanted to make workable and practical law, not because *Lyman* or any other precedent commanded it to but because the Court wanted to achieve that goal. The second court ruled as it did not because *Bouvier's Institutes* or *Waterman* commanded it to do so but because that court preferred the goal of changing past formal statements of law as little as possible.

The Pit

Five years after Sarah Hoffman's final victory, New York's highest court faced a related common law problem. A Mr. Carter, along with several other citizens of the town of Bath, maintained an alley running between their properties: Exchange Alley, people called it. The public had used the alley for twenty years as a convenient way to travel from one long block to another, but the town never acknowledged Exchange Alley as a public street or attempted to maintain it. In May 1872, Carter began excavating to erect a building on his land. The construction went slowly, so slowly in fact that on a gloomy night the next November an open pit still remained on Carter's property. That night, a Mr. Beck passed through the alley on his customary way to supper when, rather suddenly, a carriage turned into the alley and rushed toward him. Beck stepped rapidly to his left to avoid the carriage, tripped, and fell headlong into the pit, injuring himself. Although the evidence was never completely clear, since the alley had no marked border, it appeared that the pit began no fewer than seven feet away from the outermost possible edge of the "public" alley.

The lawsuit that followed brought many of the same sort of issues to the Court as had Sarah's problem. Lawyers for Carter cited the common law rule that landowners have the right to use their property as they please. They have no duty to avoid harming trespassers negligently. The lawyers

cited English cases to show that travelers who were hurt falling into pits
five, twenty, and thirty feet from a public way could not recover damages
because the danger must "adjoin" the public way.

Despite these arguments, the Court held for Beck. It had no difficulty
whatsoever determining that, even though Carter and others together pri-
vately owned Exchange Alley, allowing the public to use the property over
time created a duty to the users not to hurt them negligently.[13]

But the pit excavated truly private property. Is a seven-foot distance
from a public alley sufficient to exempt the owner from liability to the
public, or does the pit legally adjoin the alley, thereby creating a duty
of care?

The Court ruled that the alley did adjoin. It held Carter negligently responsible for Beck's injuries. It approved the idea that if the hole was "so
situated that a person lawfully using the thoroughfare, and, in a reasonable
manner, was liable to fall into it, the defendant was liable."[14]

The Court did not have to rule this way. It could have defined adjoining
pits as holes in the ground that literally touch the outer boundary of the
land. Or it could have said that seven feet was simply too far away to make
a landowner liable. But the Court offered a better decision. As in *Lyman*, it
produced a workable distinction between injuries to deliberate trespassers
and to those who reasonably attempt to use either their own space or the
public's space. Just as in the *Lyman* and *Hoffman* decisions, the judges in
Beck v. Carter chose as they did because their values—their beliefs about
desirable and undesirable social relations—led them to that conclusion. If
they deeply believed in the absolute sanctity of private property, ambiguity
in common law would certainly have given them freedom to say, "Landowners must be free to do what they wish with their land. Carter's pit was
entirely on his private land seven feet from the thoroughfare. Therefore,
Carter owed Beck no duty of care."

Before you proceed, note how these two principal cases, reduced to
their simplest terms, combine to form a seemingly comprehensive statement of law: When a court has no convincing proof that the plaintiff deliberately and intentionally trespassed on the defendant's property, then the

13. You should observe from this example that, legally speaking, property is not so
much what people hold title to as what the law says they can and cannot do with a thing,
whether they hold title to it or not.

14. *Beck v. Carter*, 68 N.Y. 283 (1876), 293. If you are dubious, measure off seven feet
from your standing place in a very dark room and mark the spot. Then imagine you
suddenly must get out of the way of a carriage by moving toward your mark in the dark.
If you pass the mark, you've fallen in the pit.

defendant owes the plaintiff a duty of care (*Hoffman*). Furthermore, when the plaintiff accidentally does trespass on the defendant's property, but the defendant should have foreseen the injury from such accidental trespass, the defendant is also liable (*Beck*). Thus arises the final question: what result should a court reach when the plaintiff knowingly and deliberately trespasses fully onto the defendant's property and is injured?

The Diving Board

On another summer day in New York—July 8, 1916—Harvey Hynes and two friends had gone swimming at a favorite spot along the Bronx bank of the then relatively unpolluted Harlem River. For five years, they and other swimmers had dived from a makeshift plank nailed to the wooden bulkhead along the river.

The electrified line of the New York Central Railroad ran along the river. The power line was suspended over the track between poles, half of which ran between the track and the river. Legally, the railroad owned the strip of riverbank containing track, poles, wires, and bulkhead. Hence, about half of the sixteen-foot diving board touched or extended over the railroad's land while the rest reached out, at a height of about three feet, over the surface of the public river.

As Harvey prepared to dive, one of the railroad's overhead supports for the power line suddenly broke loose from the pole, bringing down with it the writhing electric line that powered the trains. The wires struck Harvey, throwing him from the board. His friends pulled him, dead, from the waters of the Harlem River.

Harvey's mother sued the railroad for the damages caused by its alleged negligence in maintaining the supports for the wire. Conceding that New York Central's maintenance of the supports failed to meet the reasonable-man standard of care, the trial court and the intermediate appellate court nevertheless denied her claim. Harvey was a trespasser, a deliberate trespasser, and property owners have no duty to protect such trespassers from harm. The cherry tree and the pit cases, two rather distantly related cases among thousands that had tried to thrash out the borderline between property and tort, were about to merge as key precedents in the final *Hynes* decision.

The lawyers for the railroad presented many cases in their favor. They cited *Hoffman* to show that while perched on the board—even if he was over the river—Harvey trespassed, because the board was attached to the railroad's land. They also cited cases, *Beck* among them, to establish the point that the trespass was not a temporary and involuntary move from a public space but a sustained series of deliberate trespasses onto the defendant's land.

Three of the justices on New York's highest court agreed. The railroad had no duty of care to this trespasser. But a majority of four, led by Benjamin Cardozo, supported Harvey's mother and reversed.

Cardozo cited relatively few precedents. He did cite *Hoffman* and *Beck*, though not in the way the railroad's lawyers had hoped. The lawyers tried to convince the judges that a mechanical rule commanded a decision for the railroad. Anything, a cherry tree or a diving board, belongs to the railroad if it is affixed to the railroad's land, regardless of what it overhangs. Therefore, Harvey, at the time the wires struck him, trespassed. Since the trespass was deliberate, *Beck* commands a decision for the railroad. Cardozo, however, appealed to the deeper spirit of these cases, a spirit that rejects mechanical rules such as the root rule for determining ownership of cherry trees. The spirit requires enunciating policy—law—that corresponds to a deeper sense of how society ought to regulate rights and responsibilities in this legal, as well as physical, borderland. Cardozo wrote:

This case is a striking instance of the dangers of "a jurisprudence of conceptions" (Pound, "Mechanical Jurisprudence," 8 *Columbia Law Review*, 605, 608, 610) [1908], the extension of a maxim or a definition with relentless disregard of consequences to . . . "a dryly logical extreme." The approximate and relative become the definite and absolute. Landowners are not bound to regulate their conduct in contemplation of the presence of trespassers intruding upon private structures. Landowners *are* bound to regulate their conduct in contemplation of the presence of travelers upon the adjacent public ways. There are times when there is little trouble in marking off the field of exemption and immunity from that of liability and duty. Here structures and ways are so united and commingled, superimposed upon each other, that the fields are brought together. In such circumstances, there is little help in pursuing general maxims to ultimate conclusions. They have been framed *alio intuitu* [in a different way]. They must be reformulated and readapted to meet exceptional conditions. Rules appropriate to spheres which are conceived of as separate and distinct cannot, both, be enforced when the spheres become concentric. There must then be readjustment or collision. In one sense, and that a highly technical and artificial one, the diver at the end of the springboard is an intruder on the adjoining lands. In another sense, and one that realists will accept more readily, he is still on public waters in the exercise of public rights. The law must say whether it will subject him to the rule of the one field or of the other, of this sphere or of that. We think that considerations of analogy, of convenience, of policy, and of justice, exclude him from the field of the defendant's immunity and exemption, and place him in the field of liability and duty.[15]

Note again the effect of fact freedom on judicial choices. Although they wrote no dissenting opinion, we can make an intelligent guess that the dissenters in *Hynes* reasoned from *Hoffman* this way: "The diving board grew from the railroad's land. If ownership of the cherry tree depends on where it is rooted, then the board belongs to the railroad. Therefore, Harvey trespassed." But Cardozo refuses to rest his opinion on the simple analogy between a diving board that hangs over a river and a cherry tree that projects its branches into an adjoining yard. Cardozo in effect responds, "The important fact is that Sarah didn't really trespass. Her climb didn't really interfere with Abner's use of his backyard, just as the boys diving into the river from a board over the river didn't really interfere with the railroad's property. It's one thing to say that the railroad could have legally evicted trespassers from its land because, say, they camped out next to its tracks. It's entirely different to say that the railroad can electrocute this boy without paying for its negligence." Cardozo uses his fact freedom to draw on what he considers to be the most important aspect of the precedents. Reason in law does not allow us to say that his choice legally is right and the other legally wrong—after all, with a switch of one vote, *Hynes* would have produced a very different legal precedent. Yet by recognizing that judges have the freedom to choose among different ways of interpreting precedents, we free ourselves to say that we favor one choice over another and to justify why we feel that way.

Cardozo's opinion reflects the rise of "realism," an approach to law that rejects the view that legal conflicts can be solved just like mathematical problems, through formal logic. Instead, realism recognizes that, as Justice Holmes says in the epigraph to this chapter, "the life of the law has not been logic, but experience." Experience—changes in social background facts and changes in social values—is central to Cardozo's justification of his decision. Cardozo's opinion stresses the value of social cooperation over

15. *Hynes v. New York Central R.R.*, 231 N.Y. 229 (1921), 235–236. How should a judge, following *Hynes*, rule in a case identical to *Hoffman*, except that Abner picks cherries from the branches overhanging his yard and that, to stop him, Sarah shoots him in the leg with a .22-caliber pistol?

the values of private property and individual autonomy. Cardozo recognizes that the falling line would equally have killed Harvey if he had dived into the water just before the negligently maintained rotten wood gave way and the wire electrocuted him. Accordingly, Cardozo refuses to let the railroad off the liability hook "on a technicality." The more important point, Cardozo argues, is that the railroad had a social responsibility to be careful in its handling of hazardous electrical wires. "We think there was no moment when [Harvey] was beyond the pale of the defendant's duty—the duty of care and vigilance in the storage of destructive forces," Cardozo concluded.[16]

In this respect, the *Hynes* case foreshadowed one of the most dramatic changes in the American legal system, the shift in the twentieth century from a legal philosophy whose principles emphasize property rights and individualism to a system that promotes social caring and cooperation. In tort law, for example, judges have greatly expanded the duty of manufacturers to take care that the goods they make are safe. Lawsuits against manufacturers for injuries caused by unsafe cars, faulty tires, dangerous drugs, toxic chemicals, and even "nondefective" products such as cigarettes and guns, would not have been possible without these changes in tort doctrine.[17]

As the example of product liability indicates, realism has deeply influenced judging, so that judges today are more conscious of the importance of social background facts and changes in social values. They are less likely to hide behind a formal statement of law in a treatise, a commentary, or an abstract common law principle. Judges today are more self-conscious, too, about their ability—one might even say their duty—to make good public policy. These changes have, however, created controversy. As we'll see, judicial policy making in tort law has become particularly controversial.

Keeping the Common Law Tradition Alive

The preceding section introduces the most typical common law judicial problem, one in which precedents provide some guidance but do not automatically resolve problems. In the typical situation, the judge faces an array of precedents, some of which may seem inconsistent, some imaginative, and others wedded to past "truths" in common law. None of them automat-

16. Ibid., 235.
17. For a careful analysis of the impact of realism on tort law, see G. Edward White, *Tort Law in America: An Intellectual History* (New York: Oxford University Press, 1980).

ically controls, so the judge must make a choice. Sometimes the precedent or principle gives the judge no more than a point of departure from which to justify the unexpressed beliefs and values that determine the result.

Sometimes, however, a genuinely new problem arises, one for which precedents prove so remote, so factually different, as to give the judge no real guidance at all. The judge will see that a decision for either party in the case will create not a new variation on older law but a new and different law—a new and different definition of how people should relate to one another. In other situations, the reverse happens. The judge faces a precedent so factually similar to the one before him that he cannot distinguish or ignore it. If he chooses to reach a new result, he must overrule the precedent.

This section answers questions involving these less typical judicial problems: How should judges proceed when they cannot find common law cases that seem to apply to the case before them? When should they make common law from whole cloth? Conversely, in which circumstances should courts choose deliberately to reject a case or principle that controls the case before it? How, in other words, does stare decisis operate in common law?

Answers to these questions depend in part on what we think about the proper balance between judicial and legislative lawmaking. What kinds of problems require the kind of fact-gathering and value-balancing techniques available to legislatures but not to courts? What types of problems require, for their solution, the creation of administrative planning and enforcement mechanisms so complex that only legislatures can create, fund, and supervise them?

You may have already discerned our general approach to the problem of judicial-legislative balance. Let us make it explicit here. Courts and legislatures have much in common. They both gather evidence in a systematic way, courts through witnesses at trial and through the briefs of the parties on appeal, and legislatures through committee hearings and the many efforts of lobbyists. Both institutions gather evidence, at least formally, in an open-minded way. Courts hear both sides. The adversary system requires it. Legislatures also hear competing arguments in committee hearings and through the efforts of competing lobbyists. Furthermore, both courts and legislatures possess lawmaking power. People who look to law to plan their affairs know they should look to both institutions for legal guidance. Finally, politics influences both branches of government. Many state judges win office by election. Politicians appoint federal judges as well as state judges in unelected posts, so political restraints affect both.

In chapter 5 and appendix B we address some important political differences between judges and legislators. These differences can produce dramatically contrasting policy outcomes. Nevertheless, *judges should always presume themselves competent to take the lawmaking initiative when the legislature has not spoken clearly to them.* In other words, because as a general matter courts and legislatures have a similar authority and competence, the burden of proof always rests on the party arguing that the court should remain silent because the legislature is better qualified to speak.

Making Common Law without Close Precedents

In early March 1928, two seagoing tugboats towing barges of coal set out in good weather from Norfolk, Virginia, bound for New York. About midnight on March 8, under fair skies but with the barometer falling slightly, the tugs passed the Delaware Breakwater, a safe haven for tugs and barges caught in bad weather. The next morning, however, the wind began to freshen. By noon, gale-force winds blew up heavy seas. Early in the afternoon, two barges sprung leaks. Their crews signaled the tugs that they would proceed to anchor the barges and ride out the storm. They did so, but conditions steadily worsened. The Coast Guard heroically rescued the crews of both barges late in the day. The dawn light on March 10 revealed no trace of the barges. By then, both the barges and their cargoes rested on the ocean floor.

The coal owners sued the barge company, alleging both that the company had breached its contract of carriage and that the unseaworthiness of the barges made it liable for the loss of the coal. The barge company in turn sued the tugboat owners for the loss of both the coal and the two barges. The barge owners claimed that the two tugs had not properly handled the cargo. More precisely, they claimed that the tug owners should bear the total loss because they had not provided their tugs with conventional AM radio receivers.

At trial, the barge owners established several critical facts. On March 8, the Arlington weather bureau broadcast a 10:00 A.M. prediction calling for shifting and increasing winds the following day. Another ship in the vicinity of the tugs and barges had received this report on its AM radio. At 10:00 P.M. the same day, the Arlington bureau predicted "increasing east and southeast winds, becoming fresh to strong Friday night and increasing cloudiness followed by rain on Friday." On the basis of the morning report, one tug owner towing cargo in the vicinity had anchored at the Delaware Breakwater. Even the captain of the defendant tug conceded at trial that, had he heard the evening report, he would have done the same.

Place yourself in the position of a judge resolving this case. In your first step, aided by the arguments of the lawyers, you try to discover how much, if any, of this problem the law already makes clear. You soon find that the law of admiralty—a branch of common law for our purposes—imposes an absolute liability on ship owners for the loss of cargoes aboard their ships if unseaworthiness of the ship caused the loss. Note that this unseaworthiness doctrine does not simply extend the law of negligence to the sea. The ship owner may have no knowledge of the faulty condition. It may have been impossible even for a reasonable and prudent person to prevent the unseaworthy condition—hidden rot in some of a hull's wooden planking, for example. The rule creates a guarantee of seaworthiness.

But is a ship that does not carry a radio in 1928 unseaworthy because it can't receive weather reports? On this point the law gives no help. You find that Congress has passed a statute requiring steamers carrying more than fifty passengers to carry two-way radios so that they can call for help and receive information, but the statute does not include tugs and barges. You find no precedents whatsoever linking seaworthiness with possession of radios or any other new invention. At this point, you have several choices. You might say:

Choice One

Congress in its wisdom chose not to require two-way shortwave radios of tugs and barges. Furthermore, Congress has made no law requiring AM radios. Therefore, Congress has intended that tugs without AM radios are seaworthy and the tug owners are not liable for the loss.

Choice Two

I find no law requiring receiving sets. Since legislatures, not the courts, are the lawmakers in our democratic nation, I have no legal authority to find the tug owners liable. Therefore, they are not liable.

You can, we trust, reject both these choices immediately. We have no evidence whatsoever that Congress thought about AM receivers, much less intended or decided to pass a statute declaring that tugs without them are nevertheless seaworthy. We could just as easily conclude that the statute recognizes the general importance of radios in improving navigation safety. Therefore, the statute gives ship owners a positive signal that they should seriously examine whether radios can help them navigate better. If you have any further doubts about the weakness of the first choice, consider the fact that no congressional statute required tugs to carry compasses.

The second choice conflicts with the common law tradition. Courts do continue to make law as conditions change; over the years, courts have specifically fashioned the principles of admiralty and of seaworthiness within admiralty law. So you might instead say:

Choice Three

I admit that judges retain their general lawmaking power in admiralty. In this case, however, only a legislature can decide whether ships must carry radios. Only through legislative hearings could we learn, for example, how common it was in 1928 for people to own radios. It would hardly be fair to hold the tug owners liable if, in 1928, radios were only novel. Similarly, only legislative hearings can learn whether ship owners themselves carry radios and think it wise or necessary to do so. If they do, then the fact dictates a new policy of seaworthiness, but we can't tell. As in ancient common law, custom may hold the key to justice, but only a legislature today is equipped to find the key.

The third choice may sound like an improvement, but it's not. Its major premise, that courts can't obtain the facts, is false. The actual case from which this example is derived shows that the courts were able to make the necessary factual determinations.[18] The brief for the cargo owners documented the phenomenal growth in the sales of radios, by more than 1,000 percent between 1922 and 1928. It quoted Frederick Lewis Allen's book *Only Yesterday* (1931): "At the age of three and a half years, radio broadcasting had attained its majority. Behind those figures of radio sales lies a whole chapter of the life of the Postwar Decade: radio penetrating every third home in the country; giant broadcasting stations with nationwide hook-ups."[19] The cargo owners also elicited testimony on the witness stand from one tug captain to the effect that, although only one tug line required radios, at least 90 percent of the tugs had them, if only for entertainment.

The lesson here is critically important. As a rule, courts can find back-

18. *The T. J. Hooper*, 60 F.2d 737 (2nd Cir. 1932).

19. Quoted in Henry M. Hart and Albert M. Sacks, *The Legal Process* (Cambridge, MA: Harvard Law School, 1958), 432–433. Our selection of illustrative cases in this section draws heavily upon the much larger variety of cases that Hart and Sacks provide. Although we use these cases for somewhat different purposes, we cannot improve upon Hart and Sacks's choice of working materials; here, as elsewhere, we are much indebted to them.

ground facts as effectively as legislatures. We applaud the adversary system in courts precisely because we believe it gives lawyers the incentive to present the fullest possible range of facts to support their position. Legislatures may be superior lawmakers when complex problems require a simultaneous set of solutions and the means to coordinate them, but well-established judicial practices allow courts in cases such as this one to establish the background facts that determine whether a given legal choice is wise and fair. So might the common law tradition itself come to the rescue?

Choice Four

Custom is a time-honored source of common law. In this case, it has been convincingly shown that tugs customarily carry radios. Radio has become a part of our everyday lives. The absence of the radios in this case caused the loss.

Choice Five

Custom is a time-honored source of common law. In this case, it has been convincingly shown that a majority of tug owners do not customarily require radios. Since we cannot say that the customs of the sea require radios, we cannot conclude that the absence of a radio in this case caused the loss.

Choices four and five are improvements over earlier choices; they are better judicial choices because they do not shrink from judicial responsibility to make new law. They succeed where the other choices failed in that they create a clear rule to guide future conduct. But, of course, you should still feel unsatisfied, for custom appears to produce two contradictory results. How should you choose between them? Better to say:

Choice Six

Is it then a final answer that the business had not yet generally adopted receiving sets? There are, no doubt, cases where courts seem to make the general practice of the calling the standard of proper diligence. . . . Indeed, in most cases reasonable prudence is in fact common prudence; but strictly it is never its measure; a whole calling may have unduly lagged in the adoption of new and available devices. It may never set its own tests, however persuasive be its usages. Courts must in the end say what is required; there are precautions so imperative that even their universal disregard will not excuse their omission. . . . We hold the tugs . . . had they been properly

equipped . . . would have got the Arlington reports. The injury was a
direct consequence of this unseaworthiness.

The language of choice six speaks with a power and persuasiveness the
other choices lack because it is Judge Learned Hand's own, taken from
his opinion finally disposing of the case.[20] Hand's choice sets a clear standard, one that, anticipating the certain further growth of the radio industry, would occur sooner or later. Note, however, that with the exception
of choice four, any other choice could well have created a precedent that
would delay considerably any judicial decision requiring tugs to carry radios. These choices say that tugs don't need to carry radios. Judicial change
would require overruling any of these alternative decisions. In short, the
timid and deferential judge potentially creates a common law precedent
with just as much policy impact as does the assertive judge.

Above all, Hand's choice avoids the problem of lawmaking by default.
Judges can never know whether or when or how Congress will act on any
but dramatic national issues. Courts that wait for better legislative solutions
may wait for a solution that never comes.

Eighty years after the case of the radioless tugboat, the Supreme Court
considered another dispute arising from a shipping disaster, the wreck of
the *Exxon Valdez*, and like Judge Hand, the justices did not hesitate to take
the lawmaking initiative in their decision. The *Exxon Valdez* wreck poured
eleven billion gallons of crude oil into an otherwise pristine bay on the
Alaskan coast, an environmental catastrophe that destroyed wildlife in the
sea and on the beaches. The captain of the *Exxon Valdez* was found to
be legally intoxicated and not on the bridge during a particularly tricky
maneuver that led to the crash. A group of Native Americans, commercial
fishers, and landowners affected by the oil spill sued Exxon, claiming that
the company was responsible for the captain's conduct. A jury returned a
verdict of nearly $300 million in compensatory damages but also $5 billion
in punitive damages, later reduced by an appellate court to $2.5 billion.

Punitive damages are awarded to punish a defendant for particularly
egregious conduct and to deter the defendant and others from engaging in
that conduct. The jury's verdict—in particular the huge gap between the
compensatory and punitive award—raised a perennial problem with the
common law of damages: how should punitive damages be calculated, and
what counts as an "excessive" award? Because jurors have no knowledge

20. *The T. J. Hooper*, 740.

of damages in previous cases, juries can return widely varying punitive awards in similar cases.

The Court could have waited for Congress to weigh in on this issue, but Justice Souter's opinion noted that "courts have accepted primary responsibility for reviewing punitive damages and thus for their evolution, and if, in the absence of legislation, judicially derived standards leave the door open to outlier punitive-damages awards, it is hard to see how the judiciary can wash its hands of a problem it created." Rather than wait for Congress to address the issue, Souter's opinion explored possible rules for punitive damages, canvassing the policies of the fifty states and of other nations, as well as studies on the frequency and variability of punitive damages. Souter announced a new rule for punitive damages in maritime tort cases: punitive damage awards can be no higher than compensatory damages. He then reduced the punitive damage award from $2.5 billion to $507.5 million, the total amount of compensation paid by Exxon to the plaintiffs. Souter admitted that many other rules were possible, but he defended the Court's decision to create a limit on damages: "History certainly is no support for the notion that judges cannot use numbers," he concluded.[21] Like Judge Hand decades before, Justice Souter was confident of his ability to make law.

Horizontal Stare Decisis in Common Law

We now move to the other end of the spectrum, cases in which the judge confronts close precedents. How should judges respond to precedents that seem to state outdated or "bad" social policy but at the same time seem to completely cover and control the outcomes of cases before them? Lawyers label these precedents "precisely on point" or "on all fours with the case at bar." The existence of these precedents does not, however, contradict the concept that law remains ambiguous. Judges always choose the results. Some judges, faced with a precedent that produces an unwanted conclusion, will choose to ignore it, much to the anger of the losing lawyer. Other judges will overrule the precedent or pointedly refuse to follow it. Choices remain. In these circumstances, a judge's concerns about good social policy must be weighed against the purposes of stare decisis, which, as we have seen, are to promote legal stability, to protect honest reliance, to preserve efficient judicial administration, to maintain similar treatment of persons similarly situated, and to promote public confidence in courts. A judge

21. *Exxon Shipping v. Baker*, 554 U.S. 471 (2008).

must give weight to stare decisis only when adherence to a precedent accomplishes at least one of these goals.

Here are two sample cases, one in which stare decisis theory was used persuasively and one in which the court mindlessly botched the job.

RIGHTLY ADHERING TO PRECEDENT BECAUSE THE NEED FOR STABILITY AND RELIANCE IS PRESENT

The law of tort creates enticing moral questions because, particularly in the case of negligence, courts apply the law only when it has in fact failed to control how people behave. The negligent driver by definition does not plan to have or to avoid an accident by contemplating the law of negligence. As a result, negligence law does not generally confront a judge with the problem of upsetting someone's expectations if the judge changes the law. Negligence law defines when someone owes someone else a remedy for a past wrong, and this focus leads inevitably to the moral question of how we ought to relate to others, be they friends or strangers. As new cases arise, the moral questions they raise may lead judges to reexamine what had been settled law.

The need for stability seems much more vital in law that concerns people's business and contractual relations and the use and disposition of their property. Here we may not reach ultimate moral questions so quickly. When plans depend on law, the law's shortcomings may not justify changing it. We therefore temporarily abandon tort law and turn to one very small problem in a very complicated subject—the law of business contracts.

Contracts, among many other things, are agreements among businesspeople that allow them to formalize their buying and selling of each other's goods and services. Plans involving billions of dollars can rest on such agreements. A construction company specializing in high-rise office buildings may conditionally contract with a supplier of steel to buy steel at a given price in order to know what to bid on a construction project. If the construction company receives the award, its entire profit margin could disappear if its steel supplier at the last minute insisted on a higher price for the steel. But what legal rules convert an ordinary agreement (He: "Can you come to dinner at my place at 8:00?" She: "I'd love to! See you then.") into a legally binding contract? In early common law, if a written agreement contained the impression of a promise-making person's seal in wax, then the beneficiary of the promise could hold that person to his promise. Men wore signet rings etched with their sign (their seal) with which to impress the wax. An exception, for a time, was the king. He sealed the wax on his agreements with the impression of his front teeth. Gradually, the use of wax, seals, and front teeth declined, to the point that printing the word *seal* or the letters *L.S.* (for the Latin *locus sigilli*) created the contractual tie.

Contract law today does not require a wax seal to make the agreement binding. But in the past, in many jurisdictions when people sealed their contract (perhaps simply by adding at the end *Seal* or *L.S.*), the law made it very difficult for the contracting parties to dispute it. The law has rendered it nearly impossible to argue that the contract was made fraudulently or to prove that the promisor already performed the act he or she promised.

Long after agreements became enforceable in law without a seal, the law preserved some of the special rigidities for those contracts with seals. In one specific example, unlike an unsealed contract, only a person actually named in a sealed contract could be held liable for violating it ("breaching" it, in legal terminology). When, for example, a buyer sought to disguise his interest by having an agent write and sign the contract for him, the buyer along with the agent might find himself bound, but only if the contract of sale were to bear no seal. A sealed purchase contract, however, would bind only the agent named in it, not the buyer.

Businesspeople regularly transact business through agents. Sometimes, particularly in commercial real estate transactions, a businessperson will fund another to buy or sell property for him. The businessperson will fund the agent but insist that the agent assume all the responsibilities of the contract. The legal name for such a backer is "undisclosed principal." This technique of preserving anonymity is not necessarily unfair to the other side. If someone buys up various plots of land in an area in order to build a factory in the person's own name, the owners who are approached last may insist on a highly inflated price, knowing that if the buyer fails to get the last lot, all his other purchases will become meaningless.

Beginning in the nineteenth century, by both statute and judicial decision, the legal gap between the protections of sealed and unsealed contracts began to narrow. However, in the 1920s, this New York case arose: In a contract under seal, an agent agreed to buy land without naming an undisclosed principal. The seller agreed, but the agent shortly thereafter withdrew from the agreement. The seller, having learned the name of the principal, sued the principal. He asked the judge to order the principal to pay for the land and accept the deed.

The Court in this case, *Crowley v. Lewis*, ruled for the defendant.[22] It seems inequitable to allow the undisclosed principal to avoid keeping a promise just because of the arcane tradition of the seal, but Benjamin Car-

22. *Crowley v. Lewis*, 239 N.Y. 264 (1925).

dozo agreed with the outcome. Although he admitted that the seal system seemed an anachronism, he concluded that changing the rules about seals would be unfair:

> Men had taken title in the names of "dummies," and through them executed deeds and mortgages with the understanding, shared by the covenantees, that liability on the covenant would be confined to the apparent principal. They had done this honestly and without concealment.

Cardozo also noted that the seal arrangement had some advantages. Like the corporate form, the seal limited liability, thus facilitating business transactions. Cardozo concluded that "retrospective change would be unjust. The evil, if it was one, was to be eradicated by statute."[23] The rule may work to an unfair advantage, and it is the place of courts, not just legislatures, to minimize unfair advantages in law. However, the Court rightly left legal change to the legislature because it understood that many businesspeople, without acting unfairly, regularly employed that legal technique in planning their affairs. Judicial action would upset existing plans made by fair people, but the legislature would make law for the future. This difference, not a difference in lawmaking authority, gives the *Crowley* decision its wisdom.

The *Crowley* decision illustrates the potential unfairness of overturning a settled precedent. Every time a court makes new case law, it creates a winner and a loser in a case that happened under the older law. How can this retrospective lawmaking ever be fair and just? Judges can solve the stare decisis dilemma by asking whether it really makes sense to believe that the parties to the conflict planned their lives around the old law. In tort cases, for example, conflicts usually arise because of unplanned events, such as a car crash. In such circumstances, stare decisis dilemmas usually do not arise. But when the conflict involves a contract, breaking with precedent is much more troublesome. A primary point of any contract, after all, is to give those who make it a plan on which they can rely. Consider from this perspective a dilemma about contracts signed by elders with diminished mental capacity. At common law a contract signed by a minor cannot be enforced, but no such rule has ever applied to the elderly. Yet tests devised to assess the mental capacities of elders sometimes find that their abilities

23. Benjamin N. Cardozo, *The Paradoxes of Legal Science* (New York: Columbia University Press, 1928), 70–71.

fall in the same range as youngsters. Should courts stop enforcing contracts made by adults with diminished mental capacities—or would it be wiser to wait for legislatures to address this problem? The process of enacting new legislation, after all, would provide advance warning to seniors and their lawyers.[24]

WRONGLY ADHERING TO PRECEDENT
WHEN STABILITY IS UNNECESSARY

It would be a mistake to conclude that courts should always follow precedents in business, contract, and property matters but never in the case of negligence. It is not that simple. Tort law can, for example, influence both a person's decision to insure against loss and the rates insurance companies charge for such insurance. Precedents in tort, like precedents in contract, create expectations on which people rely. In this final illustration, however, let us look at a property problem in which a court failed to articulate a convincing reason for adhering to precedent.

The case, *Fox v. Snow*, involved New Jersey's laws of wills and of trusts, areas in which legal stability and reliance—two bedrock justifications for horizontal stare decisis—normally kick in. The decision of New Jersey's supreme court began by noting that in her will, the deceased, Rosa E. Green, stated: "I give and bequeath unto my husband, William L. Green, all of the money which I have on deposit at the Paterson Savings and Trust Company, Paterson, New Jersey, however, any money which is in the said account at the time of my said husband's death, the said sum shall be held by my niece, Catherine King Fox, absolutely and forever." William died without removing the money.

Naturally, Ms. Fox attempted to withdraw the money from the bank. However, heirs of William claimed that the conditional gift to Ms. Fox was invalid. Lawyers for the heirs cited many New Jersey precedents stating that an unconditional bequest in a will, like the one to William, gave him unconditional ownership. Any conditional gift of the same property would have to be invalid; otherwise, the first gift would not be absolute. William's heirs won. The Court said:

24. See Charles Duhigg, "Fine Line: Shielding Elders' Money, and Independence," *New York Times*, December 24, 2007. For a discussion of how American courts have increasingly refused to enforce contracts in which one party to the contract was clearly at a disadvantage, in knowledge and experience, relative to the other party, see Lief H. Carter, "Politics and the Law of Contracts," in *New Perspectives on American Law*, by Lief Carter, Austin Sarat, Mark Silverstein, and William Weaver (Durham, NC: Carolina Academic Press, 1997), 295–350.

Appellants ask this Court to explicitly and expressly overrule the
long established law of this state. This we decline to do. Such action
would be fraught with great danger in this type of case where titles
to property, held by bequests and devises, are involved. A change of
the established law by judicial decision is retrospective. It makes the
law at the time of prior decisions as it is declared in the last decision,
as to all transactions that can be reached by it. On the other hand a
change in the settled law by statute is prospective only.[25]

Think briefly about this result in terms of the reasons for stare decisis presented in chapter 2. For whom should this law remain stable? Who
could plan on the basis of this rule? Certainly not Rosa. She wanted to
make a conditional gift to Catherine but failed. William, if he wanted the
money, had only to withdraw it. Until the moment of his death (or legal
incapacitation), no one but William could make any plans based on what
might happen to "Catherine's" money. For William to have relied on New
Jersey precedents in this case, we must suppose reasoning such as this:
"I am going to die. I don't want the money, but I don't want Catherine to
obtain the money, either. I could prevent her from receiving it by depos-
iting it in another bank, but, since the clause is invalid, I'll leave it there."
Such planning is possible, but is it probable? Is it the sort of planning that
the law needs to preserve at the expense of carrying out the wishes of the
deceased? Many people do not know rules of law of this kind. Isn't it more
probable that William also intended the money to go to Catherine? Is it
plausible that, once William died leaving the money in the bank, Catherine
made plans on the assumption that she would get the money?

Consider the other purposes of stare decisis: Is the image of justice im-
proved by defeating Rosa's wishes? How important is equality of treatment
in this kind of situation? How important is it to say that because courts have
refused to carry out the wishes of past testators (creators of wills), they
must treat current testators in the same way for equality's sake?

Finally, efficiency in the judicial process does matter. Judges should not
have to question the wisdom of every point of law that arises, but that
hardly means they can never do so.

One judge disagreed with the majority in *Fox*. Chief Justice Vanderbilt's
dissent is one of the finest essays from the bench on stare decisis and more
generally on the nobility of the common law tradition. It provides a fitting
summary of this section:

25. *Fox v. Snow*, 6 N.J. 12 (1950), 14.

Vanderbilt, C. J. (dissenting)

I am constrained to dissent from the views of the majority of the court, first, because they apply to the case a technical rule of law to defeat the plain intent of the testatrix without serving any public policy whatever in so doing and, secondly—and this seems to me to be even more important—because their opinion involves a view of the judicial process, which, if it had been followed consistently in the past, would have checked irrevocably centuries ago the growth of the common law to meet changing conditions and which, if pursued now, will spell the ultimate ossification and death of the common law by depriving it of one of its most essential attributes—its inherent capacity constantly to renew its vitality and usefulness by adapting itself gradually and piecemeal to meeting the demonstrated needs of the times. . . .

By the words in the third paragraph, "any money which is in said account at the time of my said husband's death, the said sum shall be held by my niece, Catherine King Fox, absolutely and forever," the testatrix beyond any doubt intended that her husband could use up the bank account but that if he did not, the plaintiff should take what was left of it on his death. To hold otherwise is to proceed on the untenable assumption that the quoted words are meaningless and to ignore the elementary principle that the provisions of a will are not to be construed as meaningless except on the failure of every attempt to render them effective. . . . This principle is an integral part of the most fundamental rule of testamentary construction, *i.e.*, the duty of the court is to ascertain what the intent of the testator was and, then, having ascertained it, to give it effect. . . .

The opinion of the majority of the court, like every other decision in this State on the subject, makes no attempt to justify the rule it perpetuates either in reason or on grounds of public policy. Despite the deleterious effects of the rule and the lack of any sound principle to support it, the majority maintains that it should not be overthrown, because it has been the long established law of this State and because over-ruling it "would be fraught with great danger in this type of case where titles to property, held by bequests and devises, are involved" by reason of the retroactive effect of all judicial decisions. This view, if it had been consistently applied in the past, would have prevented any change whatever in property law by judicial decisions. . . . Every change in the law by judicial decision necessarily creates rights in one party to the litigation and imposes corresponding duties on the other party. This is the process by which the law grows and adjusts itself to the changing needs of the times.

The process is necessarily used not only to create new rights and corresponding duties but, where necessary, to strike down old ones. . . . "It is revolting," says Mr. Justice Holmes, "to have no better reason for a rule of law than that so it was laid down in the time of Henry IV. It is still more revolting if the grounds upon which it was laid down have vanished long since, and the rule simply persists from blind imitation of the past," and "To rest upon a formula is a slumber that, prolonged, means death." *Collected Legal Papers* (1920) 187, 306. . . .

To hold, as the majority opinion implies, that the only way to overcome the unfortunate rule of law that plagues us here is by legislation, is to put the common law in a self-imposed strait jacket. Such a theory, if followed consistently, would inevitably lead to the ultimate codification of all of our law for sheer lack of capacity in the courts to adapt the law to the needs of the living present. The doctrine of *stare decisis* neither renders the courts impotent to correct their past errors nor requires them to adhere blindly to rules that have lost their reason for being. The common law would be sapped of its life blood if *stare decisis* were to become a god instead of a guide. The doctrine when properly applied operates only to control change, not to prevent it. As Mr. Justice Cardozo has put it, "Few rules in our time are so well established that they may not be called upon any day to justify their existence as means adapted to an end. If they do not function they are diseased, . . . they must not propagate their kind. Sometimes they are cut out and extirpated altogether. Sometimes they are left with the shadow of continued life, but sterilized, truncated, impotent for harm." *Nature of the Judicial Process* (1921) 98. All lawyers as well as laymen have a perfectly natural longing to think of the law as being as steadfast and immutable as the everlasting hills, but when we face the realities, we must agree with Dean Pound when he says, "Law must be stable, and yet it cannot stand still," *Interpretations of Legal History* (1923) . . . , and with Professor Williston when he tells us, "Uniform decisions of 300 years on a particular question may, and sometimes have been overthrown in a day, and the single decision at the end of the series may establish a rule of law at variance with all that has gone before." *Some Modern Tendencies in the Law* (1929) 125. . . .

The dangers that the majority fear, it is submitted, are more apparent than real. The doctrine of *stare decisis* tends to produce certainty in our law, but it is important to realize that certainty *per se* is but a means to an end, and not an end in itself. Certainty is desirable only insofar as it operates to produce the maximum good and the minimum harm and thereby to advance justice. The courts have been reluctant to overthrow established rules when property rights are involved for the simple reason that persons in arranging their affairs have relied upon the rules as established, though outmoded or erroneous, and so to abandon them would result sometimes in greater harm than to observe them. The question whether the doctrine of *stare decisis* should be adhered to in such cases is always a choice between relative evils. When it appears that the evil resulting from a continuation of the accepted rule must be productive of greater mischief to the community than can possibly ensue from disregarding the previous adjudications on the subject, courts have frequently and wisely departed from precedent, 14 Am. Jur., Courts, Section 126.

What then, are the relative evils in the instant case? First, we should consider the evils that will result from a perpetuation of the rule here involved. It has already been demonstrated that the rule, in each and every instance in which it is applied, results in a complete frustration of the legitimate intention of the testator. It can only operate to take property from one to whom the testator intended to give it and to bestow it upon another. . . .

Having considered the evils flowing from continuing to follow the rule, let us now inquire into the evils, if any, which might result from its rejection. It is pertinent at this point to recall the words of Mr. Justice Cardozo minimizing the effect of overruling a decision: "The picture of the bewildered litigant lured into a course of action by the false light of a decision, only to meet ruin when the light is extinguished and the decision is overruled, is for the most part a figment of excited brains." *The Nature of the Judicial Process* (1921) 122.[26] The rule in question by its very nature is never relied upon by those who are seeking to make a testamentary disposition of their property, for if the rule were known to a person at the time of the drawing of his will, its operation would and could be guarded against by the choice of words appropriate to accomplish the result desired. This rule is truly subversive of the testator's intent. It is relied upon only after

26. [Judge Vanderbilt's wonderful opinion unfortunately miscited this quotation. It is from Benjamin N. Cardozo, *The Growth of the Law* (New Haven, CT: Yale University Press, 1924), 122.]

the testator's decease by those who seek, solely on the basis of its technical and arbitrary requirements, to profit from the testator's ignorance and to take his property contrary to his expressed desires. Certainly it is not unjust or inequitable to deny such persons resort to this rule. . . .[27]

The Common Law Tradition Today

Chief Justice Vanderbilt's dissent in *Fox* describes the essence of the common law tradition. Judicial choices continue to change common law today. Indeed, only within the past century have judges comes to recognize fully the inevitability and desirability of choice and change. Thus, the political consequences of choice and change have come sharply into focus.

Common law has in the past changed even when judges believed they merely chose the one applicable statute or line of precedents that "correctly" resolved the conflict before them. When judges think they solve problems by mechanically finding the one right solution from the past, the law develops in an almost thoughtless way. Judges do not grapple with moral and economic aspects of policy choices when they do not believe they choose policies. But when the point of view shifts, when judges begin believing they do make policy choices, this consciousness changes the kind and quality of law that judges make in several ways.

The first of these changes we have already studied and condemned. It occurs when judges throw up their hands and say, "In a democracy, only the legislature can make new law, not the courts. We must, therefore, deliberately avoid making changes." These decisions, in spite of themselves, do make changes, of course—just as the *Fox* decision, by rejecting Vanderbilt's powerful arguments, more deeply embedded both a mechanical view of stare decisis and the rule against conditional gifts into New Jersey's law.

A second modern view of the consequences of acknowledged judicial discretion can avoid this evil. Judges, acknowledging that they can and do make law, pay closer attention, as we are about to see, to the facts and values that help them (and us) decide that some policy choices are wiser than others. Modern decisions do tend to be less mechanistic and more concerned with the consequences for the future of various alternative choices of policy. This quality, after all, gave the *Lyman* and *Hynes* cases their modern flavor.

There is, however, a third consequence of this shift in viewpoint. Judges

27. Ibid., 14–15, 21–27.

may dramatically increase the speed of change and deliberately broaden the lengths of the legal jumps they take from old law to new. When judges realize that they rightly possess authority to remake common law, they may overreact and enact what they believe are ideal legal solutions without properly honoring competing needs for stability. Similarly, they may ignore the possibility that, while both courts and legislatures share authority to make law, they do not necessarily possess identical institutional characteristics for making wise law.

Some critics argue that this is just what has happened in tort law. Proponents of "tort reform" argue that judges have abused their common law powers by adopting doctrines that allow too many plaintiffs in personal injury lawsuits to collect too much money. The media have responded to the tort reformers' claims sympathetically by publicizing bizarre or particularly controversial tort lawsuits, such as the claim that McDonald's is legally liable for making its patrons obese. Tort reformers have successfully lobbied legislatures to reverse judge-made changes in tort policy and to limit the gains of personal injury lawsuits by, for example, capping the amount of damages a plaintiff can win. (Pro-plaintiff groups, meanwhile, have gone to court to argue that such legislation unconstitutionally interferes with the power of judges in common law cases.) Tort law has thus become a battleground not just in the courts but also in legislatures and popular culture.[28]

The rise of the tort reform movement demonstrates that judicial policy making can become the object of great controversy. The potential problems posed by judicial policy making are so central to reasoning in constitutional law that a thorough canvass of the "judicial limits" territory must be postponed until chapter 5, which deals with reasoning in constitutional interpretation. But as the example of tort reform reminds us, these same concerns are present in common law as well.

In this perspective, consider the next case. It illustrates deliberate lawmaking. It exemplifies a dramatic expansion of common law, and it faces squarely the double problem of determining whether a given policy is wise and whether the courts were the wise place to make it. The case, *Tarasoff v. Regents of the University of California*, represented a substantial jump forward in the law of negligence and duty.[29]

Tatiana Tarasoff spent the summer of 1969 in Brazil. She had, with her

28. Thomas F. Burke, *Lawyers, Lawsuits and Legal Rights: The Struggle over Litigation in American Politics* (Berkeley: University of California Press, 2002); William Haltom and Michael McCann, *Distorting the Law: Politics, Media and the Litigation Crisis* (Chicago: University of Chicago Press, 2004).

29. *Tarasoff v. Regents of the University of California*, 551 P.2d 334 (1976).

parents' consent and assistance, left her home in California, in part to escape the fanatical affections of one Prosenjit Poddar. During her absence, Poddar kept his contact alive. He persuaded Tatiana's brother to share an apartment with him near Tatiana's home in Berkeley, California.

Tatiana returned from Brazil in October. On October 27, 1969, Poddar killed her.

In due course, Tatiana's parents learned that Poddar had, during the summer, received psychological therapy on an outpatient basis from Cowell Memorial Hospital at the University of California, Berkeley. Their further investigation uncovered these facts:

- On August 20, 1969, Poddar told his therapist, Dr. Moore, that he planned to kill Tatiana when she returned from Brazil.
- When Poddar left, Dr. Moore felt Poddar should be committed for psychiatric examination in a mental hospital. He urgently consulted two of his colleagues at Cowell. They concurred.
- Moore then told two campus police officers that he would request the commitment of Poddar. He followed up with a letter of request to the campus police chief.
- Three officers, in fact, took Poddar into custody. Poddar promised them he would leave Tatiana alone in the future. The officers believed Poddar was rational and released him.
- After, and presumably in part because, the officers released Poddar, Dr. Moore's supervisor, Dr. Powelson, asked the police to return Moore's letter. Dr. Powelson also ordered destroyed all copies of the letter and of the notes Dr. Moore had taken. Dr. Powelson prohibited any further action to commit Poddar for examination or observation.
- At no point did any members of the hospital staff or the campus police attempt to notify Tatiana, her brother, or her parents of Poddar's threat.
- The staff could easily have determined Tatiana's identity as well as her location and that of her family.

The Tarasoffs sued the doctors, the officers, and the university's board of regents, claiming damages for the loss of their daughter. Among other charges, they alleged that "defendants negligently permitted Poddar to be released from police custody without 'notifying the parents of Tatiana Tarasoff that their daughter was in grave danger from Prosenjit Poddar.'"[30]

30. Ibid., 341.

They claimed, in other words, that the defendants had a duty to use reasonable care to protect Tatiana.

The California Supreme Court upheld the legality of this claim but only against the regents and the doctors. Reasoning by example played a major part in its result. The Court cited precedents from California and elsewhere holding a doctor liable for the damage caused by illness contracted by people in contact with his patient if the doctor negligently failed to diagnose the disease as contagious and to isolate the patient. It also cited a case holding a doctor liable for damages when, following his negligent refusal to admit a mental patient to a hospital, the mental patient assaulted the plaintiff.

The directly relevant case law in California, however, imposed a duty only where the defendant already assumed some responsibility for the victim. If, for example, a mental hospital failed negligently to protect one patient from another's violence, the hospital became liable. In California, no law extended the duty further.

Using fact freedom, however, the Court ignored the distinction. It said, "[W]e do not think that the duty should logically be constricted to such situations."[31] Let us review the majority's reasons for the conclusion.

The majority first stated a general framework for determining the existence or absence of a duty, a statement amply supported by recent California precedents. Note above all how different this statement is from earlier mechanical statements such as "duty owed to invitees but no duty owed to trespassers or licensees." The Court, quoting precedents, said the existence of a duty depends

> only upon the "balancing of a number of considerations"; major ones "are the foreseeability of harm to the plaintiff, the degree of certainty that the plaintiff suffered injury, the closeness of the connection between the defendant's conduct and the injury suffered, the moral blame attached to the defendant's conduct, the policy of preventing future harm, the extent of the burden to the defendant and consequences to the community of imposing a duty to exercise care with resulting liability for breach, and the availability, cost and prevalence of insurance for the risk involved."

The most important of these considerations in establishing duty is foreseeability. As a general principle, a "defendant owes a duty of care to all persons who are foreseeably endangered by his conduct,

---

31. Ibid., 344.

with respect to all risks which make the conduct unreasonably dangerous."[32]

Having said this much, the majority then noted that at common law, a duty to warn of foreseeable harm done by a dangerous person existed only when the defendant had a "special relationship" with either the source of danger or the potential victim. The Court admitted that the doctors had no special relationship to Tatiana, but it asserted that because they did have such a relationship to Poddar, they therefore owed Tatiana a duty of care.

The Court cited no convincing precedent or other authority for this expansion of law, but that did not seem to bother it. The Court did pay attention to the arguments sustaining and attacking the practical wisdom and effect of the new policy.

The Court had to deal first with the possibility that the harm was not foreseeable in the first place. The issue was made even more difficult because only a few years earlier, the Court had based an important mental health ruling on the fact that psychological and psychiatric predictions of future behavior are notoriously inaccurate.[33] To this the Court responded:

> The role of the psychiatrist, who is indeed a practitioner of medicine, and that of the psychologist who performs an allied function, are like that of the physician who must conform to the standards of the profession and who must often make diagnoses and predictions based upon such evaluations. Thus the judgment of the therapist in diagnosing emotional disorders and in predicting whether a patient presents a serious danger of violence is comparable to the judgment which doctors and professionals must regularly render under accepted rules of responsibility.
>
> We recognize the difficulty that a therapist encounters in attempting to forecast whether a patient presents a serious danger of violence. Obviously we do not require that the therapist, in making that determination, render a perfect performance; the therapist need only exercise "that reasonable degree of skill, knowledge, and care ordinarily possessed and exercised by members of [that profes-

32. Ibid., 342.

33. In this particular case, *People v. Burnick*, 14 Cal. 3d 306 (1975), the court held that a person could be committed to an institution for mentally disturbed sex offenders only after proof at trial beyond reasonable doubt that the defendant was, in fact, likely to repeat the offense.

sional specialty] under similar circumstances." (*Bardessono v. Michels* (1970) 3 Cal.3d 780, 788 . . .) Within the broad range of reasonable practice and treatment in which professional opinion and judgment may differ, the therapist is free to exercise his or her own best judgment without liability; proof, aided by hindsight, that he or she judged wrongly is insufficient to establish negligence.

In the instant case, however, the pleadings do not raise any question as to failure of defendant therapists to predict that Poddar presented a serious danger of violence. On the contrary, the present complaints allege that defendant therapists did in fact predict that Poddar would kill, but were negligent in failing to warn.[34]

The Court then turned to the most complex policy issue of all: will imposition of the duty to warn discourage patients from seeking the psychiatric help they need, thus not only preventing their own improvement but also perhaps increasing the actual incidence of violent harm to others because people don't get help? The Court insisted that such a prediction is entirely speculative. It noted that both the California code of evidence and the Principles of Medical Ethics of the American Medical Association permit a doctor to reveal information about a dangerous person if doing so could protect the patient, other individuals, or the community. The Court concluded that

the public policy favoring protection of the confidential character of patient-psychotherapist communications must yield to the extent to which disclosure is essential to avert danger to others. The protective privilege ends where the public peril begins.

Our current crowded and computerized society compels the interdependence of its members. In this risk-infested society we can hardly tolerate the further exposure to danger that would result from a concealed knowledge of the therapist that his patient was lethal. If the exercise of reasonable care to protect the threatened victim requires the therapist to warn the endangered party or those who can reasonably be expected to notify him, we see no sufficient societal interest that would protect and justify concealment. The containment of such risks lies in the public interest.[35]

34. *Tarasoff v. Regents*, 345.
35. Ibid., 347–348.

The *Tarasoff* case, like the *Hynes* case, took the common law of duty in negligence cases a large step forward. True to its nature, though, the common law did much backing and filling after *Tarasoff*; indeed, the false starts, contradictions, and inconsistencies generated in the 1970s began ironing themselves out only in the 1990s.

For example, in *Thompson v. County of Alameda*,[36] the California Supreme Court reaffirmed *Tarasoff*'s holding that one has a duty to warn only specific victims who were actually identified or were easily identifiable, as was Tatiana herself. However, the facts were different. A juvenile offender in detention told a parole officer that if he were released on furlough he would murder a child he chose at random. He was in fact released, and he did just as he predicted, but the family of the victim child lost because no specific or identifiable victim was named. Similarly in 1984, a federal appellate court affirmed that the therapist of John Hinckley Jr., who attempted to assassinate President Reagan, was not liable for the injuries that James Brady and others suffered in the attempt, because Hinckley had identified no specific or identifiable victim.[37]

The difficulty, as you may already have noted, is that such rulings contradicted California common law as it existed before *Tarasoff*. Recall that California law previously held physicians liable for the damage done by contagious patients who spread disease because they were misdiagnosed. The third-party victims in such cases were not specifically identifiable beforehand. The reality is that in some cases, we cannot reasonably expect doctors to prevent harm to a victim unless they can identify a specific victim, but in other cases we can. As the Wisconsin Supreme Court put it:

> [I]f a patient announces an intention to, for example, leave the psychotherapist's office and commit random acts of violence, the psychotherapist would be unable to warn victims of potential danger. . . . Nevertheless, notwithstanding the absence of a readily identifiable victim, warnings could, in certain instances, effectively be made to, perhaps, the patient's family or police. . . . Society must not become the victim of a dangerous patient's ambiguity.[38]

Over time new and unanticipated problems will inevitably arise, and reasoning by example will apply such precedents in new and not entirely

36. *Thompson v. County of Alameda*, 614 P.2d 728 (1980).
37. And see *DeShaney v. Winnebago County Department of Social Services*, 489 U.S. 189 (1989).
38. *Schuster v. Altenberg*, 424 N.W.2d 159 (Wis. 1988), 172–173.

predictable ways. For example, many years after *Tarasoff*, the duty to warn became an issue for doctors treating people with HIV/AIDS. Consider the case of a family practitioner who treats a husband and wife and discovers that one of the two is HIV-positive. Does she have a duty to warn the other, who is also her patient? Does any physician treating any married patient have an obligation to warn a spouse, even when the spouse is *not* her patient? Courts in many states, strongly influenced by *Tarasoff*, have ruled that doctors and other health-care workers do have such duties to third parties.[39] Indeed, *Tarasoff* has helped create an entire field of law regarding the health-care worker's duty to warn.

We conclude by returning to the underlying process by which Anglo-American common law first developed, a process akin to the way the rules of soccer also emerged during roughly the same period in England. There is intriguing evidence that something similar is currently emerging in the processes through which international trade disputes are settled by international arbitration commissions. When multinational corporations find themselves at odds over the interpretation of their often-complex business contracts, they run headlong into the tediously long and needlessly costly task of deciding which nation's contract law should govern. Indeed, such contracts are literally "supernational." In the absence of any global government with the power to set contract rules, the lawyers who practice before these commissions have found themselves much like those early soccer players or advocates before the courts of the early English kings, developing a kind of common law governing international business. They generate their own sets of private rules based on nothing more than their experiences playing the "game" of international arbitration, rules developed to resolve these disputes as quickly and efficiently as possible. In the twenty-first century the practices of international trade dispute settlement are just now being incorporated into handbooks and casebooks to guide future practitioners.[40]

---

39. Many state legislatures, in response to these court decisions, have in turn created statutes specifying the duties and privileges of health-care workers who treat HIV-positive patients. For a review of these developments, see Lawrence O. Gostin and James G. Hodge Jr., "Piercing the Veil of Secrecy in HIV/AIDS and Other Sexually Transmitted Diseases: Theories of Privacy and Disclosure in Partner Notification," *Duke Journal of Gender Law & Policy* 5 (1999): 9–88.

40. We thank Martin Shapiro for suggesting this example to us. For a fascinating study of the origins of this new legal field, see Yves Dezelay and Bryant G. Garth, *Dealing in Virtue: International Commercial Arbitration and the Construction of a Transnational Legal Order* (Chicago: University of Chicago Press, 1996).

ILLUSTRATIVE CASE

Like *Tarasoff*, the following case went to a court of appeals on a question of law before any trial had occurred to assess the facts of the case. Thus, this court's holding does not mean that defendant O'Daniels is necessarily liable to the plaintiff for damages. In a telephone conversation with Judge Andreen in July 1983, Lief Carter learned that the defendants had chosen not to appeal this ruling to the California Supreme Court. It is not clear how the dispute was resolved; the parties may have settled rather than going to trial.

Soldano v. O'Daniels
California Court of Appeals, Fifth District
190 Cal. Rptr. 310 (1983)

ANDREEN, ASSOCIATE JUSTICE

Does a business establishment incur liability for wrongful death if it denies use of its telephone to a good samaritan who explains an emergency situation occurring without and wishes to call the police? . . .

Both briefs on appeal adopt the defense averments:

"This action arises out of a shooting death occurring on August 9, 1977. Plaintiff's father [Darrell Soldano] was shot and killed by one Rudolph Villanueva on that date at defendant's Happy Jack's Saloon. This defendant owns and operates the Circle Inn which is an eating establishment located across the street from Happy Jack's. Plaintiff's second cause of action against this defendant is one for negligence.

"Plaintiff alleges that on the date of the shooting, a patron of Happy Jack's Saloon came into the Circle Inn and informed a Circle Inn employee that a man had been threatened at Happy Jack's. He requested the employee either call the police or allow him to use the Circle Inn phone to call the police. That employee allegedly refused to call the police and allegedly refused to allow the patron to use the phone to make his own call. Plaintiff alleges that the actions of the Circle Inn employee were a breach of the legal duty that the Circle Inn owed to the decedent." . . .

There is a distinction, well rooted in the common law, between action and nonaction. It has found its way into the prestigious Restatement Second of Torts (hereafter cited as Restatement), which provides in section 314: "The fact that the actor realizes or should realize that action on his part is necessary for another's aid or protection does not of itself impose upon him a duty

to take such action." . . . The distinction between malfeasance and nonfeasance, between active misconduct working positive injury and failure to act to
prevent mischief not brought on by the defendant, is founded on "that attitude
of extreme individualism so typical of anglo-saxon legal thought." [Bohlen,
The Moral Duty to Aid Others as a Basis of Tort Liability, pt. I, (1908) 56 *U. Pa.
L. Rev.* 217, 219–220.] . . .

The refusal of the law to recognize the moral obligation of one to aid another when he is in peril and when such aid may be given without danger
and at little cost in effort has been roundly criticized. Prosser describes the
case law sanctioning such inaction as a "refus[al] to recognize the moral
obligation of common decency and common humanity" and characterizes
some of these decisions as "shocking in the extreme. . . . Such decisions are
revolting to any moral sense. They have been denounced with vigor by legal
writers." [Prosser, *Law of Torts* (4th ed. 1971) § 56, pp. 340–341.] A similar rule
has been termed "morally questionable" by our Supreme Court. [*Tarasoff v.
Regents of University of California* (1976).]

Francis H. Bohlen, in his article "The Moral Duty to Aid Others as a Basis
of Tort Liability," commented:

> Nor does it follow that because the law has not as yet recognized the duty
> to repair harm innocently wrought, that it will continue indefinitely to re-
> fuse it recognition. While it is true that the common law does not attempt
> to enforce all moral, ethical, or humanitarian duties, it is, it is submitted,
> equally true that all ethical and moral conceptions, which are not the
> mere temporary manifestations of a passing wave of sentimentalism or
> puritanism, but on the contrary, find a real and permanent place in the
> settled convictions of a race and become part of the normal habit of
> thought thereof, of necessity do in time color the judicial conception of
> legal obligation. . . . [Bohlen, 56 *U. Pa. L. Rev.* 316, 334–337.]

As noted in *Tarasoff v. Regents of University of California, supra*, the courts
have increased the instances in which affirmative duties are imposed not by
direct rejection of the common law rule, but by expanding the list of special
relationships which will justify departure from that rule. . . .

Here there was no special relationship between the defendant and the
deceased. It would be stretching the concept beyond recognition to assert
there was a relationship between the defendant and the patron from Happy
Jack's Saloon who wished to summon aid. But this does not end the matter.

It is time to reexamine the common law rule of nonliability for nonfeasance in the special circumstances of the instant case. . . .

The Legislature has recognized the importance of the telephone system in reporting crime and in summoning emergency aid. Penal Code section 384 makes it a misdemeanor to refuse to relinquish a party line when informed that it is needed to call a police department or obtain other specified emergency services. This requirement, which the Legislature has mandated to be printed in virtually every telephone book in this state, may have wider printed distribution in this state than even the Ten Commandments. It creates an affirmative duty to do something—to clear the line for another user of the party line—in certain circumstances.

In 1972 the Legislature enacted the Warren-911-Emergency Assistance Act. This act expressly recognizes the importance of the telephone system in procuring emergency aid. . . .

The above statutes are cited without the suggestion that the defendant violated a statute which would result in a presumption of a failure to use due care under Evidence Code section 669. Instead, they, and the quotations from the prestigious national commissions, demonstrate that "that attitude of extreme individualism so typical of anglo-saxon legal thought" may need limited reexamination in the light of current societal conditions and the facts of this case to determine whether the defendant owed a duty to the deceased to permit the use of the telephone.

We turn now to the concept of duty in a tort case. The Supreme Court has identified certain factors to be considered in determining whether a duty is owed to third persons. These factors include:

> the foreseeability of harm to the plaintiff, the degree of certainty that the plaintiff suffered injury, the closeness of the connection between the defendant's conduct and the injury suffered, the moral blame attached to the defendant's conduct, the policy of preventing future harm, the extent of the burden to the defendant and consequences to the community of imposing a duty to exercise care with resulting liability for breach, and the availability, cost, and prevalence of insurance for the risk involved. (*Rowland v. Christian*, 1968, 443 P.2d 561.)

We examine those factors in reference to this case. (1) The harm to the decedent was abundantly foreseeable; it was imminent. The employee was expressly told that a man had been threatened. The employee was a bartender. As such he knew it is foreseeable that some people who drink alcohol in the milieu of a bar setting are prone to violence. (2) The certainty of decedent's injury is undisputed. (3) There is arguably a close connection between the employee's conduct and the injury: the patron wanted to use the phone to summon the police to intervene. The employee's refusal to allow the use of the phone prevented this anticipated intervention. If permitted to go to trial, the plaintiff may be able to show that the probable response time of the police would have been shorter than the time between the prohibited telephone call and the fatal shot. (4) The employee's conduct displayed a disregard for human life that can be characterized as morally wrong: he was callously indifferent to the possibility that Darrell Soldano would die as the result of his refusal to allow a person to use the telephone. Under the circumstances before us the bartender's burden was minimal and exposed him to no risk: all he had to do was allow the use of the telephone. It would have cost him or his employer nothing. It could have saved a life. (5) Finding a duty in these circumstances would promote a policy of preventing future harm. A citizen would not be required to summon the police but would be required, in circumstances such as those before us, not to impede another who has chosen to summon aid. (6) We have no information on the question of the availability, cost, and prevalence of insurance for the risk, but note that the liability which is sought to be imposed here is that of employee negligence, which is covered by many insurance policies. (7) The extent of the burden on the defendant was minimal, as noted.

The consequences to the community of imposing a duty, the remaining factor mentioned in *Rowland v. Christian, supra,* is termed "the administrative [141 Cal. App. 3d 452] factor" by Professor Green in his analysis of determining whether a duty exists in a given case. (Green, The Duty Problem in Negligence Cases, I (1929) 28 *Colum. L. Rev.* 1014, 1035–1045. . . .) The administrative factor is simply the pragmatic concern of fashioning a workable rule and the impact of such a rule on the judicial machinery. It is the policy of major concern in this case.

As the Supreme Court has noted, the reluctance of the law to impose liability for nonfeasance, as distinguished from misfeasance, is in part due to the difficulties in setting standards and of making rules workable. (*Tarasoff v. Regents of University of California, supra* . . . .)

Many citizens simply "don't want to get involved." No rule should be adopted which would require a citizen to open up his or her house to a stranger so that the latter may use the telephone to call for emergency assistance. As Mrs. Alexander in Anthony Burgess' *A Clockwork Orange* learned to her horror, such an action may be fraught with danger. It does not follow, however, that use of a telephone in a public portion of a business should be refused for a legitimate emergency call. Imposing liability for such a refusal would not subject innocent citizens to possible attack by the "good samaritan," for it would be limited to an establishment open to the public during times when it is open to business, and to places within the establishment ordinarily accessible to the public. Nor would a stranger's mere assertion that an "emergency" situation is occurring create the duty to utilize an accessible telephone because the duty would arise if and only if it were clearly conveyed that there exists an imminent danger of physical harm. . . .

We acknowledge that defendant contracted for the use of his telephone, and its use is a species of property. But if it exists in a public place as defined above, there is no privacy or ownership interest in it such that the owner should be permitted to interfere with a good faith attempt to use it by a third person to come to the aid of another. . . .

We conclude that the bartender owed a duty to the plaintiff's decedent to permit the patron from Happy Jack's to place a call to the police or to place the call himself.

It bears emphasizing that the duty in this case does not require that one must go to the aid of another. That is not the issue here. The employee was not the good samaritan intent on aiding another. The patron was. . . .

The creative and regenerative power of the law has been strong enough to break chains imposed by outmoded former decisions. What the courts have power to create, they also have power to modify, reject and re-create in response to the needs of a dynamic society. The exercise of this power is an imperative function of the courts and is the strength of the common law. It cannot be surrendered to legislative inaction. Prosser puts it this way:

> New and nameless torts are being recognized constantly, and the progress of the common law is marked by many cases of first impression, in which the court has struck out boldly to create a new cause of action, where none had been recognized before. . . . The law of torts is anything but static, and the limits of its development are never set. When it becomes clear that the plaintiff's interests are entitled to legal protection against the conduct of the defendant, the mere fact that the claim is novel will not of itself operate as a bar to the remedy.

The possible imposition of liability on the defendant in this case is not a global change in the law. It is but a slight departure from the "morally questionable" rule of nonliability for inaction absent a special relationship. . . . It is a logical extension of Restatement section 327 which imposes liability for negligent interference with a third person who the defendant knows is attempting to render necessary aid. However small it may be, it is a step which should be taken.

We conclude there are sufficient justiciable issues to permit the case to go to trial and therefore reverse.

FRANSON, ACTING P.J., AND STANTON, J., CONCUR.

QUESTIONS ABOUT THE CASE

---

1. Judge Andreen explicitly disregards a common law rule of long standing. Do you agree that the old rule was "bad law"? (Remember that for the doctrine of stare decisis to come into play, a judge presumably believes that the old rule states unwise public policy, at least when applied to facts like Soldano's. Do the principles of stare decisis, then, permit ignoring the line of precedents in this case? Why or why not?)

2. Judge Andreen cites *Tarasoff*. Is that case really a precedent for the holding in this case? In what sense?

3. Is this case really only a "slight departure" from prior law? Why or why not?

4. Judge Andreen sent Lief Carter copies of the briefs in this case. The bulk of Judge Andreen's reasoning appears nowhere in either brief. That is, despite the adversary system, this judge felt no hesitation to go beyond the parties' arguments to decide according to the reasons he and his unanimous court felt best. Is this a violation of the basic spirit of the adversary system?

CHAPTER 4

Statutory Interpretation

Whoever hath an absolute authority to interpret any written or spoken laws, it is he who is truly the Law-giver to all intents and purposes, and not the person who first spoke or wrote them.

—BENJAMIN HOADLY

It is of course dangerous that judges be philosophers—almost as dangerous as if they were not.

—PAUL FREUND

Text without context often invites confusion and judicial adventurism.

—ORRIN HATCH

The Problem with Statutes

Previous chapters have described the struggle over the constitutionality of the Patient Protection and Affordable Care Act (ACA), also known as Obamacare. The resolution of this issue in *National Federation of Independent Business v. Sebelius* (2012) did not, however, end the legal conflict over the ACA; a second struggle developed, this one a dispute over the meaning of the law itself.

The dispute was complex and consequential. A provision in Obamacare empowers states to create a health-care insurance exchange, an online marketplace for health insurance, but many states chose not to do this. Under Obamacare the federal government was required to create an exchange in their place, and so the federal government ended up operating the system in a majority of states. Critics of Obamacare contended that this had implications for another provision in the law, one that provides subsidies to individuals and families to enable them to buy health insurance. The subsidies, that provision says, are to be given to individuals and families who bought insurance from exchanges "established by the State." The Internal Revenue Service (IRS), which administers the subsidies, interpreted this as applying to all the exchanges, reasoning that it would have been nonsensical for Congress to discriminate against people who happened to live in states that had failed to create an exchange. Obamacare opponents, however, contended that the IRS's position ignored the words of the statute, which they argued granted subsidies only for exchanges created by states, not for the ones "established" by the federal government.

The opponents challenged the IRS's position in federal courts across the nation, and that challenge eventually reached the Supreme Court in *King v. Burwell*. At stake were the subsidies of millions of individuals seeking health insurance, many of whom would be unable to afford coverage without help. But the implications swept even further: if all those people were unable to buy health insurance, they would be unable to pay for health care when they needed it. The results might destabilize the entire Obamacare reform. So the question was left to the Supreme Court: Did Congress, by specifying that the subsidies were for exchanges "established by the State," deny them in the federal exchanges? Or should the IRS's interpretation of the law, which had concluded that this interpretation made no sense, prevail?

As *King* demonstrates, the choices judges make about how to interpret statutes can have profound consequences. Statutes are the muscles of the body politic. In political systems that honor the rule of law, statutes empower the government to take our property, our freedom, and even our lives. Political campaigns and elections—indeed, much in public life that does excite us—matter because they directly influence the making of statutes. And it is in cases of statutory interpretation that judges decide what exactly those statutes do.

When judges interpret statutes, they encounter issues that differ significantly from those we discussed in the previous chapter. As chapter 3 demonstrated, common law judges are, whether or not they think of themselves this way, policy makers. They often resolve controversies in which no legislature has gone before, for example, whether therapists owe a duty to warn to potential victims of their patients or whether tugboats should be required to carry AM radios. In the twentieth century, judges in common law cases became more explicit and self-conscious about their policy-making role, and their choices have occasionally created a legislative backlash, as we saw in the case of tort reform. Judges in common law cases, then, must wrestle with the proper balance of legislative and judicial lawmaking, but they do so knowing they are empowered to decide for themselves how to resolve public policy issues.

In statutory disputes the proper balance between legislative and judicial power is necessarily quite different. Judges who interpret statutes must remember that even in common law systems such as the United States, legislatures are the primary lawmakers, so when legislatures try to correct a problem by writing a statute, they are supreme. Hence, in matters of statutory interpretation, judges must follow the legislature's policy, not their own, to resolve the case.

The history of statutory interpretation from the twentieth century on has been a series of attempts to respect the supremacy of legislative policy making by devising some technique for keeping judges within their proper bounds. The practice of statutory interpretation has been haunted by the fear that judges will, in deciding disputes over what statutes mean, substitute their own policy views for those of democratically elected legislators.[1] Chapter 5 on constitutional law assesses more carefully the claim that judicial policy making violates fundamental principles of democracy. For now, the important point is that concerns about judicial policy making have led legal theorists, and judges themselves, to try to find ways to limit the role of courts in interpreting statutes. In particular, judges and legal theorists have adopted several approaches to statutory interpretation aimed at neatly separating policy making and judging.[2]

In this chapter we argue that these approaches are misguided. Each of them involves an attempt to constrain judges by giving them a formula that ensures they do exactly what the law commands. But as you should see by now, law does not work that way. Legal disputes usually come to court when the law is uncertain, so that two parties have opposing interpretations of the law. No formula of interpretation can magically dissolve the ambiguities inherent in law. And statutory law, like common law, has many sources of uncertainty.

---

1. See William Popkin, *Statutes in Court: The History and Theory of Statutory Interpretation* (Durham, NC: Duke University Press, 1999).

2. Among the many recent studies of statutory interpretation that explore this problem, see Robert Katzmann, *Judging Statutes* (New York: Oxford University Press 2014); Antonin Scalia and Bryan A. Garner, *Reading Law: The Interpretation of Legal Texts* (St. Paul, MN: Thomson/West Publishing, 2012); Ken Greenawalt, *Statutory and Common Law Interpretation* (New York: Oxford University Press, 2013); Lawrence Solan, *The Language of Statutes: Laws and Their Interpretation* (Chicago: University of Chicago Press, 2010); and John Manning, "What Divides Textualists from Purposivists?" *Columbia Law Review* 106 (2006): 70–111.

First, statutes are written in words, and as we have already seen, the words of everyday life and of law are often slippery and ambiguous. Judges who arm themselves with dictionaries and expect to find a single, unproblematic interpretation of a statute expect too much of language—and too little of themselves.

Second, the process by which legislatures make statutes is complex and multilayered. Attempts to isolate particular moments from the legislative process and glean from them a single correct answer to a statutory dispute usually do injustice to the complexity of legislating. Committee reports, floor speeches, and the rest of the legislative process may help us make sense of a statute, but only the duly enacted statute has the force of law. Legislatures can communicate their chosen policies in a legally binding way only by voting favorably on a written proposal. Without the vote by the legislature, no matter how forcefully individual legislators or political parties advocate a policy decision, they create no law. Judges who fruitlessly search dictionaries for a single right answer to a statutory question will be just as frustrated when they turn to the legislative process.

Third, statutes are written in general terms and so do not neatly resolve particular disputes. There are, of course, some statutes that have extremely detailed rules. Tax laws take literally thousands of pages of rules and regulations to specify how government shall raise revenues. But other statutes are incredibly general. Early antitrust statutes said that society has a problem preserving effective business competition, and made it illegal to restrain competition. In 1890, a nearly unanimous Congress passed with very little debate the Sherman Antitrust Act. Its first two sections state: (1) "Every contract, combination in the form of a trust or otherwise, or conspiracy, in restraint of trade or commerce among the several States, or with foreign nations, is hereby declared to be illegal"; and (2) "Every person who shall monopolize, or attempt to monopolize . . . any part of the trade or commerce among the several States, or with foreign nations, shall be deemed guilty of a misdemeanor." Such general language (Just what is "commerce"? Just what counts as a "restraint"?) leaves judges much freedom to shape and refine law.

Finally, even if they wished to make all statutes as lengthy and detailed as tax codes, legislatures could not possibly anticipate every conflict that might arise under a statute. Legislators are not soothsayers, so they cannot, for example, write laws for technologies that have not yet been invented. The Congress that in 1939 enacted a law granting Social Security benefits to children of workers who have died could not have anticipated the creation of new reproductive technologies like the freezing of sperm and in vitro fertilization. Yet seventy-two years later, judges were deciding whether twin children conceived using these technologies and born eighteen months after their father died were eligible for Social Security survivor benefits.[3] Similarly, the Congress that enacted the Clean Air Act in 1970 did not anticipate that the preeminent threat to the environment would arise out of a gas necessary for life, carbon dioxide, yet four decades later judges had to interpret the Act to decide whether carbon dioxide, an otherwise beneficial substance, was an "air pollutant."[4] In statutory law, as in common law, judges must grapple with new kinds of conflicts using old legal rules.

Given all these difficulties, how should judges decide in concrete cases what statutes mean? Because chapters 2 and 3 have focused on the role of precedents in judging, one preliminary answer to this question should be familiar to you: judges in statutory cases should first seek the guidance of precedents dealing with the same interpretive problem. Then, as in the common law, judges can be guided—though of course not bound—by the principle of stare decisis and by the discipline of reasoning by example.

But what if a particular kind of dispute has never arisen before? We call this *statutory interpretation in the first instance*. When judges decide what uncertain statutes "really" mean the first time, all the problems of statutory interpretation we have just sketched out become particularly acute. In *McBoyle*, the airplane theft case discussed in chapter 1 and reproduced in appendix A, and in *Caminetti*, the "weekend affair in Reno" case mentioned in chapter 2, judges had to unravel the uncertain commands of Congress with no close precedent to guide them. Judge Richard Posner likens their challenge to that of a field commander in combat who radios his superiors for instructions. He hears the instruction, "Go . . ." but immediately loses contact with headquarters. The field commander must decide to go forward or backward, but he knows he cannot stay where he is, even if that seems the wisest course to him.[5]

What can judges do in such a messy situation? We argue that judges best interpret statutes when they pay attention to the purposes of legislation, an approach some scholars refer to as "purposivism."[6] A judge must address directly such questions as these: What kind of problem does this statute

---

3. In *Astrue v. Capato*, 566 U.S. ___ (2012), the Supreme Court ruled that they were not.

4. *Massachusetts v. EPA*, 549 U.S. 497 (2007). As mentioned in chapter 1, the Court ruled that carbon dioxide was in fact an "air pollutant" that the EPA could regulate.

5. See Richard Posner's "Legal Formalism, Legal Realism, and the Interpretation of Statutes and the Constitution," *Case Western Reserve Law Review* 37 (1986–1987): 179–217.

6. Popkin, *Statutes in Court*, 125–149.

try to solve? Is the case before me an example of such a problem? If so, how does this statute tell me to solve it? These questions will not yield a single right answer to the legal problem the judge confronts, nor will they wholly eliminate the influence of the judge's worldviews on the answer she reaches. Nevertheless, the purpose-oriented approach strikes the best balance between legislative and judicial power in statutory interpretation. Judges who approach statutory interpretation as a matter of purpose acknowledge legislative supremacy, but they do so in a way that does not oversimplify the complexity of legislation or the difficulty of the task before them.

Judges who approach statutes wisely know that they cannot treat the words as a series of definitions from *Webster*'s strung together. They intuitively appreciate the saying, "The greatest difficulty with communication is the illusion that it has been achieved." They know that words gain meaning not from dictionaries but from context. They realize that a sign on an outdoor escalator reading Dogs Must Be Carried does not mean that everyone riding the escalator must carry a dog.[7] They know, as Judge Learned Hand has written, that the words of statutes become meaningful only when they are applied sensibly to the solution of public problems:

> [I]t is one of the surest indexes of a mature and developed jurisprudence not to make a fortress out of the dictionary; but to remember that statutes always have some purpose or object to accomplish, whose sympathetic and imaginative discovery is the surest guide to their meaning.[8]

Four Misguided Approaches to "First Instance" Statutory Interpretation

We have just outlined how judges should interpret statutes in the first instance and why we think other approaches to statutory interpretation are misguided. The rest of the chapter fills in the details. As we demonstrate, in attempting to evade the responsibility inherent in statutory interpretation, judges end up on the wrong path—and sometimes get downright silly.[9]

7. Our thanks to Professor Allan Hutchinson for this illustration.

8. This is from Learned Hand's opinion in *Cabell v. Markham*, 148 F.2d 737 (1945), 739, as quoted in Popkin, *Statutes in Court*, 133.

9. The persistence of what verges on downright silliness in statutory interpretation thus illustrates a critical point made near the beginning of chapter 2: the law's language, practices, and traditions, like those in any field of organized human action, tend to per-

Literalism: Sticking to the Words

Perhaps the most celebrated problem of statutory interpretation in American jurisprudence involves the seemingly straightforward and rather boring statutes governing inheritances. When someone with property dies with a valid will, statutes direct that the property go to the heirs named in the will. (The decision in *Fox v. Snow* in the previous chapter seems wrong in part because its result did not send Rosa's property where Rosa's will said it should go.) When a person dies without a will, statutes designate which relatives—spouses, children, parents, siblings, and so on—take priority and in which order. In Ohio, a statute made children whose parents died without a spouse and without a will the inheritors of the parents' estate. When one Elmer Sharkey murdered his mother, an Ohio court held that the law entitled him—or rather his creditors, since Ohio had already hanged Elmer—to the money because the statute did not, by its literal words, forbid murderers from inheriting from their victims. The Court reviewed a New York case holding that a grandson named to inherit in his grandfather's will should, despite the law, *not* inherit after he poisoned his grandfather. The Ohio court nevertheless reasoned: "[W]hen the legislature, not transcending the limits of its power, speaks in clear language upon a question of policy, it becomes the judicial tribunals to remain silent." Is this good legal reasoning? The New York court had reasoned that it would not serve any valid statutory purpose to let someone inherit who had murdered to do so.[10]

In 1912, Lord Atkinson, speaking for the British House of Lords in its appellate judicial role, said:

> If the language of a statute be plain, admitting of only one meaning, the Legislature must be taken to have meant and intended what it has plainly expressed, and whatever it has in clear terms enacted must be enforced though it should lead to absurd or mischievous results.[11]

---

petuate themselves even when they no longer square well with contemporary social background facts and values; that is, they perpetuate bad legal reasoning.

10. *Deem v. Milliken*, 6 Ohio C.C. 357 (1892), 360, and 53 Ohio St. 668 (1895); *Riggs v. Palmer*, 115 N.Y. 506 (1889). See also Richard Posner, *The Problems of Jurisprudence* (Cambridge, MA: Harvard University Press, 1990), 105–107. For Ronald Dworkin's famous discussion of this classic problem, see his *Taking Rights Seriously* (Cambridge, MA: Harvard University Press, 1977), 23–31. And see Joel Levin's discussion of the same problem in his *How Judges Reason* (New York: Peter Lang, 1992), chap. 6.

11. *Vacher and Sons, Ltd., v. London Society of Compositors*, (1913) A.C. 107, 121.

Lord Atkinson, no doubt, respected legislative powers and responsibilities—in this case, those of the House of Commons. The problem he presumably perceived is this: if courts can go beyond the words at all, they can go anywhere they want, setting their own limits and destroying legislative supremacy in the process. This is the classic rationale for the literal, sometimes absurd, reading of statutes.

Legislative supremacy deserves our deepest respect. But how would the good Lord Atkinson react to this hypothetical statute: "A uniformed police officer may require any person driving a motor vehicle in a public place to provide a specimen of breath for a breath test if the officer has reasonable cause to suspect him of having alcohol in his body." Presumably, Lord Atkinson would not exempt women from this law just because the last sentence reads "him" rather than "him or her." The earlier use of the word *person*, even to a literalist, can cover both genders. But how would Lord Atkinson handle the following argument by an equally literalistic defendant? "The statute plainly says the officer may require the specimen from a 'person driving.' I may have been slightly inebriated when the officer pulled me over, but when the officer required the specimen I was *not* 'driving a motor vehicle.' I wasn't even in my car. I was doing my imitation of a pig in the middle of the pavement when the officer requested the specimen."[12] This result is absurd, but Lord Atkinson seems willing to accept absurd results. Should he be, especially in light of the knowledge that language rarely, if ever, admits "of only one meaning"?

American judges have also been seduced by the appeal of adhering to the words. A Virginia statute stated: "No cemetery shall be hereafter established within the corporate limits of any city or town; nor shall any cemetery be established within two hundred and fifty yards of any residence without the consent of the owner." In 1942, after the legislature passed this statute, the town of Petersburg, Virginia, bought an acre of land within its corporate limits on which to relocate bodies exhumed during a road-widening project. The acre adjoined and would be incorporated into a long-established cemetery. A city resident well within the proscribed distance of the added acre brought suit to prevent the expansion and cited the statute.

He lost. Justice Gregory wrote for the appellate court:

---

12. See Sir Rupert Cross, *Statutory Interpretation* (London: Butterworths, 1976), 59. Or imagine a city ordinance requiring all liquor stores "to cease doing business at 10:00 P.M." Does the ordinance permit them to reopen at 10:01 P.M.?

If the language of a statute is plain and unambiguous, and its meaning perfectly clear and definite, effect must be given to it regardless of what courts think of its wisdom or policy. . . .

The word "established" is defined in *Webster's New International Dictionary*, second edition, 1936, thus: "To originate and secure the permanent existence of; to found; to institute; to create and regulate. . . ."

Just why the Legislature, in its wisdom, saw fit to prohibit the establishment of cemeteries in cities and towns, and did not see fit to prohibit enlargements or additions, is no concern of ours. Certain it is that language could not be plainer than that employed to express the legislative will. From it we can see with certainty that . . . a cemetery . . . may be added to or enlarged without running counter to the inhibition found in [the statute]. . . . Our duty is to construe the statute as written.[13]

Judges such as Justice Gregory who cling to the literal meaning of words fail to appreciate that the Virginia legislature is filled with politicians, not dictionary writers.[14] By sticking to the words, the judges prevent themselves from asking what problem the legislature sought to address. Just why the legislature might purposely allow enlargement but not establishment of cemeteries in cities and towns *is* Justice Gregory's concern. Unless he tries to solve that puzzle, we can have no confidence that he has applied the statute to achieve its purpose.

---

13. *Temple v. City of Petersburg*, 182 Va. 418, 423–424 (1944). In 1988 Congress authorized the automatic deportation of all noncitizens who were found guilty of an "aggravated felony," which Congress defined as including "crimes of violence." Did Josue Leocal, for twenty years a legal resident of the United States, commit an "aggravated felony" when he, while driving drunk, struck and injured two people? The vague words of the statute simply do not provide us with an answer. In 2004 the U.S. Supreme Court ruled that Leocal did not commit a "crime of violence" and so should not have been deported. *Leocal v. Ashcroft*, 543 U.S. 1 (2004). In the case featured at the end of this chapter, *Begay v. United States*, the Court wrestles with a similar question: is drunk driving a "violent felony" under federal law?

14. "[No] one uses a freaking dictionary," one congressional staff member who drafts legislation told researchers when asked about this. Said another: "I have tried to get an Oxford English Dictionary but people over at finance say we aren't spending money to buy you a dictionary." In a survey of congressional statute drafters, only 15 percent said dictionaries were always or often used; more than half said dictionaries were rarely or never used. Abbe R. Gluck and Lisa Schultz Bressman, "Statutory Interpretation from the Inside—An Empirical Study of Congressional Drafting, Delegation and the Canons: Part I," *Stanford Law Review* 65 (2013): 901–1026, at 938.

The Golden Rule

Of course, Lord Atkinson could have solved his problem another way, by sticking to the words except when they produce absurd results. The "golden rule of statutory interpretation" holds that judges should follow

> the grammatical and ordinary sense of the words . . . unless that would lead to some absurdity, or some repugnance or inconsistency with the rest of the instrument, in which case the grammatical and ordinary sense of the words may be modified, so as to avoid the absurdity and inconsistency, but no farther.[15]

The golden rule thus would solve the problem of the clever intoxicated driver. It would be absurd and possibly dangerous to require that the officer ride with him and collect the specimen while weaving down the road. But the golden rule, unfortunately, does not solve much more because it does not tell us how to separate the absurd from the merely questionable.[16]

Take, for example, *King v. Burwell*, the Obamacare case with which this chapter began. It might seem ridiculous that the Democrats in Congress who enacted the Affordable Care Act, a law aimed at expanding health insurance coverage, would choose to subsidize only those who happened to live in a state that created its own health exchange while denying subsidies to people in other states. But is this interpretation truly "absurd"—or just puzzling?

Or consider the case of Elián González, the six-year-old Cuban boy who in 2000 was found clinging to an inner tube in the Atlantic Ocean off the coast of Florida. Elián had been traveling by boat with his mother in an attempt to flee Cuba. When the boat capsized, eleven passengers died, including Elián's mother. Elián was brought to the United States and put in

15. *Grey v. Pearson*, 6 H.L. Cas. 61 (1857), 106, quoted in Cross, *Statutory Interpretation*, 15.

16. Justice Scalia similarly distinguishes "hyperliteralism," which he says is misguided, from literalism, which he says is an appropriate approach to statutory interpretation. But how do we know if an interpretation is "hyperliteral" rather than literal? Scalia says a literal meaning, unlike a hyperliteral one, is "sensible" and consistent with the canons of construction (which we discuss later in this chapter). Scalia says that an interpretation is hyperliteral if it is "inconsistent with the textually manifest purpose of the act." As with the golden rule, it's not clear how these formulations solve the issue of ambiguity: they replace one question (what does the statute command?) with a whole set of questions (how should one decide whether an interpretation is "sensible" and consistent with the "textually manifest purpose of the act" in line with the canons of construction?) that seem equally difficult and open to dispute. Scalia and Garner, *Reading Law*, 39–40.

the temporary custody of his great uncle, Lázaro González. When Elián's Cuban father requested that his son be returned to him in Cuba, Lázaro González asked the Immigration and Naturalization Service (INS) to grant the child asylum in the United States. The INS refused, concluding that since a six-year-old would be incompetent to apply for asylum on his own, only Elián's father could submit an application for him. Lázaro González then sued the INS in federal court, claiming that he had acted at the request of Elián and noting that federal law fails to restrict asylum applications by age, providing only that "any alien . . . may apply for asylum." In a preliminary order barring the removal of Elián from the United States before a final decision in the case could be made, three federal appeals court judges ruled in favor of Lázaro González. The judges agreed that the meaning of "any alien" is "pretty clear," and that if Congress had wanted to restrict asylum applications by age, it would not have written the statute to include "any alien":

> To some people, the idea that a six-year-old child may file for asylum in the United States, contrary to the express wishes of his parents, may seem a strange or even foolish policy. But this Court does not make immigration policy, and we cannot review the wisdom of statutes duly enacted by Congress.[17]

Is it absurd to let a six-year-old apply for asylum or merely unwise? The golden rule provides no help, and so the Court simply throws up its hands.[18]

To further test the weakness of the golden rule, ask yourself two questions: (1) Is it absurd, or only questionable, to allow expansion of existing graveyards while prohibiting the creation of new ones? (2) Is it absurd, or merely questionable, to use the Mann Act to prevent the transportation of willing girlfriends and mistresses across state lines along with unwilling "white slaves" and prostitutes? The golden rule provides no answer.

17. *Gonzalez v. Reno*, No. 90-11424-D, 2000 U.S. App. Lexis 7025 (11th Cir., April 19, 2000), n. 9.

18. Two months later, the same judges decided that, since "Congress ha[d] left a gap in the statutory scheme" by failing to describe *how* an alien should apply for asylum, the INS could reasonably fill that gap by deciding that a six-year-old could not go through the process of applying for asylum without the assistance of his parents. The final decision in *Gonzalez* ordered Elián to be returned to his father in Cuba. It rested on a basic principle of administrative law, deference to executive agencies. The opinion in this case concluded that the Court should not second-guess the way the INS had interpreted the statute; only if the agency's interpretation was "unreasonable" should the Court step in. *Gonzalez v. Reno*, 212 F.3d 1338 (11th Cir., June 1, 2000).

Both the literal approach and the superficially more sensible golden rule fail. They deceive judges into believing that words in isolation can be and usually are clear and that the words communicate by themselves. But they don't. The word *establish* in *Temple* (the graveyard case), the phrase *immoral purpose* in *Caminetti* (the Mann Act case "weekend in Reno"), and the word *vehicle* in *McBoyle* (the airplane theft case) simply are not clear, and no blunt assertion to the contrary will make them so.

That, of course, doesn't stop judges from insisting that the definition they happen to prefer is the only correct one. To give their preferred definitions the sheen of objectivity, judges have increasingly turned to dictionaries, with sometimes hilarious results. Supreme Court justices, for example, have consulted dictionaries to define words such as *now, also, any*, and *if*.[19] Alas, dictionaries are a particularly problematic way to resolve matters of interpretation because they are simply catalogs of the various ways in which people use words. For nearly every word, most dictionary entries offer multiple definitions. Moreover, judges can choose from many competing dictionaries.[20] No surprise, then, that some cases feature "dueling dictionaries" in which judges brandish their own preferred definition of a word and scorn rival definitions. In *Begay v. United States*, the illustrative case at the end of this chapter, the justices fight over the meaning of *otherwise*, invoking differing definitions and citing competing dictionaries.

Even if judges could, through dictionaries, come to agree on the single best meaning of a word, they would still face the task that is typically much more difficult in disputes over statutory interpretation: applying their agreed meaning to the facts of a particular case. In the Elián González case, the words "any alien . . . may apply" seem straightforward until the judge contemplates the mental world of a six-year-old, who may not be able to understand what it means to apply for asylum, let alone fill out the application forms on his own. The judge who asserts that the words "any alien" by themselves resolve the case fails to honestly confront these difficulties. Interpreting words in isolation is a danger because it leads judges to believe that they have thought a problem through to its end when they have only reached its beginning.

To summarize, words become meaningful only in their contexts. In statutory interpretation, judges must analyze two contexts. The first is the

---

19. Jeffrey L. Kirchmeier and Samuel A. Thumma, "Scaling the Lexicon Fortress: The United States Supreme Court's Use of Dictionaries in the Twenty First Century," *Marquette Law Review* 94, no. 1 (2010): 77–259, at 101–102.

20. Supreme Court justices have cited more than 120 different dictionaries in their opinions. See ibid., 82.

legislative context—the general problem that existed when the statute was passed and the policy solution to it the legislature created. The second is the case context—what the litigants are disputing and whether their dispute involves the problem the statute addresses. The words of a statute become clearer to the extent that the case facts line up with the legislative context in which the statute was produced. If Elián González had been twenty-five years old, or if Mr. McBoyle had stolen a car rather than a plane, judges would have had no difficulty concluding that the statutory words clearly and unambiguously determine the case. For the most part statutes work in just this way, giving individuals enough clarity about legal rules that they can resolve matters long before they reach the courthouse. It is precisely when the words of a statute as applied to the facts of a case are ambiguous that legal reasoning becomes necessary.

Canons of Statutory Construction

Judges have defended themselves against the imprecision of words by arming themselves with interpretive weapons called "canons of construction." As part of a broader interpretative approach, canons of construction can be useful. The problem comes when judges use canons as if they were mathematical equations that can provide precise answers to problems in statutory interpretation.

A canon of construction or interpretation (which are, for our purposes, the same) is really a rule for interpreting rules. These canons, developed over hundreds of years by judges in statutory cases (a process similar to common law), provide rules for resolving ambiguities in the language of laws.

Take, for example, the *McBoyle* case that is reproduced in appendix A. The relevant statute forbade transportation across state lines of a stolen "automobile, automobile truck, automobile wagon, motorcycle or any other self-propelled vehicle not designed for running on rails." The question raised by the case is whether an airplane is a vehicle. Can the canons help?

One of the canons of construction says:

> Where general words follow a statutory specification, they are to be held as applying only to persons and things of the same general kind or class of thing to which the specified things belong.

By invoking this canon, called *ejusdem generis* ("of the same kind"), a judge could conclude that the general words "or any other self-propelled vehicle" refer only to items *like* (in the same genus as) the objects that the statute specifically mentions (the species). In this case, all the specific items run on land. Therefore, an airplane is not a vehicle.

Similarly, in *Caminetti*, Justice Day invoked the *ejusdem generis* canon in reaching the conclusion that the Mann Act did cover mistresses. He said that the general words "other immoral purposes" referred only to sexual immorality because all the specific examples fit that genus. If you take your mother or a female friend across a state line to help you rob a bank, you will not violate the Mann Act even though the word *immoral*, by its plain meaning, surely includes robbery.

One frequently cited canon, the rule of lenity, instructs judges to interpret criminal statutes narrowly. This means that when a judge finds that the statute does not clearly resolve his case, he should resolve it in favor of the defendant. Again *McBoyle* can illustrate. Justice Holmes wrote for the Supreme Court in that case:

> [I]t is reasonable that a fair warning should be given to the world in language that the common world will understand of what the law intends to do if a certain line is passed. To make the warning fair, so far as possible the line should be clear.

Holmes argues, in other words, that unless judges interpret criminal statutes narrowly, judges will send to jail people who had no clear notice that they had committed a crime.[21] Reflect a bit and you will see how the rule of lenity empowers judges to resist the tendency of government officials, in police-state fashion, to abuse their powers.

Holmes's concern for fairness in *McBoyle* reminds us that the canons are not totally ineffective or undesirable weapons. Supreme Court justice Felix Frankfurter said that "even generalized restatements from time to time may not be wholly wasteful. Out of them may come a sharper rephrasing of the conscious factors of interpretation; new instances may make them more vivid but also disclose more clearly their limitations."[22] Nearly every canon that judges have created contains at least a small charge of sensibility.

21. *McBoyle v. United States.* A narrow interpretation may produce a very different decision from that of a literal interpretation. As noted in chapter 2, a literal interpretation of the words "other immoral purposes" in the Mann Act might even make traveling with our wives to Colorado (where marijuana is legal) to smoke pot an illegal act. A narrow interpretation would not.

22. Felix Frankfurter, "Some Reflections on the Reading of Statutes," *Columbia Law Review* 47, no. 4 (1947): 527–546, at 544–545.

Canons exist to support each of the principles of proper interpretation that this chapter covers. For example, the canon *noscitur a sociis* ("it is known by its associates") states that words should be interpreted in the context of the whole statute. One British court used this canon to confine a statute regulating houses "for public refreshment, resort and entertainment" only to places where people received food and drink, excluding music halls and theaters, refreshing though their shows might be. The statute bore the title Refreshment House Act.[23]

So what's the problem with canons? By making disorderly words appear orderly, canons can deceive judges into thinking they have found the one and only correct application of the statute to the case. This can lead judges to think they can evade the difficult task of untangling statutory purpose and of weighing all four elements of legal reasoning.

One example of this judicial evasion of purpose occurred after Congress passed a statute in 1893 designed to promote railway safety.[24] In part, Section 2 of the statute reads:

[I]t shall be unlawful for any . . . common carrier [engaged in interstate commerce] to haul or permit to be hauled or used on its line any car . . . not equipped with couplers coupling automatically by impact, and which can be uncoupled without the necessity of men going between the ends of the cars.

Section 8 of the Act placed the right to sue for damages in the hands of "any employee of any such common carrier who may be injured by any locomotive, car or train in use contrary to the provisions of this act." Additionally, the Act imposed criminal penalties on railroads that failed to comply.

A worker was injured while positioned between a locomotive and a car. Because the locomotive did not have an automatic coupler, he tried to couple them by hand. He sued for damages and lost, both in the trial court and in the U.S. Court of Appeals, the latter holding that while the statute required railroad cars to have automatic couplers, this requirement did not apply to locomotives. Judge Sanborn fired canon after canon in defense of his conclusion that the statutory word *cars* did not include locomotives. Here are three examples:

23. Cross, *Statutory Interpretation*, 118. The list of canons is lengthy. Karl Llewellyn provides judicial citations for fifty-six canons in "Remarks on the Theory of Appellate Decision and the Rules or Canons about How Statutes Are to Be Construed," *Vanderbilt Law Review* 3 (1950): 395–405, at 401–405.

24. 27 Stat. c. 196, 531.

- "The familiar rule that the expression of one thing is the exclusion of the others leads to [this] conclusion."
- "This is a penal statute, and it may not be so broadened by judicial construction as to make it cover and permit the punishment of an act which is not denounced by the fair import of its terms."
- "The intention of the legislature and the meaning of a penal statute must be found in the language actually used."[25]

Do any of these canons convince you that this statute does not require locomotives to have automatic couplers? Again, the canons are not themselves absurd; the damage occurs when they seduce judges into applying them simplistically and into thinking the canon gives *the* answer when the canon only justifies *an* answer. Does not Judge Sanborn's reasoning at least create the suspicion in your mind that he wanted, for whatever reasons, to rule for the railroads, and that the easy availability of canons only provided convenient camouflage for his personal preferences?[26]

The vice of the canons resembles the familiar law of mechanics. For each and every canon, there is an equal and opposite canon. Llewellyn organizes fifty-six canons he collected into twenty-eight sets of opposing canons: "THRUST BUT PARRY," he calls them.[27] The judge who, for whatever reason, reaches any conclusion can usually find a canon to defend it.

Consider this example of Llewellyn's point: A federal statute prohibits the interstate shipment of any "obscene . . . book, pamphlet, picture, motion-picture film, paper, letter, writing, print or other matter of indecent character." One Mr. Alpers shipped interstate some phonograph records that, admitted for the sake of argument, were obscene. On the basis of the canons *ejusdem generis* ("of the same kind") and the rule of lenity (narrow construction of criminal statutes), we might expect Mr. Alpers to win his case. After all, the genus to which all the species belong is "things comprehended through sight." Instead, Justice Minton, for the Supreme Court, alluded to *noscitur a sociis* ("it is known by its associates"), another canon, and upheld the conviction.[28]

In short, the canons war against themselves. In *Caminetti*, *ejusdem generis* pushes toward conviction, but the rule of lenity pushes toward acquit-

25. *Johnson v. Southern Pacific Co.*, 117 F. 462 (8th Cir. 1902). Fortunately, the U. S. Supreme Court reversed, at 196 U.S. 1 (1904).

26. See Richard Posner, "Statutory Interpretation—in the Classroom and in the Courtroom," *University of Chicago Law Review* 50 (1983): 800–822, at 816.

27. Llewellyn, "Remarks on the Theory of Appellate Decision," 401–405.

28. *United States v. Alpers*, 338 U.S. 680 (1950).

tal. In the illustrative case at the end of this chapter, *Begay v. United States*, each of the three justices who wrote an opinion fires a canon in defending his interpretation of a statute, but the canons shoot in three different directions. Clearly, canons, whatever their virtues, cannot provide the "right answer" to questions of statutory interpretation.

Legislative Intent

Another common way in which judges attempt to justify their interpretations of statutes is to try to discover what the legislature "intended" its statutory words to mean. We can define an *intention* as a conscious mental commitment to act in some specific way. According to this definition, judges who follow a "legislative intent" approach can resolve statutory conflicts by studying the intentions of legislators who voted for a statute (and the executives who sign them). They try to figure out how the legislators thought the statute should apply to the case in question. In *King v. Burwell*, the Obamacare case that began this chapter, a judge would attempt to figure out whether the 60 senators and 219 representatives who voted for the law (as well as President Obama, who signed it) intended to deny insurance subsidies to people living in states that failed to establish their own health insurance exchanges. We shall try in a moment to persuade you that legislative intent by this definition is a mirage and that the quest for it almost inevitably leads judges astray. For now, consider the following use of legislative intent.

Shortly after it became a state, and long before the Nineteenth Amendment to the U.S. Constitution guaranteed women the right to vote, Massachusetts passed a statute providing that "a person qualified to vote for representative to the General Court [the official name of the Massachusetts legislature] shall be liable to serve as a juror." Ten years after the passage of the Nineteenth Amendment, one Genevieve Welosky, a criminal defendant, found herself facing a Massachusetts jury that excluded all women. Welosky protested the exclusion, appealed, and lost. Under the literal or golden rule approaches, she would surely have won, for *person* includes women, and women were "qualified to vote." Even before the days of women's liberation, we would hardly label it absurd to seat women on juries.

But Massachusetts Chief Justice Rugg invoked the intent of the legislature:

> It is clear beyond peradventure that the words of [the statute] when originally enacted could not by any possibility have included or been intended by the General Court to include women among those liable

to jury duty. . . . Manifestly, therefore, the intent of the Legislature must have been, in using the word "person" in statutes concerning jurors and jury lists, to confine its meaning to men.[29]

The legislature didn't intend women to become jurors when they passed the statute, because at that time women could not vote. Despite the literal meaning of the words, women cannot therefore sit on juries.

The title of this section offered the hope that judges can find statutory truth by discovering legislative intent. The Massachusetts court has identified an uncontested social background fact—that women could not vote when the statute was passed—and concluded logically that the legislature did not intend women to sit on juries. This logic is straightforward enough, but the *Welosky* opinion is a virtual fraud. Rugg says the simple sequence of historical events reveals the legislature's intent; because the statute came before the suffrage amendment, the legislature did not intend to include women. But Rugg's first quoted sentence sends us on a wild goose chase. It is plausible that the legislature did not consider the possibility of women—or for that matter, immigrant Martians—becoming jurors. But it is simultaneously plausible that the Massachusetts legislature "intended" to settle the problem of who may sit as a juror once and for all by simply tying jury service to voting eligibility, so that anyone legally entitled to vote could be called for jury duty. A legislature that did so would hardly act absurdly. Rugg completely fails to show that it did not so act.

Does the hope that legislative intent will reveal the meaning of statutory language hence fail? Yes, but not because of poorly reasoned cases such as *Welosky*. The quest for legislative intent is a search for hard evidence. It is detective work in the legal field, not Rugg's idle armchair speculations, so we should not abandon the field of legislative intent so quickly. Judges have many sleuthing techniques for discovering evidence of intent, of which we now review three of the most prominent. What do you think of them?

OTHER WORDS IN THE STATUTE

The brief excerpt from the cemetery case, discussed earlier in this chapter, may have treated Justice Gregory unfairly, for he did not simply rest his opinion on *Webster*'s dictionary. He continued by pointing out that another section of the cemetery statute of Virginia

29. *Commonwealth v. Welosky*, 276 Mass. 398, 402–406 (1931).

affords a complete answer to the question of legislative intent in the use of the word "established" in Section 56, for the former section [Section 53] makes a distinction between "establish" and "enlarge" in these words: "If it be desired at any time to establish a cemetery, for the use of a city, town, county, or magisterial district, or to enlarge any such already established, and the title to land needed cannot be otherwise acquired, land sufficient for the purpose may be condemned. . . ."

The foregoing language, taken from Section 53, completely demonstrates that the legislature did not intend the words "establish" and "enlarge" to be used interchangeably, but that the use of one excluded any idea that it embraced or meant the other.[30]

Similarly, Justice McKenna, dissenting in *Caminetti*, found support in the official title of the Mann Act:

For the context I must refer to the statute; of the purpose of the statute Congress itself has given us illumination. It devotes a section to the declaration that the "Act shall be known and referred to as the 'White Slave Traffic Act.'" And its prominence gives it prevalence in the construction of the statute. It cannot be pushed aside or subordinated by indefinite words in other sentences, limited even there by the context.[31]

The title of the statute tells Justice McKenna that Congress did not intend to police the activities of willing girlfriends. Willing girlfriends are not white slaves; the conclusion sounds sensible.

THE EXPRESSED INTENT OF INDIVIDUAL LEGISLATORS AND COMMITTEE REPORTS

Like Justice Gregory, Justice McKenna, in his *Caminetti* dissent, made more than one argument to support his conclusion.[32] In fact, he went directly to the words of the bill's author and quoted extensively from Representative Mann:

---

30. *Temple v. City of Petersburg*, 424.
31. *Caminetti v. United States*, 242 U.S. 470, 497 (1917).
32. Appellate judges often give multiple arguments for the conclusions in their opinions, but they do not always articulate whether one argument, by itself, would justify the same result. They don't always, in other words, spell out the relative importance of the arguments they use.

"The White Slave Trade—A material portion of the legislation suggested and proposed is necessary to meet conditions which have
arisen within the past few years. The legislation is needed to put a
stop to the villainous interstate and international traffic in women
and girls. The legislation is not needed or intended as an aid to the
states in the exercise of their police powers in the suppression or
regulation of immorality in general. It does not attempt to regulate
the practice of voluntary prostitution, but aims solely to prevent pan-
derers and procurers from compelling thousands of women and girls
against their will and desire to enter and continue in a life of prostitution." *Congressional Record*, vol. 50, pp. 3368, 3370.

In other words, it is vice as a business at which the law is directed,
using interstate commerce as a facility to procure or distribute its
victims.

Judges rarely argue that the expressed views of any one legislator necessarily convey legislative intent, but they frequently cite committee reports
and statements of authors as proof of intent. This allows the words of
one legislator, or of a small minority, to determine what the law holds,
despite the fact that in a legislature, only a voting majority has the power
to make law.[33]

OTHER ACTIONS, EVENTS, AND
DECISIONS IN THE LEGISLATURE

To establish legislative intent, judges may also look at how the legislature
handled related legislation. In *Welosky*, Chief Justice Rugg noted that the
Massachusetts legislature had in 1920 changed several laws relating to
women in order to make them conform to the Eighteenth and Nineteenth

---

33. Federal Judge Robert A. Katzmann, in his treatise on statutory interpretation,
strongly defends the use of legislative history, particularly committee reports. See
Katzmann, *Judging Statutes*, 35–49. Katzmann notes that empirical research on the legislative process suggests that the average member of Congress is far more likely to read
the committee report on a statute rather than the statute itself—statutes are voluminous
and difficult for nonspecialists in legislative drafting to understand. A survey of congressional staffers involved in drafting legislation found bipartisan and overwhelming
support for the use of committee reports in interpreting statutes. These staffers argued
that members of Congress are far more involved in the drafting of committee reports
than in the writing of statutes! See Gluck and Bressman, "Statutory Interpretation from
the Inside . . . Part I," 964–969. Former Supreme Court Justice John Paul Stevens has
been an outspoken advocate of the use of legislative history. See his appreciative review
of Katzmann's book, "Law without History?" *New York Review of Books*, October 23,
2014, 22–26.

Amendments but did nothing about the problem of female jurors. He argued regarding the 1920 legislation:

> It is most unlikely that the Legislature should, for the first time require women to serve as jurors without making provision respecting the exemption of the considerable numbers of women who ought not to be required to serve as jurors, and without directing that changes for the convenience of women be made in court houses, some of which are notoriously over-crowded and unfit for their accommodation as jurors.

Judges may even find in the physical evidence presented to committees the key to intent. In the 1940s, the postmaster general refused to grant the preferential lower postage rate to books that contained many blank pages, such as workbooks and notebooks. Congress then amended the relevant statute to grant the preferential postal rates to books with space for notes. However, the postmaster general continued to refuse the rate to so-called loose-leaf notebooks with blank pages on the basis that they were not permanently bound. A shipper of such notebooks eager for the cheaper postage rate sued for an order granting the preferential rate. The opinion of Judge Groner concluded that Congress did intend to give the preferential rate to loose-leaf notebooks because the many physical exhibits placed before the committee that handled the bill included some such notebooks. Groner wrote, "[I]t follows logically that textbooks of the make and quality of those of appellant were considered and purposely included by Congress in the list of publications entitled to the book rate."[34]

The list of possibilities in this category could continue for pages. For example, judges are fond of finding legislative intent by discovering that one house's version of a bill contained a clause that does not appear in the final law that was approved by both houses. The judges conclude from this discovery that the legislature intended that the remaining words *not* mean what the dropped clause meant.

Superficially, these discoveries about legislative intent are appealing, but as evidence of what the legislators who voted for the statute actually intended by their vote, they fall far short. When, for example, Judge Groner concludes "logically" that the legislature intended to include loose-leaf

---

34. *McCormick-Mathers Publishing Co. v. Hannegan*, 161 F.2d 873, 875 (D.C. Cir. 1947).

notebooks for the preferential rate, he is logically completely incorrect. He does not give one shred of evidence that any legislator, much less the majority, actually thought about the physical exhibits when he or she voted. Of course, Representative Mann's thoughts give us some clue to his intent, but we do not know that a majority heard or read his thoughts. Even if a majority in the House and Senate did know what Mann intended, we don't know that they agreed with him. After all, the statute uses the word *prostitution* without Mann's qualifications. Maybe the majority voted for the Act because they wanted a tougher response to the sex-trade problem than did Mann.

THE PERILS OF LEGISLATIVE INTENT

Why, then, precisely, does legislative intent fail as a tool of statutory interpretation? A legislature is an organizational unit of government. By itself, a legislature can no more intend something than can a car or an office building. *People* intend things, and because the elected representatives in a legislature are people, they may intend something when they vote. If all members of the voting majority intended the same thing, then that might well state the intent of the statute. However, here two difficulties fatal to the cause of legislative intent arise.

First, we know enough about politics to know that in all likelihood the people making up the voting majority do not intend the same thing. Most will not have read the statute they vote on. By casting their vote, some will intend to repay a political debt, or to be a loyal follower of their party leaders, or to encourage a campaign contribution from a private source in the future. If we want to deduce collective intent on anything, we must take a poll, and the only poll we ever take of legislators is when the presiding officers of the House and Senate call for the vote to enact or defeat a bill (and when the president or governor decides whether to sign or veto legislation). "Yes" voters intend to vote yes, and "no" voters intend to vote no, but that's about all we can accurately say about their intentions.

Second, even if we somehow knew that those legislators who voted for a bill intended the same thing about a statute, it is highly unlikely, if not absolutely impossible, that they intended anything about the unique facts of the case before the court. Legislators simply do not confront the concrete and always-unique case. In this sense, as former attorney general Edward H. Levi once said, "Despite much gospel to the contrary, a legislature is not a fact-finding body. There is no mechanism, as there is with a court, to require the legislature to sift facts and to make a decision about specific situations."[35] In all probability, no one in the legislature foresaw the precise problem facing the judge, and it is even less likely that the legislature consciously intended to resolve the case one way or another. Pose to the politicians who enacted the Mann Act the problems of migrating Mormons or vacationing prostitutes, and you would probably get a gruff instruction to "ask a judge about the details." And if you were to somehow bring back to life the makers of the 1939 amendments to the Social Security Act to ask about whether children conceived after their father's death should receive survivors' benefits, you would undoubtedly get blank stares.

Those are just the most basic problems with using legislative history to discern legislative intent. Consider a few more:

- Legislators and lobbyists can "cook" legislative history, inserting comments and planting evidence in the legislative record solely for the purpose of persuading judges later on in litigation that the legislature had a particular intent. The loose-leaf notebooks that Judge Groner put so much weight on in the postal-rate case might well have been planted there by a lobbyist. As long ago as 1947, Archibald Cox wrote, "[I]t is becoming increasingly common to manufacture 'legislative history' during the course of legislation."[36]
- Public policy is increasingly complex and political polarization increasingly intense. Complexity and polarization augment the tendency of legislatures to make garbled policy and send conflicting messages to the courts and executive agencies charged with implementing legislation. Indeed, judges often ignore the possibility that the lawmaking process might purposely create unclear law because legislatures *want* courts (or more often, executive agencies, such as the Environmental Protection Administration) to fill in the details.[37]

35. Edward H. Levi, *An Introduction to Legal Reasoning* (Chicago: University of Chicago Press, 2013), 31.

36. Archibald Cox, "Some Aspects of the Labor Management Relations Act, 1947," *Harvard Law Review* 61 (1947): 55–103, at 44. Justice Antonin Scalia, who describes himself as a "textualist" in the battle over statutory interpretation, has made this point one of his main arguments against legislative history. See Scalia, *A Matter of Interpretation* (Princeton, NJ: Princeton University Press, 1997), 32–36. Senators Jon Kyl and Lindsey Graham allegedly planted evidence in the *Congressional Record* to suggest that Congress intended to strip the federal courts of jurisdiction to hear cases of Guantánamo detainees under the Detainee Treatment Act. See Emily Bazelon, "Invisible Men: Did Lindsey Graham and Jon Kyl Mislead the Supreme Court?" *Slate*, March 27, 2006.

37. In a survey of congressional staffers involved in drafting statutes, 39 percent said Congress intentionally leaves gaps in statutes hoping that courts will fill them, but 91 percent said this about executive agencies. Abbe R. Gluck and Lisa Schultz Bressman,

This may amount to buck-passing in the hope that courts or agencies will take the pressure for an unpopular result. But legislators may also believe that the everyday processes of agency implementation and case-by-case judicial action are the best way to decide precisely what the statute should include and exclude.

- Often there is no real legislative history at all. Most state legislatures still do not produce complete documentation of proceedings that most lawyers can access. At the federal level, Congress increasingly engages in what the political scientist Barbara Sinclair has labeled "unorthodox lawmaking,"[38] in which the textbook steps of the legislative process—hearings, committee deliberations, debates over amendments—are truncated or skipped. Legislative gridlock has led Congress increasingly to rely on omnibus bills, massive appropriations measures that fold together all kinds of legislation into one package.[39] The searcher for legislative intent in such cases has little with which to work.

Much can be (and has been) said for abandoning the concept of legislative intent. The ever-skeptical Holmes wrote, "I don't care what their intention was, I only want to know what the words mean." And Frankfurter added, "You may have observed that I have not yet used the word 'intention.' All these years I have avoided speaking of the 'legislative intent' and I shall continue to be on my guard against using it."[40] The candid judge looking for firm evidence of intent simply won't find it very often. A candid Rugg would, for example, have concluded, "I simply can't say whether the Massachusetts legislature thought about women becoming jurors or not." The names Holmes and Frankfurter endure more prominently than Rugg because they were intellectually rigorous enough to make such candid judgments.[41] Given the realities of the legislative process, judges should be wary of concluding that legislators ever collectively intended anything.

"Statutory Interpretation from the Inside—An Empirical Study of Congressional Drafting, Delegation and the Canons: Part II," *Stanford Law Review* 66 (2014) 725–801, 774.

38. Barbara Sinclair, *Unorthodox Lawmaking: New Legislative Processes in the U.S. Congress*, 4th ed. (Washington, DC: CQ Press, 2011).

39. In the 112th Congress (2011–2013), for example, Gluck and Bressman find that only seven of the ninety-one measures enacted followed a "textbook" process. Many bills are negotiated by the leaderships of each chamber and then simply passed without further deliberation. See Gluck and Bressman, "Statutory Interpretation from the Inside . . . Part II," 762.

40. Frankfurter, "Some Reflections," 227–228.

41. The eminent jurisprudent John Gray wrote, "The fact is that the difficulties of so-called interpretation arise when the Legislature has had no meaning at all; when the

To summarize, the ultimate danger in all the methods of statutory inter-pretation we've described—the literal and golden rule approaches, the use of canons, and the search for legislative intent in legislative history—is that each allows the judge to reach a conclusion without ever struggling with the fundamental question of whether one interpretation or another actually copes with social problems effectively. These methods, in other words, per-petuate decisions that may not promote law's basic goal—social coopera-tion. The next section describes a better way for judges to interpret statutes.

Purpose: The Key to Wise Statutory Interpretation

Statutory interpretation so frequently seems inadequate because judges face an unavoidable necessity. Judges must say what the law "is" in order to resolve the case before them. This is necessary because our society, our culture, believes that judges act unfairly when they do not decide on the basis of what the law says and is. Judges cannot hear a case and then refuse to render a decision because they cannot determine the legal answer.[42] We do not pay judges to say, "Maybe the law is X. Maybe the law is Y. I'll guess Y. You lose!" (Or worse, "I don't care if it's X or Y. You still lose!") To render justice in our culture, judges must persuade us to believe with certainty that which is inherently uncertain.

Making the murky and muddled appear, within its own particular frame, "composed" (which is the art in judging and in everything else) is par-ticularly difficult in statutory interpretation. In common law, the courts know that they have authority to make law. In these realms, judges can say, "The law ought to be X, not Y. Therefore, the law is X." But legislative supremacy bars judges from interpreting statutes so boldly. They must try to make sense of the messy and often mysterious political processes in a legislature—processes in which the judges themselves did not participate.

Despite the generality, vagueness, and ambiguity of words in statutes, and despite the disorderliness of the legislative process that produces those words, judges can nevertheless arrive at persuasive interpretations of stat-utes. They can do so by identifying the *purpose* of the statute, the problem statutory language tries to solve.

---

question which is raised on the statute never occurred to it." *The Nature and Sources of the Law* (New York: Macmillan, 1927), 173.

42. This is true of most formal legal systems. For example, the French Civil Code, dating from 1804, states, "A judge who refuses to enter judgment on the pretext of si-lence, obscurity, or inadequacy of the statute is subject to prosecution for the denial of justice."

This approach is often confused with the search for legislative intent. Indeed, many who use the word *intent* and defend the use of legislative history are not in fact literally searching for the motivations of all the actors involved in creating a statute. These proponents of intent don't worry that the vast majority of legislators have intentions about statutes that are either irrelevant (placating one's party or an interest group to which one is aligned) or nonexistent. Instead, these wiser proponents focus on the more constructive elements of the legislative process, the aspects of legislative history that can help the judge, in cases when the meaning of a statute is under dispute, go beyond the ambiguous words of the statute to better understand the context in which it was enacted. We believe that this approach is better labeled as "purposive" or "purpose oriented" because it treats legislation as a social institution, the product of a collective entity, rather than as the mere sum of individual choices. Where individual decision making is typically ascribed to one's "intentions," social institutions (think, for example, of colleges, museums, and charities) are typically described as having "purposes." Indeed, social institutions often have purposes that transcend the individual motivations of the people who created them.[43] A purposive approach treats legislation in just such a way.[44]

The Centrality of Statutory Purpose

The questions judges should ask themselves in statutory cases always begin with legislative purpose: What kind of societal problem does this statute try to correct? Does the case before the court represent the problem the statute addresses? Imagine, for example, that an FBI agent drives a recovered stolen car across a state line back to its owner. Has the agent violated the National Motor Vehicle Theft Act? The answer is easy—if a judge focuses on legislative purpose. If the purpose of the Act is to stop interstate

43. Consider, for example, Wellesley College, the employer of one of your authors, which was founded by Pauline and Henry Fowle Durant partly with the intention of doing a "special work for God" in memory of their son Henry, who had died of diphtheria at the age of eight. Thus, one *intent* behind the creation of Wellesley College was to memorialize Henry Durant. Yet the *purpose* of Wellesley College is best described as educating women, another expressed intention of the Durants. See Jean Glasscock, ed., *Wellesley College 1875–1975: A Century of Women* (Wellesley, MA: Wellesley College, 1975).

44. Kent Greenawalt suggests one potential problem with the purposive approach, its breadth. He asks, can't different parts of a statute have different aims, reflecting legislative compromise among factions of legislators? See Greenawalt, *Statutory Interpretation*, 98–103; and Manning, "What Divides Textualists from Purposivists?"

vehicle theft, then the FBI agent is part of the solution, not part of the problem.

Dictionaries and legislative histories may aid judges in the search for legislative purpose, but they can never substitute for it. The problem the statute addresses always gives direction to the search for purpose. A dictionary alone never does. Think of the difference it makes in *Johnson* (the locomotive-coupling case) if the judge asks (1) "Is a locomotive a railroad car?" versus (2) "Is protecting the safety of workers coupling locomotives to cars as well as cars to cars a sensible part of the problem this law tries to cope with?" Staring intently at the words "railroad car" or looking them up in the dictionary won't help the judge make a better ruling. Thinking about how a ruling implements statutory purpose can. Notice that whenever judges inquire into the purpose of the legislation, they inevitably inquire into the social background facts to discover the nature of the broader problems raised by the case and how the statute tries to cope with them.

Determining Purpose: Words Can Help

It is the language of a statute that alone has the force of law. Nothing else that individual legislators and legislative bodies say or do legally binds a judge. When, for example, Congress included the word *prostitution* in the Mann Act, it unambiguously prohibited something aside from white slavery; prostitutes after all are not necessarily more "enslaved" in their occupation than other workers who do dirty or dangerous jobs. Except for the Mann Act's euphemistic title, the "White Slave Act," the statute contains not one word to indicate that the women whose transportation it forbids must be "slaves" or, for that matter, "white." It is in this context that the word *prostitution* unambiguously shapes the Mann Act's meaning.

Context is always crucial. Some contexts require courts to follow precisely the opposite of the literal command of words. If, through some printing error, the officially published version of a statute omits a key word, judges properly include the word if the context makes such a purpose clear. Suppose that a statute prohibiting some very undesirable behavior omits in its official version the key prohibitory word *not*. Although the statute would then literally permit or even require the unwarranted behavior, judges may apply the statute as if it contained the missing and critical *not*.

Canons of interpretation may help reassure judges that a given word, phrase, or sentence has a certain meaning in a specific context. They may serve as shorthand reminders of ways of thinking about purpose. But a canon should never dictate to a judge that words must have only one meaning regardless of context. The canons of *ejusdem generis* ("of the same kind") and the rule of lenity (narrow construction) in criminal law may help a judge exclude airplanes and obscene records from the reach of two of the statutes we have looked at here, but they do not compel that conclusion, as the next section illustrates. *Noscitur a sociis* ("it is known by its associates") can also help a judge think more clearly about statutory purpose. The context of neighboring words may crystallize the meaning of an ambiguous phrase. What, for example, is "indecent conduct"? In the abstract, we might agree that it depends on individual perceptions and moralities, and that we can't really tell what it is. But consider two statutes, one that prohibits "indecent conduct at a divine service of worship" and another that prohibits "indecent conduct at a public beach or bathing place." The contexts of worship and beach could both classify having sex in public as indecent conduct, but only one context would classify strolling about in string bikinis as indecent. In life, as in law, things don't exist "in the abstract." In the abstract, there is no such objective thing as "indecent conduct." We might, trying to pick an extreme and hence conclusive example, say that cannibalism is automatically indecent conduct. But when the survivors of a plane crash high in the Andes consume the flesh of the dead in the hope of staying alive, does not the specific context, the specter of imminent death by starvation, change our feelings drastically about the "indecency" of cannibalism?

Determining Purpose: The Audience

Legislatures direct different statutes to different kinds of audiences. Some statutes, especially criminal statutes, communicate to the community at large. Criminal statutes thus have the purpose of communicating general standards of conduct to large populations that contain people of widely varying degrees of literacy and local customs and habits. Judges properly interpret such words according to the common meanings they may expect these words to convey to this diverse population. Other perhaps highly technical laws may communicate only to special classes of people, such as radio and television stations or insurance underwriters. Here the words may assume technical meanings that only the special audience understands. Similarly, judges should hold that a statute purposely changes a long-held principle of common law or the legality of a behavior widely believed proper in the past only when they think a statute makes that purpose unambiguously clear.

Determining Purpose: The Assumption of Legislative
Rationality and the Uses of Legislative History

In determining whether an issue in a lawsuit is part of the problem that a statute purposely tries to address, judges should treat the people who make laws
and the process of lawmaking as rational and sensible "reasonable persons
pursuing reasonable purposes reasonably," as Hart and Sacks put it.[45] This
assumption helps judges determine purpose because it forces them to determine which portion of the law, prior to the enactment of the statute, worked
so poorly that a rational legislature wanted to change it.[46] Again, think about
how the result in the locomotive-coupling case would differ if the Court had
approached the problem this way. Isn't the purpose to allow injured railroad workers to recover compensation for their on-the-job losses? Finally,
what purposes would a rational legislator have for inserting the "good moral
character" test in our naturalization laws? Is such a purpose well served by
making moral judgments about cannibalism or incest or mercy killing in the
abstract? (See the "Illustrative Case" section in chapter 2.)

The judge who thinks about lawmaking as a reasonable process also
recognizes that no statute exists in isolation, for rational lawmakers understand that no one act can completely define where the statute's policy
stops and another competing policy ought, instead, to govern. Members
of Congress realize that state law, not federal law, assumes the major responsibility for defining and policing criminal behavior, an issue that the
illustrative case at the end of this chapter squarely confronts. Knowing that
state laws define and prohibit sexual immorality limited the purpose the
Court attributed to the Mann Act in *Mortensen*, the case of the vacationing
prostitutes that was described in chapter 2.

Sometimes no helpful legislative history exists at all. But other times,
courts can generate sensible conclusions about the purpose of statutes
from the statements of legislative committees, sponsors of the bill, and
so forth. This history may allow a judge to understand which aspects or
consequences of prior law failed to cope with a social problem so that the
legislature needed to create a new law. Legislative history may also clarify
where one policy should give way to another. Legislative history relating
to specific applications of the statute, as in the loose-leaf notebook case,
helps the judge only to the extent that it provides good evidence of the
legislation's general purpose.

45. Henry M. Hart and Albert M. Sacks, *The Legal Process* (Cambridge, MA: Harvard Law School, 1958), 1415.

46. Lord Coke originated this helpful approach, sometimes labeled the "mischief
rule," in 1584.

Illustrations of Statutory Purpose: Two Easy Cases

You should now have little difficulty resolving some of this chapter's cases. Despite the ambiguities in the statutory language, you should not hesitate (1) to allow the officer to collect the breath specimen from a driver standing on the shoulder of the road, not while the driver weaves down the highway, and (2) to prohibit the liquor store from reopening at 10:01.[47] The words don't require these conclusions, and judges probably lack any legislative history for these state and local laws, but judges can still reach sensible results. Notice, by the way, how the solution to both of these cases hinges on the judge's realistic assessment of the social background facts and widespread public values that bear on these cases, not merely on the rules and case facts alone.

Of course, other cases could arise under these same statutes in which the words themselves would not bear the interpretation claimed for them. Our police officer cannot collect breath specimens in parking lots and driveways outside cocktail parties at midnight, even if he rightly assumes that many will soon drive home and even if we believe it a highly wise social policy to prevent intoxicated drivers from driving in the first place. This action might be an effective preventive, but it is not found in the meaning and purpose of this law because the words make "driving" a prerequisite for demanding the specimen.

THE CASE OF THE LADY JURORS; OR, WHY LEGISLATIVE INTENT DOES NOT DETERMINE STATUTORY PURPOSE

Recall briefly Chief Justice Rugg's justification for excluding women from jury liability despite the fact that they could vote and despite the fact that the statute required jury duty of "persons" (not "men") qualified to vote. The legislature did not intend the word *person* to include females, because females could not then vote, Rugg said.

Like the case of the automatic train couplers, *Welosky* offers a classic example of a judge reaching the right answer to the wrong question. Of course the legislature did not intend to include women, but that doesn't answer the right question. The proper question is, what purpose is served by legislation that ties jury service to voter eligibility?

Efficiency is one possible answer, because this policy spares the legislature from repeatedly rehashing the question of who should sit on juries. Quality is another, for this policy provides a test of qualifications that will ensure at least the same minimum degree of responsibility, compe-

---

47. See note 12, *supra*.

tence, education, and permanence of residence for both jurors and voters. Both voting and jury duty are general civic functions of citizens, but
gearing the right to practice medicine, for instance, to voting eligibility
would not make much sense. Does it serve a purpose, however, to pass
a statute saying, in effect, the following: "If you are qualified to vote, you
are qualified to serve as a juror; however, any changes in voter eligibility
hereafter enacted won't count because we haven't thought of them yet"?
If the legislature had this purpose, why didn't it simply list the desirable
qualifications for jurors? Read the statute as Rugg did and the gearing loses
purpose. Rugg did not treat the policy process as rational and sensible. He
did not admit that juror qualifications could have been purposely designed
to change with the times.

The difference between a search for legislative intent and a search for
purpose, then, is the difference in the evidence judges seek. Judges who
believe they must show intent will examine reports, speeches, and prior
drafts of bills. This evidence probably won't give clear meaning to the statute because it will contain internal inconsistencies or raise issues only in
general terms—yet judges who think they must find intent can fool themselves into believing that they have found it. Judges who believe that they
must articulate a sensible statement of purpose, however, will necessarily
search much further, into dictionaries, canons, and competing social policies as well as history itself. They will coordinate the materials to reach a
confident articulation of purpose. They will perform the judicial function
as Benjamin Cardozo described it (see the epigraph that opens this book).
They will work harder than will judges who stop when they have found a
nugget of legislative history, which is why so many judges, possessing the
all-too-human tendency to laziness, are satisfied with the nugget.

STATUTORY PURPOSE IN THE CASES OF CRIMINAL
COMMERCE: CAMINETTI, MCBOYLE, AND ALPERS
In each of the three cases of *Caminetti*, *McBoyle*, and *Alpers*, Congress,
under the authority of the commerce clause of the U.S. Constitution, forbade citizens from moving what Congress deemed evil from one state to
another. Let us assume that every state had laws to deal with each of the
evil things—theft, prostitution, and pornography, respectively. What purpose, then, does additional *federal* legislation on these matters serve? For
each of the federal statutes, there are records of committee reports, floor
speeches, and other legislative history. In no case, however, does the solid
data of legislative history reveal whether the purpose of the statute does or
does not include the cases of our defendants. After a delightfully detailed

review of the House and Senate reports on the Mann Act and of the discussions reported in the *Congressional Record*—showing, if not total confusion about the Act, at least much disagreement about its specific meaning—Levi concludes, "The Mann Act was passed after there had been many extensive governmental investigations. Yet there was no common understanding of the facts, and whatever understanding seems to have been achieved concerning the white-slave trade seems incorrectly based. The words used were broad and ambiguous."[48]

Given this ambiguity, perhaps judges could use the canons of construction to resolve the three cases. The rule of lenity dictating narrow construction of criminal statutes, for example, could allow judges to reverse the three convictions because in each case, the law does not unambiguously apply to the special facts involved. A judge who adopted Holmes's belief that criminal laws must communicate to a general lay audience with a clarity the average person can understand would reach the same result. Of course it depends on which canon the judge used to resolve the case. Following the canon of *ejusdem generis* ("of the same kind"), Mr. Caminetti, who took his girlfriend to Reno, might go to jail, but Mr. McBoyle, the airplane thief, and Mr. Alpers, the seller of obscene records, might go free.

These cases, however, do not come out this way. The smut peddler Alpers and the boyfriend Caminetti went to jail. The airplane thief McBoyle had his conviction reversed. Worse, the judicial opinions in these cases articulate no coherent linkages between purposes and outcomes. To create that linkage, one must begin with the right question: Why would Congress, "reasonable persons pursuing reasonable purposes reasonably," pass laws creating federal crimes when all the states already have, through their criminal laws, punished these same evils? Does not the purpose lie in the fact that movement from state to state makes it more difficult for the states to detect or enforce the violation? A car owner who has his car stolen may have trouble tracking it in another state. The prosecutor in the state where citizens receive wanted or unwanted pornography has no jurisdiction over the man who peddles by mail from another state. Men who hustle girls far from home may make impossible both detection and social pressure to resist prostitution. Movement has consequences. It makes objects and behaviors physically harder to locate. It makes apprehension and prosecution more difficult, because police and prosecutors in one jurisdiction don't have authority in another. The presence of physical movement thus helps to reveal purpose.

48. Levi, *Introduction to Legal Reasoning*, 40.

In *McBoyle*, then, the proper questions ought to look something like this: (1) Do airplanes, because they are movable, complicate the task of catching the people who steal them? (2) Does it serve any purpose to assume that McBoyle thought flying a stolen airplane to another state was legal because of the ambiguities in the word *vehicle*? Is it, in other words, unfair to McBoyle to convict him under this act because it does not unambiguously include airplanes? You should reach your own conclusion, but we would answer the first question with a yes, the second with a no, and respectfully dissent from Justice Holmes.

You should ask one other question about *McBoyle*. Suppose McBoyle's lawyer had argued that when the National Motor Vehicle Theft Act was passed, air travel was in such infancy that Congress probably did not intend to include airplanes. Notice that this argument should matter to you only if you think it important to ask what Congress intended. If you instead consider legislation as policy designed to adjust to future technological and other changes that lawmakers cannot in the present foresee, and if you ask instead which kinds of crimes call for the kind of law enforcement help that this act provides, you would find McBoyle's lawyer's legislative intent argument trivial.

Is *Alpers* any different? It might be, particularly if you see the case as presenting a constitutional problem of free expression. The purpose of the statute forbidding the interstate shipment of obscenity might be said to be preventing the exposure of children or unwilling people—people who open mail or see magazines left around—to visual pornography. Is this purpose served by prohibiting the shipment of obscene records, or today, CDs?

Alpers is an especially difficult case. Unlike Mr. McBoyle, Mr. Alpers could reasonably have interpreted the Act as not banning records for two reasons. First, the competing principle of free expression sets limits on government interference with the communication of ideas. No such principle limits governmental interference with the movement of property known to be stolen. Second, the purpose of the National Motor Vehicle Theft Act seems to apply specifically to airplanes. They are very transportable. The Act's purpose may therefore especially apply to airplanes. However, one reading of the purpose of the statute in *Alpers*—visual pornography left around may offend, whereas a phonograph record lying around does not—reduces its applicability to *Alpers*. That said, the recipient might play the offensive record for an unwilling person. But consider again the rule of lenity, which favors the narrow construction of criminal statutes. If Mr. McBoyle went free, why not Mr. Alpers?

Finally, consider the married man who brings in a willing girlfriend from out of state for a night of debauchery. Conceivably, the "White Slave" statute could purposely try to police all forms of sexual immorality somehow involving interstate transportation. But what are the probabilities that this legislation has such purpose in light of (1) the title of the Act; (2) the canons of narrow construction of, and clear communication in, criminal statutes; (3) the problem arousing public concern at the time; (4) the fact that states, if they so choose, are just as able as is the FBI to discover and crack down on noncommercial illegal sex (or to decriminalize it, as most states have); and (5) Representative Mann's report as well as the widespread belief that the general police powers reside in state and not federal hands?

Notice how it is only by weaving together many different techniques of interpretation that we begin to develop confidence about the purpose of the Mann Act.

A Final Complication

This summary of sensible judicial approaches to statutes may have misled you in one critical respect. You may now feel that in every case, the "right-thinking" judge will find the one "right" solution simply by uncovering a single purpose of the statute. This chapter's illustrations all make sense when we analyze them in terms of purpose. *We may, however, still honestly disagree about purpose.* The task of judging is choosing among plausible alternative possibilities, not solving an algebra problem. A purpose-oriented approach does not eliminate judicial discretion in statutory interpretation. Judges who thoughtfully and diligently consider legislative purpose may nonetheless disagree about the resolution of a specific case.

To illustrate, suppose Holmes had said in *McBoyle*:

> The purpose of this act is to permit federal assistance to states in finding easily moved and hidden vehicles. But airplanes, while easily moved, are really like trains, which the Act expressly excludes, because, like trains, they are tied to places where they cannot be hidden—airports. What goes up must come down, and only in certain places. One black Ford may look like a thousand other black Fords almost anywhere, but an airplane is much more like a train in this respect. Therefore, since we believe states, not the federal government, possess primary police powers, this act does not cover airplanes.

Finally, suppose in the cemetery case Justice Gregory argued:

> Establishment and expansion of cemeteries differ because the people
> near an expanded cemetery are already used to its presence, but to
> create a new cemetery in a place where residents had not planned on
> seeing funeral processions and graves and other unwanted reminders
> of life's transience is another matter.

Or imagine in *King v. Burwell*, the Obamacare case, these two possible
readings of statutory purpose:

1. The purpose of the Affordable Care Act is to expand health care to
   the uninsured and, as all insurance does, to spread the risk of unfore-
   seen harm more evenly through society. All provisions of the statute
   reflect this purpose, and except for the provision regarding subsidies,
   each part of the statute clearly treats states that create their own insurance marketplaces the same as those in which the federal government establishes the marketplaces. The only way to make sense of
   the statute, therefore, is to interpret it as providing subsidies to all
   who qualify, no matter where they happen to live.
2. The purpose of the Affordable Care Act is to expand health care
   to the uninsured, and the statute aims to do this through a system
   in which the federal government and the states work together. By
   withholding subsidies from states that refuse to create their own insurance exchanges, the statute encourages the cooperation among
   states and the federal government that is at the heart of the statute.
   Therefore, the statute is best interpreted as providing subsidies only
   in states that have established their own exchanges.

Whether we agree or disagree with these analyses, at least they rest on
purpose. We should prefer them to the automatic citation of a canon, a
quotation from a dictionary, or to any technique of interpretation that allows judges to evade the difficult task of determining the societal problems
the statute is meant to address.

Critics of a purpose-oriented approach make much of the fact that
judges with different worldviews can find different purposes in the same
statute. Justice Scalia, for example, has contended that purposivism is "a
rhetorical ploy that allows the judge to disregard text" and so create the
outcome the judge desires. Scalia contrasts this with his own more literalistic approach, which he claims binds him to vote without regard to his

political beliefs.[49] Scalia and other proponents of literalism, however, don't bother to examine whether in fact this approach really directs judges in the way they imagine. Fortunately, social scientists are increasingly studying what judges actually do in cases of statutory interpretation. Their studies have found that conservative judges like Scalia tend to find "literal" meanings that happen to justify conservative outcomes, whereas more liberal justices tend find "literal" meanings that justify liberal outcomes.[50] The same goes for the use of canons of construction, which as we have seen are available to justify many possible lines of legal reasoning.[51] In the terminology of social scientists, literalist and canonist approaches fail to constrain the judges' worldviews from affecting their legal reasoning. Nor do they appear to create consensus on the one right answer to questions of statutory interpretation.[52] Do these findings surprise you? We think them deeply

49. Scalia and Garner, *Reading Law*, 19, 17. Scalia, a proponent of "textualism," starts with what he calls a "fair meaning" interpretation of statutory language, and where this interpretation is ambiguous, he uses the canons of construction to try to resolve the ambiguities. Scalia's extensive use of court-created canons means that his approach, despite his "textualist" label, can in some cases take him far afield from the "plain meaning" of a statute—see Bradley C. Karkkainen, "'Plain Meaning': Justice Scalia's Jurisprudence of Strict Statutory Construction," *Harvard Journal of Law and Public Policy* 17 (1994): 401–477. In practice Scalia, like other working judges, uses a variety of approaches to statutory interpretation, perhaps in part to fend off the arguments of justices who disagree with him. See Miranda Oshige McGowan, "Do as I Do, Not as I Say: An Empirical Investigation of Justice Scalia's Ordinary Meaning Method of Statutory Interpretation" *Mississippi Law Journal* 78 (2008): 129–198; and Frank Cross, *The Theory and Practice of Statutory Interpretation* (Stanford, CA: Stanford University Press, 2009), 149–155.

50. Frank Cross, for example, finds that in a sample of cases in which Scalia employed a "plain meaning" approach to statutory interpretation, he voted conservatively 71.4 percent of the time; in a comparison sample of civil liberties cases, Scalia voted conservatively 71.6 percent of the time. Ruth Bader Ginsburg, by contrast, voted conservatively in 39.8 percent of her "plain meaning" cases and 35.5 percent of civil liberties cases. See Cross, *Theory and Practice of Statutory Interpretation*, table 7.1, 165, and more generally 166–179.

51. In their study James Brudney and Corey Ditslear found not only that judges relied on different canons that justified outcomes consistent with their worldviews but also that judges with different worldviews often disagreed on the outcome while citing the same canon. See Brudney and Ditslear, "Canons of Construction and the Elusive Quest for Neutral Reasoning," *Vanderbilt Law Review* (2005): 1–120.

52. Cross finds that Supreme Court justices who employ "textualist" analysis in their opinions do not create consensus among justices on the Court at any greater rate than those who use legislative intent or canons of construction; in fact, the only approach associated with greater consensus was a "pragmatist" approach, in which policy outcomes were considered. See Cross, *Theory and Practice of Statutory Interpretation*, 156–158. Cross also finds that Supreme Court opinions that use a "textualist" approach are particularly divisive within the lower federal courts, garnering both more positive and more negative citations than opinions with other approaches (see 191–199).

unsurprising considering all the sources of ambiguity in both statutory language and theories of statutory interpretation this chapter has described.

Stare Decisis in Statutory Interpretation

We have thus far studied an atypical occurrence in statutory interpretation, interpretation in the first instance. This may have puzzled you, for in the previous chapters we have seen that reasoning by example—using precedents as guides for resolving legal conflicts—is a fundamental component of legal reasoning. In fact, judges in statutory cases rarely go where no judge has gone before: in the vast majority of cases they follow in the footsteps of many other judges. So judges in statutory interpretation cases usually must wrestle, just as they do in common law cases, with the weight of stare decisis. When should a court follow what another court has said about a statute? When, conversely, should courts prefer a different interpretation and ignore or overrule an earlier court's first effort to make sense of the statute's meaning?

Assume that the *McBoyle* decision wrongly interpreted the National Motor Vehicle Theft Act because the statute's purpose does cover the theft of airplanes. Or assume that *Caminetti* wrongly applied the Mann Act to include the transportation of girlfriends. Should a court facing a new airplane or girlfriend case feel bound to accept that interpretation? Once a precedent or series of precedents gives a clear answer on a point of law, should courts leave it to legislatures to change that questionable interpretation by statutory amendment? In which circumstances should judges adhere to precedents?

It might seem sensible, and indeed, it *is* sensible, to answer these questions by referring to the justifications for stare decisis that appear near the end of chapter 2. When adherence to a prior interpretation or series of cases interpreting a statute promotes stability in law, and that stability in turn allows citizens to plan their affairs by relying on specific legal rules—in short, when stability promotes the paramount social goal of cooperation—courts should not abandon stare decisis. Similarly, if a citizen now deserves to receive the same treatment a citizen in a precedent did, or if stare decisis would preserve efficient judicial administration or a positive public image of justice, then courts should honor it. When stare decisis does not promote these goals, courts should freely ignore it. Thus, assuming a court felt that both *McBoyle* and *Caminetti* were wrongly decided, normal stare decisis theory would permit overruling *Caminetti* but not *McBoyle*. It injures no citizen to declare that something once held criminal is no longer so, but it does seem unfair to convict someone after declaring that his or her actions were not crimes.

Unfortunately, some judges and legal scholars believe that judges should invariably follow the first judicial attempt to find statutory meaning, even when they have doubts about the wisdom of the first attempt and, worse, when the characteristics of the problem do not call for stare decisis. We shall first review an example of this "one-shot theory" of statutory interpretation in action.[53] We then evaluate its shortcomings. In short, the "one-shot theory" fails because it is based on myths about how legislatures operate. The following legal story also reveals considerable judicial ignorance about the purposes of stare decisis.

Major League Baseball, Haviland's Dog and Pony Show, and Government Regulation of Business

Much of the power of the federal government to regulate business derives from the constitutional clause empowering Congress to make laws that regulate commerce "among the several States." This is one of the provisions of the Constitution, you might remember from chapter 2, that was argued over in the legal struggle over Obamacare. Armed with this authority, Congress has passed many statutes regulating businesses and businesspersons who physically cross state lines or transact business among states. But the interstate commerce clause has also been interpreted to empower Congress to regulate businesses operating within one state entirely, on the theory that those businesses nevertheless may compete with and affect businesses operating from other states.[54]

Among the many federal statutes whose authority rests on the commerce clause, we consider only two. The more substantial of the two, federal antitrust law, such as the Sherman Antitrust Act mentioned earlier in this chapter, was a response to the huge cartels and monopolies that emerged in the nineteenth century. Federal antitrust law prohibits businesses from engaging in anticompetitive practices, such as agreements

53. William Eskridge calls the theory "the super-strong presumption against overruling statutory precedents." "Overruling Statutory Precedents," *Georgetown Law Journal* 76 (1988): 1361–1439, at 1363. Eskridge's very thorough analysis agrees in nearly all respects with the position we take in this chapter. Calling the notion "a very odd doctrine," he analyzes cases from 1961 to 1987 and finds that "in only twenty-six instances (or one per term) has the Court explicitly repudiated both the reasoning and the result of a statutory precedent" (1368). He concurs with Justice Scalia's statement that "vindication by Congressional inaction is a canard" (1405n).

54. Recall *Wickard v. Filburn*, 317 U.S. 111 (1942), in which a farmer grew grain for his own family's use.

among rival companies to set prices or salaries at a certain level. Antitrust laws authorize the government and private citizens to bring criminal and civil lawsuits against businesses that engage in anticompetitive behavior.

The Animal Welfare Act of 1970, our second statutory example, specifies a variety of requirements for handling animals humanely. The statute requires "exhibitors" of animals "purchased in commerce or the intended distribution of which affects commerce or will affect commerce" to obtain an exhibitor's license. The statute explicitly includes carnivals, circuses, and zoos. It empowers the Department of Agriculture to administer its regulatory provisions.

Put these two statutes together and consider a truly wondrous phenomenon in contemporary law. Within the past half century, courts have held (1) that the multimillion-dollar industry of professional baseball, with all its national commercial television coverage and travel from state to state and to foreign countries, is *not* a business in interstate commerce and thus cannot be regulated by antitrust laws, and (2) that Haviland's Dog and Pony Show, consisting of a maximum of two ponies and five dogs traveling the rural byways of the American Midwest and earning a handful of dollars weekly, *is* a business in interstate commerce that must therefore meet the requirements of the Animal Welfare Act.[55]

We need say little more about the *Haviland* case. Haviland refused to obtain an exhibitor's license as required by the Animal Welfare Act, arguing that the well-being of his tiny troupe of dogs and ponies had little to do with interstate commerce. A federal appeals court disagreed—a win for the animals, as owners of dog-and-pony shows, we can assume, are no less likely than the staff of the San Diego Zoo to abuse their charges; rather more likely, we would bet.

But why don't antitrust statutes regulate Major League Baseball? Rigid adherence to stare decisis in statutory interpretation provides the answer, as the following chronology of decisions illustrates:

1922 The Federal Baseball Club of Baltimore, a member of a short-lived third major league, sued the National and American Leagues, claiming that the two leagues had, in violation of antitrust laws, colluded to destroy the third league by buying some of its clubs and convincing other owners not to join. The case reached the U.S. Supreme Court, where Justice Holmes's opinion held that the

---

55. *Flood v. Kuhn*, 407 U.S. 258 (1972); *Haviland v. Butz*, 543 F.2d 169 (D.C. Cir. 1976).

playing of baseball did not involve interstate commerce any more than, say, a lecturer traveling from town to town, so that Congress could not regulate it.[56] Holmes's ruling was in line with the prevailing view of Congress's commerce power at the time; it was two decades later that the Supreme Court enlarged this power in cases like *Wickard v. Filburn* (the case of the farmer who grew wheat in his garden). For its time, *Federal Baseball* rested on defensible, if not indisputable, reasoning.

1948 An outfielder, Danny Gardella, sued the professional baseball leagues after they banned him from playing for any of their teams for five years. The ban punished Gardella for leaving the New York Giants to play in the Mexican League, where salaries were higher. Gardella argued that the ban violated federal antitrust law because it stopped baseball owners from competing to hire him. The Second Circuit Court of Appeals ruled that, in part as a result of increased radio and television revenues, baseball was part of interstate commerce and so subject to antitrust law. One of the judges on the Court, Jerome Frank, called the major league's treatment of players "shockingly repugnant" and akin to slavery, outlawed by the Thirteenth Amendment after the Civil War.[57]

1953 Minor league pitcher George Toolson, perhaps buoyed by the *Gardella* decision, brought a lawsuit arguing that baseball's "reserve clause" violated federal antitrust laws. Under the reserve clause, players were bound to their teams even after their contracts ran out; this stopped the owners from competing for players and so kept players' salaries down. Toolson felt stuck in the Yankees' organization and wanted to move to another team. The reserve clause seemed like just the kind of anticompetitive practice targeted by antitrust laws, yet the Supreme Court, in *Toolson v. New York Yankees*, followed the *Federal Baseball* precedent in ruling that baseball was not covered by the laws. The majority opinion stressed stare decisis:

> Congress has had the [*Federal Baseball*] ruling under consideration but has not seen fit to bring such business under these laws by legislation having prospective effect. The business has

56. *Federal Baseball Club of Baltimore v. National League of Professional Baseball Clubs*, 259 U.S. 200 (1922).

57. *Gardella v. Chandler*, 172 F.2d 402 (2nd Cir., 1949). See Andrew Zimbalist, *Baseball and Billions* (New York: Basic Books, 1992), 13.

thus been left for thirty years to develop, on the understanding that it was not subject to existing antitrust legislation. The present cases ask us to overrule the prior decision and, with retrospective effect, hold the legislation applicable. . . . Without reexamination of the underlying issues, the judgments below are affirmed on the authority of *Federal Baseball* . . . so far as that decision determines that Congress had no intention of including the business of baseball within the scope of the federal antitrust laws.[58]

The majority's last sentence was a complete fabrication; Justice Holmes never contended in 1922 that Congress intended to leave baseball out of antitrust laws. And for good reason: The notion that members of Congress even thought about baseball when they were writing the Sherman Antitrust Act in 1890 is laughable. But beyond that, the *Toolson* opinion discounts a key social background fact, the growth of baseball as a national sport between 1922 and 1953, as well as a key change in legal rules, the growth of Congress's commerce power in cases decided in the 1930s and 1940s. After *Toolson*, things get downright silly.

1955   The Supreme Court rules that both the movie business and professional boxing are part of interstate commerce and so fall under federal antitrust law. It distinguishes *Toolson* as a "narrow application of the rule of stare decisis."[59]

1957   A befuddled lower appellate court, mystified by the distinction between baseball and boxing that the Supreme Court had created, decided that football did not fall under the antitrust laws because football, like baseball but unlike boxing, was a team sport. The Supreme Court reversed![60]

1971   The Supreme Court held that the antitrust laws governed professional basketball.[61]

1972   Having ruled that boxing, football, and basketball were all governed by antitrust law, the Supreme Court once again faced a antitrust lawsuit brought by a baseball player, Curt Flood, challenging the reserve clause, the rule preventing players from leaving their teams. After a panegyric review of baseball's history, replete with

58. *Toolson v. New York Yankees*, 346 U.S. 356 (1953).
59. *United States v. Shubert*, 348 U.S. 222 (1955).
60. *Radovich v. National Football League*, 352 U.S. 445 (1957).
61. *Heywood v. National Basketball Association*, 401 U.S. 1204 (1971).

references to Ernest Thayer's "Casey at the Bat" and a long and curious list of baseball's greats,[62] Justice Blackmun ruled once again that baseball was immune from antitrust law. Though he admitted the precedents were illogical, he followed them:

> [W]e adhere once again to *Federal Baseball* and *Toolson* and to their application to professional baseball. We adhere also to *International Boxing* and *Radovich* and to their respective applications to professional boxing and professional football. If there is any inconsistency or illogic in all this, it is an inconsistency and illogic of long-standing that is to be remedied by the Congress and not by this Court. If we were to act otherwise, we would be withdrawing from the conclusion as to congressional intent made in *Toolson* and from the concerns as to retrospectivity therein expressed. Under these circumstances, there is merit in consistency even though some might claim that beneath that consistency is a layer of inconsistency.[63]

Justice Douglas dissented. He wrote, "The unbroken silence of Congress should not prevent us from correcting our own mistakes."[64]

Curt Flood, who sacrificed the remainder of his career to challenge the owners, eventually became a hero to the players, who formed their own union and got the reserve rule eliminated.[65] In 1998, Congress enacted the Curt Flood Act (Curt Flood, alas, had died the previous year), which specified that when it comes to their relations with major league players, baseball owners are governed by antitrust laws just like their colleagues in football and basketball. Does this mean that for all other purposes professional baseball remains exempt from federal antitrust law? Courts continue to disagree over this question, resulting in a stream of litigation over, for example, whether Major League Baseball can control where

62. The list includes such immortals as Three-Finger Brown and Hans Lobert but omits Hall of Famers Stan Musial, Joe DiMaggio, Ted Williams, and Hank Aaron.

63. *Flood v. Kuhn*, 407 U.S. 258 (1972), 284.

64. The mess created by these decisions will not go away. In 1996 the Court returned to them in *Brown v. Washington Redskins*, 518 U.S. 231 (1996). See particularly Justice Stevens's dissent, in which he cites *Federal Baseball, Toolson, Radovich*, and *Flood*. The lawsuit alleged that the National Football League's unilateral arrangement to pay "taxi squad" members a flat rate of $1,000 per week violated the Sherman Antitrust Act.

65. Robert M. Goldman, *One Man Out: Curt Flood versus Baseball* (Lawrence: University Press of Kansas 2008).

baseball franchises are located—a power that would normally violate antitrust laws.[66]

What did the Supreme Court get wrong here? In the immediate case of sports and the antitrust laws, *Toolson*'s utterly inaccurate insistence that *Federal Baseball* means that Congress did not intend to include baseball wreaked the most havoc. *Toolson*, to paraphrase, says, "The highest law-making body in the country, Congress, has determined that the antitrust laws should not apply to professional baseball. Therefore, the owners of baseball teams have made many business arrangements in reliance on this state of the law. It would be wrong to upset these expectations legitimized by the intent of Congress." This position is pure nonsense. Congress did not intend to exclude baseball. Holmes in *Federal Baseball* never said Congress so intended. The baseball owners had no reason to rely on *Federal Baseball*, at least not in 1953, given intervening precedents. Stability and reliance do not in this instance require the Court to invoke stare decisis and follow *Federal Baseball*. *Toolson* reached that different result by merely saying, without supporting evidence, that Congress in its silence so commanded.

Unfortunately, the Supreme Court's reasoning in these cases is worse than that. At least, you might say, baseball owners probably did honestly believe that they had a good chance of escaping the antitrust laws and acted on that basis. There is some merit in the reliance argument. But if stare decisis seeks to assist people in making plans in reliance on stable law, then surely owners of football, basketball, and boxing franchises and athletes had every bit as much reason for relying on *Federal Baseball* or *Toolson* as did the baseball owners. After all, in terms of the antitrust law, there is no difference among these sports that ought to induce baseball owners to rely on the original precedent while preventing those in the other sports from doing so.

In the name of stare decisis, then, we have a series of decisions that hardly seems stable, that violates reliance expectations to the extent that there are any, and that does not treat equals equally. To complete the list of justifications for adhering to precedent, do these decisions strike you as efficient judicial administration? What image of justice do these cases flash in your mind?

Fortunately, we have deliberately chosen an extreme example. Faced

---

66. Justin B. Bryant, "Note: Analyzing the Scope of Major League Baseball's Antitrust Exemption in Light of San Jose v. Office of the Commissioner of Baseball," *Notre Dame Law Review* 89 (2014): 1841–1874. For the most recent addition to the now-venerable literature on baseball as a business, see Stuart Banner, *The Baseball Trust* (New York: Oxford University Press), 2014.

with statutory precedents, courts do not invariably invoke stare decisis in order to wreak havoc on the very justifications for stare decisis. Nevertheless, this critical question remains: *if* judges think that an existing judicial interpretation of a statute is erroneous, and *if* they also think that they may overrule it without doing violence to the five justifications of stare decisis, should such judges hesitate because the legislature has failed to act? Put differently, should judges, out of a concern for interfering with the work of legislatures, treat stare decisis any differently in statutory law than in common law? We believe the proper answer to this question is no. Let us, however, review the arguments given for what has been called the "one-shot theory" of statutory interpretation.

The Case against Increased Adherence to Precedent in Statutory Interpretation

Proponents of the one-shot theory sometimes argue that the failure of a legislature to change a statute is a signal to courts to stick with precedents. In *Toolson*, for example, the Supreme Court seemed to say that because Congress had not passed a statute to cover baseball by the antitrust laws, Congress had somehow converted *Federal Baseball* into statutory law. Would any of the following events in Congress, or in any legislature, strengthen such a conclusion?

- Many bills were introduced to cover baseball, but none of them passed.
- Many bills were introduced to exempt baseball, but none of them passed.
- Congress reenacted the relevant antitrust provisions, with some modifications, none of which attempted to cover or exempt baseball specifically.
- Congress passed a statute explicitly placing, say, professional boxing prior to 1955, under the antitrust laws, and the statute makes no mention of baseball's status.
- Congress passed a joint resolution that officially states that baseball is hereinafter to be considered "the national pastime of the United States."

Judges often buttress their adherence to precedents on such grounds, but this is unwarranted. Congress possesses no power to make law other than by passing statutes. Statutes are, among other items, subject to presidential veto power. Therefore, not even joint resolutions, which escape presidential veto, create law. To say that any of the legislative acts we just listed creates law is to give Congress a lawmaking power not found in the Constitution.

Furthermore, consider these reasons that a legislature might not, in fact, directly respond to a judicial interpretation by law:[67]

- Legislators never learn of the judicial interpretation in the first place.
- Legislators don't care about the issue the interpretation raises.
- Legislators care but feel they must spend their limited time and political resources on other more important matters.
- Legislators like the proposed new statute or amendment but feel it politically unwise to vote for it.
- Legislators decide to vote against the bill because they do not like another unrelated provision of the bill.
- Legislators feel that the bill does not go far enough and vote against it in hopes of promulgating more comprehensive law later.
- Legislators don't like the bill's sponsor personally and therefore vote negatively.
- Legislators believe, in the words of Hart and Sacks, "that the matter should be left to be handled by the normal process of judicial development of decisional law, including the overruling of outstanding decisions to the extent that the sound growth of the law requires."[68]

Do not all these possibilities, especially the last, convince you that courts should not speculate about the meaning of legislative silence? Recent scholarship suggests the complexity of court-Congress interactions in statutory interpretation. Sometimes members of Congress are so outraged by a judicial decision that they immediately override it, but as Jeb Barnes has found, there are many other possible scenarios: Some overrides are matters of great controversy, with interest groups on both sides highly mobilized. Many others are quiet and consensual.[69] And most times, Congress, for a variety of reasons, does not override. Lawrence Baum and Lori Hausegger found in their study that from 1978 to 1989, Congress overrode only about 6 percent of the statutory decisions made by the Supreme Court.[70]

67. Hart and Sacks, *Legal Process*, 1395–1396.
68. Ibid., 1396.
69. Jeb Barnes, *Overruled? Legislative Overrides, Pluralism and Contemporary Court-Congress Relations* (Palo Alto, CA: Stanford University Press, 2004).
70. Cited in Lawrence Baum and Lori Hausegger, "The Supreme Court and Congress: Reconsidering the Relationship," in *Putting the Pieces Together: Lawmaking from an Interbranch Perspective*, ed. Mark Miller and Jeb Barnes (Washington, DC: Georgetown University Press, 2004). Growing polarization between the parties in Congress

Sophisticated proponents of the one-shot theory of statutory interpretation admit that legislative silence is meaningless.[71] They worry instead about the proper apportionment of legislative and judicial responsibilities. Their argument goes this way: Legislatures deliberately use ambiguous language in statutes, not simply to bring many somewhat different, specific events under one policy roof but also to allow room for the compromises necessary to generate a majority vote. Once written, the words of a statute will not change; but because they are general, vague, and ambiguous, courts will certainly have the opportunity to interpret those same words in many different ways.

If, the argument continues, words have different meanings at different times and places, the legislature's power to make law becomes pointless, or at least quite subordinate to the judicial power of interpretation. Courts must find one meaning. They do so by determining legislative intent. The judiciary insults the legislature if it says that at one time the legislature intended the words to carry one meaning and at another time another meaning. To say this is to say of the legislature that it had no intent and that it did not understand its actions. That assertion would embarrass the legislature, to say the least.

The argument thus holds that part of the judicial responsibility to the legislature is to reinforce the concept that the legislature did in fact have a specific intention, because that is what the public expects of legislatures. In the first half of this chapter, we explained why this argument fails.

Fortunately, the argument does not stop there. Levi asserts:

> Legislatures and courts are cooperative law-making bodies. It is important to know where the responsibility lies. If legislation which is disfavored can be interpreted away from time to time, then it is not to be expected, particularly if controversy is high, that the legislature will ever act. It will always be possible to say that new legislation is not needed because the court in the future will make a more appropriate interpretation. If the court is to have freedom to reinterpret legislation, the result will be to relieve the legislature from pressure. The legislation needs judicial consistency. Moreover, the court's own

---

resulting in legislative gridlock may be reducing still further the rate of overrides and so creating more "legislative silences," although the pattern of congressional activity in recent years is complex. See Matthew R. Christiansen and William N. Eskridge Jr., "Congressional Overrides of Supreme Court Statutory Interpretation Decisions, 1967–2011," *Texas Law Review* 92 (2014): 1317–1541.

71. See especially Levi, *Introduction to Legal Reasoning*, 31–33.

behavior in the face of pressure is likely to be indecisive. In all likelihood it will do enough to prevent legislative revision and not much
more. Therefore it seems better to say that once a decisive interpretation of legislative intent has been made, and in that sense a direction
has been fixed within the gap of ambiguity, the court should take that
direction as given. In this sense a court's interpretation of legislation
is not dictum. The words it uses do more than decide the case. They
give broad direction to the statute.[72]

Levi's argument cuts too deeply. Indeed, there are instances in which
legislators breathe sighs of relief that courts have taken delicate political
problems from them. (Curiously enough, courts most often do so by applying constitutional standards to legislation, and in this area, Levi does
not demand similarly strict stare decisis.) But Levi's position is simply inaccurate in its assumption that most questions of interpretation raise highly
charged public issues that legislatures ought to deal with but won't if courts
do it for them. For the most part, judicial errors in statutory interpretation involve borderline application of statutes. The interpretations may
do considerable injustice to the parties who find themselves in borderline
situations without, in any significant way, damaging the central purposes
of the statutory policy as a whole. In the large majority of cases, then, it
is wholly unrealistic to assume that either overruling or adherence will
affect how legislators perform. Try to imagine, for example, how Congress
would have reacted had the Supreme Court held in 1946 that the traveling
bigamous Mormons did not violate the Mann Act. Probably with a yawn.[73]

A Summary Statement of the Appropriate Judicial
Approach to Statutory Interpretation

To conclude, notice how many of the problems that courts have created
for themselves regarding the place of stare decisis in statutory interpre-

---

72. Ibid., 32.

73. However, nearly three-quarters of a century after the *Caminetti* decision, Congress quietly altered key provisions of the Mann Act when it enacted the Child Sexual
Abuse and Pornography Act of 1986. The amendments eliminated the reference to white
slavery, substituted *individual* for *female* and *woman or girl*, and instead of debauchery
or immoral purpose, specified "any sexual activity for which any person can be charged
with a criminal offense." New York Governor Eliot Spitzer was forced from office in
March 2008 after he admitted to liaisons with prostitutes who had traveled to New York
from other states to tryst with him, in part because he had allegedly violated the revised
Mann Act, although federal prosecutors ultimately decided not to prosecute him.

tations would evaporate if only judges convinced themselves to seek out the purpose of a statute and not speculate about legislative intent from inconclusive legislative evidence. The inadequate conclusions that judges reach when they reason on the first and more superficial analytical level would disappear altogether. At the more sophisticated level, the concept that the courts embarrass legislatures by implying the rather obvious truth that the legislators probably had no intent regarding the precise issue before the court would also disappear. Is this truth so awful? Of course not. That statutes speak in general terms is a simple necessity in political life. Such generality explains and justifies the existence of courts.

Just as in common law cases, judges in statutory interpretation should follow precedents when one or more of the five justifications for stare decisis we listed in chapter 2 so dictate. Their primary obligation to the legislature is to apply the statutes it creates so as to achieve, as best judges can determine it, the intelligible solution of problems the statute exists to solve. Judges should try to determine purpose accurately, but they will err from time to time. It is no embarrassment to the legislature for judges to admit that they erred in determining statutory purpose and in properly applying it to cases before them. They should therefore give stare decisis no special weight in statutory interpretation. They should do so with the confidence that, to the extent that they can predict legislative behavior at all, they can assume that the legislature is no less likely to correct them if they err today than if they erred yesterday. Of course, legislation needs judicial consistency. Affixing proper legislative responsibility will occur only when courts sensibly articulate statutory purposes.

ILLUSTRATIVE CASE

After a night of heavy drinking, Larry Begay first threatened his aunt and then his sister with an unloaded rifle. Begay's possession of the rifle violated federal statutory law because he was a convicted felon; he had been convicted a dozen times for driving under the influence (DUI), and under New Mexico law, the fourth and all succeeding DUI convictions are punishable as felonies. Ordinarily, Begay would have received ten years for possessing a gun, but a federal judge sentenced him under the Armed Career Criminal Act, which imposes a mandatory fifteen-year sentence on an offender who has had three prior convictions for a "violent felony or a serious drug offense."

The act defines a "violent felony" as "any crime punishable by imprisonment for a term exceeding one year that

(i) has as an element the use, attempted use, or threatened use of physical force against the person of another; or

(ii) is burglary, arson, or extortion, involves use of explosives, or otherwise involves conduct that presents a serious potential risk of physical injury to another."

Begay appealed his sentence, arguing that his DUI convictions did not fall under either of the two specified descriptions of a "violent felony."

Begay v. United States
U.S. Supreme Court
553 U.S. 137 (2008)

JUSTICE BREYER delivered the opinion of the Court:

. . . In our view, the provision's listed examples—burglary, arson, extortion, or crimes involving the use of explosives—illustrate the kinds of crimes that fall within the statute's scope. Their presence indicates that the statute covers only *similar* crimes, rather than *every* crime that "presents a serious potential risk of physical injury to another." (ii). If Congress meant the latter, *i.e.*, if it meant the statute to be all-encompassing, it is hard to see why it would have needed to include the examples at all. Without them, clause (ii) would cover *all* crimes that present a "serious potential risk of physical injury." Additionally, if Congress meant clause (ii) to include *all* risky crimes, why would it have included clause (i)? A crime which has as an element the "use, attempted use, or threatened use of physical force" against the person (as clause (i) specifies) is likely to create "a serious potential risk of physical injury" and would seem to fall within the scope of clause (ii). . . .

These considerations taken together convince us that, "'to give effect . . . to every clause and word'" of this statute, we should read the examples as limiting the crimes that clause (ii) covers to crimes that are roughly similar, in kind as well as in degree of risk posed, to the examples themselves. . . . Of course, the statute places the word "otherwise" just after the examples, so that the provision covers a felony that is one of the example crimes "or *otherwise* involves conduct that presents a serious potential risk of physical injury." (ii) [Emphasis added.] But we cannot agree with the Government that the word "otherwise" is *sufficient* to demonstrate that the examples do not limit the scope of the clause. That is because the word "otherwise" *can* (we do not say *must* [Scalia, J., concurring in judgment]) refer to a crime that is similar to the listed examples in some respects but different in others—similar say in respect to the degree of risk it produces, but different in respect to the "way or manner" in which it produces that risk. Webster's Third New International Dictionary 1598 (1961) (defining "otherwise" to mean "in a different way or manner"). . . .

In our view, DUI differs from the example crimes—burglary, arson, extortion, and crimes involving the use of explosives—in at least one pertinent, and important, respect. The listed crimes all typically involve purposeful, "violent," and "aggressive" conduct. See *Taylor v. United States*, 495 U.S. 575, 598 (1990) ("burglary" is an unlawful or unprivileged entry into a building or other structure with "intent to commit a crime"); ALI Model Penal Code §220.1(1) (1985) ("arson" is causing a fire or explosion with "the purpose of," *e.g.*, "destroying a building . . . of another" or "damaging any property . . . to collect insurance"); *id.*, §223.4 (extortion is "purposely" obtaining property of another through threat of, *e.g.*, inflicting "bodily injury"); *Leocal v. Ashcroft*, 543 U.S. 1, 9 (2004) (the word "'use' . . . most naturally suggests a higher degree of intent than negligent or merely accidental conduct which fact helps bring it outside the scope of the statutory term 'crime of violence'"). That conduct is such that it makes more likely that an offender, later possessing a gun, will use that gun deliberately to harm a victim. Crimes committed in such a purposeful, violent, and aggressive manner are "potentially more dangerous when firearms are involved." And such crimes are "characteristic of the armed career criminal, the eponym of the statute."

By way of contrast, statutes that forbid driving under the influence, such as the statute before us, typically do not insist on purposeful, violent, and aggressive conduct; rather, they are, or are most nearly comparable to, crimes that impose strict liability, criminalizing conduct in respect to which the offender need not have had any criminal intent at all. . . .

When viewed in terms of the Act's basic purposes, this distinction matters considerably. As suggested by its title, the Armed Career Criminal Act focuses upon the special danger created when a particular type of offender—a violent criminal or drug trafficker—possesses a gun. . . . In order to determine which offenders fall into this category, the Act looks to past crimes. This is because an offender's criminal history is relevant to the question whether he is a career criminal, or, more precisely, to the kind or degree of danger the offender would pose were he to possess a gun.

In this respect—namely, a prior crime's relevance to the possibility of future danger with a gun—crimes involving intentional or purposeful conduct (as in burglary and arson) are different than DUI, a strict liability crime. In both instances, the offender's prior crimes reveal a degree of callousness toward risk, but in the former instance they also show an increased likelihood that the offender is the kind of person who might deliberately point the gun and pull the trigger. We have no reason to believe that Congress intended a 15-year mandatory prison term where that increased likelihood does not exist. . . .

SCALIA, CONCURRING:

. . . [T]he problem with the Court's holding today is that it is not remotely faithful to the statute that Congress wrote. There is simply no basis (other than the necessity of resolving the present case) for holding that the enumerated and unenumerated crimes must be similar in respects *other than the degree of risk that they pose*.

The Court is correct that the clause "otherwise involves conduct that presents a serious potential risk of physical injury to another" signifies a similarity between the enumerated and unenumerated crimes. It is not, however, *any* old similarity, such as (to take a random example) "purposeful, 'violent,' and 'aggressive' conduct." Rather, it is the *particular* similarity specified after the "otherwise"—*i.e.*, that they all pose a serious potential risk of physical injury to another. They need not be similar in any other way. As the Court correctly notes, the word "otherwise" in this context means "in a different way or manner." Webster's New International Dictionary 1729 (2d ed. 1957) ("in another way or in other ways"). Therefore, by using the word "otherwise" the writer draws a substantive connection between two sets only on one specific dimension—*i.e.*, whatever follows "otherwise." What that means here is that "committing one of the enumerated crimes . . . is *one way* to commit a crime 'involv[ing] a serious potential risk of physical injury to another'; and that *other ways* of committing a crime of that character similarly constitute 'violent felon[ies].'"

The Court rejects this seemingly straightforward statutory analysis, reading the residual clause to mean that the unenumerated offenses must be similar to the enumerated offenses not only in the degree of risk they pose, but also "in kind," despite the fact that "otherwise" means that the *common* element of risk must be presented "'in a *different* way or manner.'" . . .

The Court supports its argument with that ever-ready refuge from the hardships of statutory text, the (judicially) perceived statutory purpose. According to the Court, because the Armed Career Criminal Act is concerned with "the special danger created when a particular type of offender—a violent criminal or drug trafficker—possesses a gun," the statutory purpose favors applying [the statute's] enhanced penalty only to those criminals "who might deliberately point the gun and pull the trigger." I cannot possibly infer that purpose from the statute. For all I know, the statute was meant to punish those who are indifferent to human life, or who are undeterred by the criminal penalties attached to the commission of other crimes (after all, the statute enhances penalties for drug traffickers). While the Court's asserted purpose would surely be a reasonable one, it has no more grounding in the statutory text than do these other possibilities. And what is more, the Court's posited purpose is positively contradicted by the fact that one of the enumerated crimes—the unlawful use of explosives—may involve merely negligent or reckless conduct. See ALI, Model Penal Code §220.2(2) (1985) ("A person is guilty of a misdemeanor if he recklessly creates a risk of catastrophe in the employment of fire, explosives or other dangerous means"); ("A person is guilty of criminal mischief if he . . . damages tangible property of another purposely, recklessly, or by negligence in the employment of fire, explosives, or other dangerous means"). . . .

Under my interpretation of [the statute], I must answer one question: Does drunk driving pose at least as serious a risk of physical injury to another as burglary? From the evidence presented by the Government, I cannot conclude so. Because of that, the rule of lenity requires that I resolve this case in favor of the defendant. . . .

ALITO, DISSENTING:

The Court holds that an offense does not fall within the residual clause unless it is "roughly similar, in kind as well as in degree of risked posed," to the crimes specifically listed in [the statute,] i.e., burglary, extortion, arson, and crimes involving the use of explosives. These crimes, according to the Court, "all typically involve purposeful, 'violent,' and 'aggressive' conduct."

This interpretation cannot be squared with the text of the statute, which simply does not provide that an offense must be "purposeful," "violent," or "aggressive" in order to fall within the residual clause. Rather, after listing burglary, arson, extortion, and explosives offenses, the statute provides (in the residual clause) that an offense qualifies if it "otherwise involves conduct that presents a serious potential risk of physical injury to another." Therefore, offenses falling within the residual clause must be similar to the named offenses in one respect only: They must, "otherwise"—which is to say, "in a different manner," 10 OED 984 (def. B(1)); see also Webster's 1598—"involve[] conduct that presents a serious potential risk of physical injury to another." Requiring that an offense must also be "purposeful," "violent," or "aggressive" amounts to adding new elements to the statute, but we "ordinarily resist

reading words or elements into a statute that do not appear on its face."
Bates v. United States, 522 U.S. 23, 29 (1997). . . .

The Court defends its new statutory element on the ground that a defendant who merely engages in felony drunk driving is not likely to be "the kind of person who might deliberately point the gun and pull the trigger." The Court cites no empirical support for this conclusion, and its accuracy is not self-evident. . . .

Justice Scalia, like the Court, does not follow the statutory language. The statute says that offenses falling within the residual clause must present "a serious potential risk of physical injury to another." The statute does not say that these offenses must present at least as much risk as the enumerated offenses. . . .

QUESTIONS ABOUT THE CASE

1. What purpose does Justice Breyer see in the statute? That is, what problem does Breyer think this statute aims to solve, and why does he conclude that Mr. Begay is not part of the problem? What evidence does Breyer use to convince us that his reading of statutory purpose is plausible?

2. Besides statutory purpose, a theme of this chapter, this case also involves *criminal* purpose, or the intent behind various criminal acts. How does Breyer use criminal purpose to distinguish DUI from burglary, arson, and extortion?

3. Scalia criticizes Breyer's purposive approach. Why? Do you agree with his criticisms? Which approach to interpreting the statute does Scalia use?

4. On what basis does Alito disagree with Breyer's purposive interpretation of the statute? With Scalia's nonpurposive interpretation?

5. If Scalia and Alito see no purpose in the statute, how do they make sense of it? For example, imagine that Begay had no history of drunk driving but had been repeatedly ticketed for speeding so far above the limit as to constitute the felony of reckless driving. How would Scalia and Alito apply the statute to that case? (Keep in mind that, as the common phrase has it, "speed kills.") Don't we have to figure out the purposes of statutes before we can make sense of them?

6. Each of the justices uses a canon of statutory construction, but the canons lead the justices in different directions. What canon of statutory interpretation does Breyer cite? (Hint: Holmes used it in interpreting the National Motor Vehicle Theft Act.) What canon of statutory interpretation does Scalia cite? (Hint: He calls it the "rule of lenity," but we have also referred to it using a

more descriptive phrase.) What canon of statutory construction does Alito cite? (Hint: He draws it from *Bates v. United States*.) Does the simultaneous firing of three canons in three different directions suggest that canons, as tools of statutory interpretation, are useless?

7. The interpretation of just one sentence in a federal statute split the Court into three contending groups. What exactly made this sentence so befuddling to the Court? After reading the opinions, do you believe that one interpretation is "correct" and the others "incorrect"? If not, do you nonetheless believe one of the justices nonetheless did a better job of writing a persuasive opinion? Why?

CHAPTER 5

Interpreting the U.S. Constitution

We are under a Constitution—but the Constitution is what the Judges say it is.

—CHARLES EVANS HUGHES

A provision of the Constitution, it is hardly necessary to say, does not admit of two distinctly opposite interpretations. It does not mean one thing at one time and an entirely different thing at another time.

—JUSTICE GEORGE SUTHERLAND

I look forward to seeing my plays staged so that I can find out what they mean.

—TOM STOPPARD, PLAYWRIGHT

Chapter 1 described legal reasoning as the way in which courts and judges justify their use of political power. Our argument has proceeded in four steps. First, in a political system committed to the rule of law, the law must in fact rule—people must act consistently with the law. Second, courts have unquestioned power to interpret what the law means in the cases that come before them. Third, general rules and principles of law are often unclear when applied to the ever-new factual details of individual cases, so the time will never come when all law becomes "clear and settled." Thus, leaving aside the easy cases brought by foolish or apathetic litigants who have no chance of prevailing, appellate judges resolve disputes by choosing what the law means.

But now the obvious question arises: how can judges follow the law if at the same time they choose what the law means? Hence the fourth step: judges who exercise political power under the rule of law must justify their choices. In common law nations, judges do this through the medium of legal reasoning, published justifications that fit together, or harmonize, rules of law, facts of cases, social background facts, and widespread social values. (This is not expected of most judges in civil law nations such as France, where courts do not traditionally give extensive justifications for their decisions.)

In constitutional law, the final source of law this text examines, we encounter what is conventionally considered the most "political" field of law, in which politicians and bloggers rant about controversial rulings and debate the virtues or vices of the judges who make them. Political science has historically paid close attention to constitutional law even as it has largely ignored common law and statutory law. It has also largely ignored state constitutions, although all fifty states have them and they also play a role in important political controversies.[1] Why?

The U.S. Constitution does two important things. First, it allocates specific powers both among the branches of the national government and between national and state governments. (For example, only the national government may coin money; the states have primary but not exclusive power over alcohol regulation.) Second, the Constitution declares rights over which no branch of government at any level can exert power—freedom of speech or the free exercise of religion, for example. But state constitutions simultaneously convey powers and provide rights. Early victories in the effort to legalize same-sex marriage were won using language in Massachusetts and California state constitutions.[2] So what makes the U.S. Constitution uniquely important?

---

1. A fine exception is political scientist Emily Zackin's *Looking for Rights in All the Wrong Places* (Princeton, NJ: Princeton University Press, 2013). See also law professor Sanford Levinson's *Framed: America's 51 Constitutions and the Crisis of Governance* (New York: Oxford University Press, 2012).

2. The California Supreme Court ruled in 2008 that laws defining marriage as between a man and a woman violated state constitutional guarantees of privacy, equality, and due process. *In re Marriage Cases*, 43 Cal. 4th 757 (2008). That ruling was later overturned by California voters, who approved Proposition 8, amending the state constitution to define marriage as between a man and a woman. Proposition 8 was in turn struck down by a federal district court judge as a violation of the Fourteenth Amendment of the U.S. Constitution, in *Perry v. Schwarzenegger*, 704 F. Supp. 2d 921 (N.D. Cal. 2010). The California decision followed that of the Massachusetts Supreme Judicial Court, which in 2003 ruled that state constitutional guarantees of due process and equal protection gave same-sex couples the right to marry. *Goodridge v. Department of Public Health*, 440 Mass. 309 (2003).

The Supreme Law of the Land

The short answer to the question, What makes the U.S. Constitution so important? is that the Constitution of the United States declares itself, in Article VI, to be "the supreme law of the land." If the Constitution is supreme, it presumably overrides all state constitutions and all statutes and common law rulings. In other words, when a law or executive action is inconsistent with the Constitution, the law or action has got to go.

The supremacy clause is the constitutional equivalent of the familiar saying "The buck stops here." As we have seen, rules of law do not necessarily provide one and only one obviously "right" answer to concrete legal conflicts. Because only the scarcity of time and money curb the ingenuity of lawyers in creating legal arguments, virtually every question of governmental operation and of civil rights and liberties can become the subject of constitutional litigation. Major constitutional decisions, like the Supreme Court's 5–4 ruling upholding the constitutionality of Obamacare, regularly become leading stories in the news media. But countless other constitutional issues, less headline-worthy but of deep importance to somebody, also arise. Here are three examples:

- In 1999 Congress enacted a law prohibiting the creation and sale of materials depicting cruelty to animals. The law excluded from coverage "any depiction that has serious religious, political, scientific, educational, journalistic, historical, or artistic value." In 2004, Robert J. Stevens was convicted for creating and selling three videotapes, two of which showed pit bulls engaged in vicious fighting, the third a gruesome attack by a dog on a domestic pig. Stevens didn't shoot the material; he merely collected tapes from others, packaged them with his own introduction and commentary, and sold them for profit. Did Stevens's conviction violate his First Amendment right to freedom of speech?[3]
- Section 4 of Article I of the U.S. Constitution begins with this seemingly plain and unambiguous sentence: "The Times, Places, and Manner of holding Elections for Senators and Representatives, shall be prescribed in each State by the Legislature thereof." In the early

---

3. In *United States v. Stevens*, 550 U.S. 460 (2010), eight of the nine justices ruled for Stevens and overturned his conviction. Only Justice Alito dissented, using his fact freedom to conclude that depictions of animal cruelty are comparable to child pornography, which according to the precedent *New York v. Ferber*, 458 U.S. 747 (1982), is not protected by the First Amendment.

twenty-first century, voters in Arizona and California, disgusted by partisan attempts by legislative majorities to gerrymander (creatively shape) electoral districts so as permanently to retain their hold on power, voted to strip redistricting power from their state legislatures and give it to bipartisan commissions. But the Republican majority in Arizona's state legislature sued, insisting that under the language of Article I, only "the Legislature" could determine electoral districts. Defendants responded that the phrase "the Legislature" in the Constitution can plausibly include all legislative bodies, and other state laws unambiguously authorized the people to "legislate" by voting on initiatives and referenda, as they did in this case. Can the voters of a state determine how their own legislative districts are drawn?[4]

- A wedding photographer, Elaine Huguenin, politely refused to photograph a lesbian "commitment ceremony" because of her opposition to same-sex marriage (though not, she insisted, to homosexual relationships) and to her religious beliefs. Her would-be customers, a lesbian couple, sued her under a New Mexico law forbidding discrimination against gay men and lesbian women. Does Ms. Huguenin have a First Amendment right to discriminate on the basis of her religious beliefs?[5]

All of these constitutional questions, if fully litigated, end up in one place—the federal judicial system. The Constitution in Article III gives the U.S. Supreme Court, and all federal courts, jurisdiction to hear cases "arising under this Constitution." In the famous case of *Marbury v. Madison* in 1803, Chief Justice John Marshall, a lifetime appointee from the repudiated Federalist Party government of John Adams, put the jurisdiction clause and the supremacy clause together and announced that the federal courts

---

4. In *Arizona State Legislature v. Arizona Independent Redistricting Commission* 576 U.S. ___ (2015), the Court, by a 5–4 vote, upheld the right of Arizona voters to create a redistricting commission through a ballot initiative.

5. The New Mexico Supreme Court did not think so, ruling against her in *Elane Photography LLC v. Willock*, 309 P.3d 53 (N.M. 2013). Justice Richard Bosson concurred in the decision:

> That sense of respect we owe others, whether or not we believe as they do, illuminates this country, setting it apart from the discord that afflicts much of the rest of the world. In short, I would say to the Huguenins, with the utmost respect: it is the price of citizenship. (*Elane Photography v. Willock*, 92)

The U.S. Supreme Court declined to hear Ms. Huguenin's appeal.

could declare null and void the acts of democratically elected Congress—in 1803, a very decidedly anti-Federalist and pro-Republican Congress. We call this process "judicial review."

Judicial review of constitutionality puts U.S. courts in an unusually strong position. Legislatures, as previous chapters demonstrated, can overturn court decisions based on either statutory or common law. There's no such democratic backstopping for constitutions. Those who oppose a constitutional ruling must either persuade the Court to change its mind or amend the Constitution. But a constitutional amendment requires the approval of two-thirds of both houses of Congress and three-fourths of the states.[6] This means that relatively small minorities can block passage of a proposed amendment. Only two of the eleven amendments ratified in the twentieth century (the Sixteenth Amendment, authorizing a federal income tax, and the Nineteenth, granting women's suffrage) can be said to have corrected controversial Supreme Court readings of the Constitution. To a large extent, then, constitutional provisions "ain't nuthin" until the Supreme Court "calls 'em," or as Charles Evans Hughes put it in this chapter's epigraph, they are "what the Judges say."[7]

Interpretations of the Constitution lie at the center of many of our most urgent political controversies. On the basis of their reading of the Constitution, courts tell cities what rules they can make to regulate guns. Courts strike down or uphold laws prohibiting abortion. Courts tell the federal government what it can and can't do to regulate the Internet. Courts reverse the convictions of killers because of what some critics call "technicalities." Courts decide who can marry whom.

Why, in a democracy, should decisions such as these be made by judges who do not subject themselves to the rigors of the electoral process? As we discuss later in this chapter, that question has created an entire academic industry of legal theorists and social scientists who have attempted to square judicial review with democratic theory. Just as with statutory

6. Article V of the Constitution provides a second route to amending the Constitution: two-thirds of the state legislatures can call for a constitutional convention, at which one or more amendments could be considered. Any amendments approved by the convention, however, would require ratification by three-quarters of the states. This second route to amending the Constitution has never been used. The U.S. Constitution has been called the world's most difficult to amend. See Donald Lutz, "Toward a Theory of Constitutional Amendment," *American Political Science Review* 88(1994): 355–370.

7. H. J. Powell, "Constitutional Virtues," *Green Bag* 9 (2006): 379–389, quoting Charles Evans Hughes, *Addresses of Charles Evan Hughes* (1916), 185. Hughes, in fact, did not literally believe that the Supreme Court controlled the meaning of the Constitution and came to regret the way this famous quotation was used.

interpretation, the subject of the previous chapter, the enterprise of constitutional interpretation is haunted by the fear that judges, insulated from the people, will use their position to remake society according to their own visions. Yet when disputes arise over what the Constitution requires, some group or individual must settle them. And, as more and more of the nations of the world are deciding, courts are appropriate institutions for that task.[8]

The desire for an authoritative interpretation of constitutional language is especially acute in the United States because of the "openness" of the U.S. Constitution. The Constitution speaks in some instances with considerable clarity, but in many others only in broad and ambiguous terms. As you would expect, the clear parts of the Constitution rarely create much dispute. For example, the Constitution says that the president must be at least thirty-five years old. While we can imagine hypothetical cases—an eighteen-year-old presidential candidate, invoking his right to freely exercise his religion under the First Amendment, claims to be a reincarnated spiritual guru and "really" one hundred—in fact no one has ever litigated that clause. But the Constitution's most frequently litigated clauses do little more than command the courts to *care* about basic political and governmental values, without specifying with any precision the values or the problems to which the provisions apply:

- The Fifth Amendment reads, "No person shall be . . . deprived of life, liberty or property without due process of law," but what does that mean? Something like this: "Care that government not become too zealous in fighting crime. Respect people's homes and property. Give them a fair chance to prove their innocence in court. In short, avoid the evils of a police state. But it's up to you to decide what's fair, and where the genuine evils of a police state begin."
- The First Amendment prohibits Congress from making a law "respecting an establishment of religion, or prohibiting the free exercise thereof." Those words, practically, mean: "Care that the government

8. On the growing importance of judicial review around the world, see Diana Kapiszewski, Gordon Silverstein, and Robert A. Kagan, *Consequential Courts: Judicial Roles in Global Perspective* (New York: Cambridge University Press, 2013); Tom Ginsburg, *Judicial Review in New Democracies* (New York: Cambridge University Press, 2003); Ran Hirschl, *Towards Juristocracy* (Cambridge, MA: Harvard University Press, 2004); and Alex Stone Sweet, *Governing with Judges: Constitutional Politics in Europe* (New York: Oxford University Press, 2000).

not take sides on religious matters or constrain religious freedom unduly. But it's up to you to define *religion* and *establishment*, and to decide what counts as either improper government support for or constraint of religion."

- The commerce clause, described in earlier chapters, says Congress has the power to "regulate Commerce with foreign Nations, and among the several States, and with the Indian Tribes." That amounts to little more than this: "People must be able to trade effectively. Work it out so they can—and don't let governments, state or federal, arbitrarily restrict trade."

The Constitution omits references to some rights that the structure of our government seems to require. For example, the Constitution contains no guarantee of a right to vote. Obviously, the Constitution's framers could not anticipate some violations of liberty and privacy, such as thermal imaging or surveillance by drones, or wiretapping and cell phone eavesdropping by the National Security Agency. Conversely, the Constitution omits reference to some rights that we assume the framers knew about and took for granted—rights that are so much a part of our liberty as to "go without saying." The right to marry may well fall in this category. Thus, interpreting the Constitution only according to what its words may have meant to the people who wrote them (even if they all agreed, which in fact they did not—compromises abounded) seems to defeat its purpose. And once we accept that there are some liberties that the Constitution protects yet never specifies, someone has to decide where to draw the line.[9]

The Supreme Court has declared that the right to an abortion is an unspecified liberty. Similarly, the Court declared in 2000 that parents had a constitutional right to raise children as they wish, though no provision in the Constitution mentions child rearing.[10] In 2003 the Supreme Court declared that the right of persons to freely associate with each other, another unspecified right, made Texas's law banning homosexual sodomy unconstitutional.[11] The scope of the right of privacy, or of the right to raise children without interference from the state, or of the freedom of association is unclear. So, even if we could assume that every governmental representative—whether a legislator before voting for a statute or a police

9. See Judge Richard Posner's case against "strict constructionism," aptly titled, "What Am I? A Potted Plant?" *New Republic*, September 28, 1987, 23–25.

10. *Troxel v. Granville*, 530 U.S. 65 (2000).

11. *Lawrence v. Texas*, 539 U.S. 558 (2003).

officer before deciding to arrest—stopped and made a conscientious determination of the constitutionality of a decision, under our Constitution, we would still need a constitution-interpreting organization such as the courts. The Constitution is so vague, general, and ambiguous that people with the best of legal training and intentions may not reach the same interpretations of it.

Federalism also seems to require a Supreme Court to interpret the Constitution. The United States has one national constitution but many state constitutions. If we take its legal status seriously, then the U.S. Constitution should mean the same everywhere, just as the Mann Act should not have one meaning in Utah and another in the District of Columbia. If the United States was a unitary nation, without a division of authority between the national government and the states, then maybe (but only maybe) we could count on a conscientious Congress to determine uniform constitutional applications. Under our Constitution, however, Congress is neither structured nor empowered to review the constitutionality of the actions of state and local governments.

For all these reasons—the finality of the Supreme Court, the importance of constitutional issues, the inconclusiveness of the Constitution's text, and the need for constitutional uniformity—we might expect the Supreme Court to take particular care to use the familiar tools of good legal reasoning to persuade us that it has done justice. The bulk of this chapter explains why just the opposite happens. Indeed, justifications in constitutional law can differ dramatically from the practices of legal reasoning described in previous chapters.

Readers will have to put up with a higher level of abstraction in this chapter than in chapters 3 and 4. In part, it is necessary to move toward the general and the abstract in order to say anything at all about such an immense subject, one on which books about the Supreme Court, the judicial selection process, and constitutional interpretation itself flow steadily forth.[12] But there is a much more profound reason for the abstraction to

12. Here is a small sampling of recent books on the subject: Thomas M. Keck, *Judicial Politics in Polarized Times* (Chicago: University of Chicago Press, 2014); Jack Balkin, *Living Originalism* (Cambridge, MA: Belknap Press of Harvard University Press, 2014); Mark Tushnet, *In the Balance: Law and Politics on the Supreme Court* (New York: W. W. Norton, 2013); Marcia Coyle, *The Roberts Court: The Struggle for the Constitution* (New York: Simon & Schuster, 2014) Jeffrey Toobin, *The Oath: The Obama White House and the Supreme Court* (New York: Anchor Press, 2013); Matthew E. K. Hall, *The Nature of Supreme Court Power* (New York: Cambridge University Press 2011); Michael Bailey and Forest Maltzman, *The Constrained Court: Law, Politics and the Decisions Justices Make* (Princeton, NJ: Princeton University Press, 2011).

follow, and this reason itself will seem difficult and abstract at first: because the Constitution is supreme and because we believe we should follow it, we have throughout the many turbulent changes in our history worked very hard to make the Constitution fit and harmonize with what we do and what we believe. Bruce Ackerman's *We the People: Foundations* emphasizes that the United States has had—under one written document—two constitutional revolutions, the Civil War and the New Deal, both of which radically transformed American government. Though we have not changed many of the Constitution's words, we have profoundly altered its meaning.[13] Like it or not, and contrary to Justice Sutherland's epigraph to this chapter, the Constitution inevitably *does* mean one thing at one time and something very different at another. New cases with unique facts raise new questions that prior cases never answered.

Constitutional law, then, is abstract because most of the Constitution's meaning is symbolic rather than specific. We need the security of believing we are one political community with a continuous history, so we say we are living under one Constitution when in fact we work hard to change our interpretations of it to legitimate contemporary realities. The fluidity of constitutional interpretation, and thus the capacity of law to adapt as facts and values change, reflects the broader American common law tradition of judge-made law.

Conventional Legal Reasoning in Constitutional Interpretation

The inconclusiveness of the constitutional text, the centrality of constitutional issues in American politics, and the need for uniform constitutional meaning both within the national government and among all the states might seem to call for especially stable and clear patterns of legal reasoning and justification, yet this is precisely what more than two hundred years of constitutional interpretation has never achieved, and for good reason. As in statutory interpretation, the formulas (literalism and intent, for example) that some judges use in a vain attempt to avoid making public policy are doomed to fail. But in constitutional law, the more open-ended, purpose-oriented techniques we recommended for interpreting statutory commands fall short as well.

---

13. Bruce Ackerman, *Foundations*, vol. 1 of *We the People* (Cambridge, MA: Belknap Press of Harvard University Press, 1991), and *Transformations*, vol. 2 of *We the People* (Cambridge, MA: Belknap Press of Harvard University Press, 1997).

Words as Channels of Meaning

Four words drawn from the Constitution loomed over the battle over the impeachment of Bill Clinton. "High crimes and misdemeanors," the Constitution says, are impeachable offenses, but what exactly are "high crimes and misdemeanors"? Naturally, Republicans and Democrats in Congress had different views. Democrats argued that even if Bill Clinton lied in a deposition about his sexual relationship with Monica Lewinsky, this did not relate closely enough to his performance in office to qualify as "high crimes and misdemeanors." Republicans, however, believed that Clinton had broken the law, betrayed the trust of the American people, and demeaned the office of the presidency, certainly high crimes and misdemeanors. As usual in political conflicts, legal language divided rather than united.[14] Similarly in 2008, the Supreme Court fought over the language of the Second Amendment, which speaks both of the states' need to maintain a "well regulated militia" and the "right of the people to keep and bear arms." One side argued that the Second Amendment conferred an individual right to own and carry firearms, whereas the other concluded that it simply protected the right of states to organize their armed militias as they see fit.[15]

Constitutional language by itself rarely resolves disputes that reach the Supreme Court. As in statutory law, many cases turn on arguments about the meaning of key phrases—"due process," "establishment of religion," "cruel and unusual punishment," and so forth. These symbolic phrases are broad and general, making literalism a particularly unsatisfactory method of constitutional interpretation.

Moreover, even in cases in which the constitutional language seems specific and unambiguous, the Supreme Court sometimes ignores it. Consider, for example, Article I, Section 10 of the Constitution, which prohibits states from making treaties, coining money, or keeping a militia during times of peace without congressional permission. The section also includes these words: "No state shall . . . pass any . . . law impairing the obligation of contracts."

Debts provide the best example of the kind of contract the state may not impair under the contract clause. In the typical case of such a contract— "executory" contracts in legal language—Pauline borrows money, say from

14. For a provocative analysis of the impeachment battle, see Howard Gillman, *The Votes That Counted: How the Court Decided the 2000 Presidential Election* (Chicago: University of Chicago Press, 2001).

15. The "individual" view of the Second Amendment prevailed, and by a 5–4 vote, the Supreme Court struck down a District of Columbia handgun ban as unconstitutional. *District of Columbia v. Heller*, 554 U.S. 570 (2008).

a bank, and promises to pay the money back some time in the future. Until she pays the money back, she has a contractual obligation to do so and within the schedule the contract specifies. The contract clause prevents the state from impairing Pauline's "obligation" to repay. In short, the state can't pass a law saying that people don't have to pay back when they owe money, even if a popularly elected legislature—many more voters are debtors than creditors, after all—voted to do so. Thus, the word *impairing* would seem to prevent the state from allowing Pauline to forget about paying the interest or to pay back years later than she promised.

But during the Great Depression, a number of states passed laws allowing owners of homes and land to postpone making their mortgage payments. These statutes forbade banks and other mortgage holders from using their contractual right to foreclose, that is, to take back properties when the mortgage on them hadn't been paid. The Depression, of course, destroyed the financial ability of hundreds of thousands of Paulines to repay mortgages on time, but the mortgage moratorium laws spared the Paulines from this peril by impairing the bank's ability to recover the debt. Yet the Supreme Court ruled, in *Home Building and Loan Association v. Blaisdell*, that the laws did not violate the contract clause.[16]

The political context of the case was volatile. In Brest and Levinson's words, "[A]ngry farmers denounced and in some instances forcibly stopped foreclosure of their farms. In Iowa, a local judge who refused to suspend foreclosure proceedings was dragged from a courtroom and had a rope put around his neck before the crowd let him go."[17] Yet surely the Supreme Court should not decide cases simply to minimize violence. That only invites constitutional blackmail.

We *can*, however, defend this decision even though it ignores the clear words of the Constitution. Just as with survival in nature, the survival of economic and political values depends on adaptation, on the ability to reevaluate policies in light of new information. The Supreme Court rejected the contract clause's words and upheld the Depression's mortgage moratorium laws because the laws were based on economic knowledge not fully available to the framers of the Constitution. With the forced-panic sale of land following massive numbers of foreclosures of mortgages, what would happen to the price of land? Supply-and-demand analysis predicted that

16. *Home Building and Loan Association v. Blaisdell*, 290 U.S. 398 (1934). See also *East New York Savings Bank v. Hahn*, 326 U.S. 230 (1945), and *El Paso v. Simmons*, 379 U.S. 497 (1965).

17. Paul Brest and Sanford Levinson, *Processes of Constitutional Decisionmaking*, 3rd ed. (Boston: Little, Brown, 1992), 352.

the price would drastically decline—quite possibly to a point at which the creditors, the bankers, as well as the debtors, the farmers, would all lose because the land could be sold for only a fraction of what the banks had originally loaned on it. The Court upheld the law as a defensible method by which to prevent further collapse of the economy. Indeed, more than seventy years later, in 2008, policy makers, facing another plunge in housing prices that threatened to spiral out of control, once again considered loan moratoriums to forestall foreclosures.[18]

A decision in the monumental school desegregation cases of the 1950s provides another example of prudent judicial flight from constitutional words. In its celebrated decision, *Brown v. Board of Education*, the Court held that the equal protection clause of the Fourteenth Amendment prohibited laws and policies designed to maintain segregation in public schools of the then forty-eight states.[19] A case decided the same day as *Brown, Bolling v. Sharpe*, concerned the problem of segregation of schools in the nation's capital. The Fourteenth Amendment's sentence containing the equal protection clause begins with the words "no state shall." It does not govern the District of Columbia. The original Bill of Rights does govern the national government and hence the District, but it contains no equal protection clause. Nonetheless, the Court in *Bolling* forbade segregation in the District's public schools by substituting for the equal protection clause in its analysis the due process clause of the Fifth Amendment.[20] The Court did this even though the due process clause does not address the problem of equality. Its words, quoted earlier, seem to address the problem of the fairness of procedures, the "process due" in the courts. The Fourteenth Amendment contains both due process and equal protection clauses, which further suggests that the clauses convey different messages.

Yet the Court was right to go beyond the words of the Fifth and Fourteenth Amendments. If the Constitution denies government the power to segregate schools by race, it would be absurd to permit segregation only

18. As in the Great Depression, housing prices beginning in 2006 began a sharp decline. People who had taken out "teaser loans," home mortgage loans with low initial payments but much higher charges in later years, found themselves unable to make payments or to get a new loan on more favorable terms. As a result, foreclosures spiked, pushing home prices down. The Bush administration at one point proposed postponing mortgage payments to try to avoid a deluge of home foreclosures, just as states had down in the 1930s. See Michael Grynbaum, "Plan to Aid Borrowers Is Greeted by Criticism," *New York Times*, February 13, 2008.

19. *Brown v. Board of Education*, 347 U.S. 483 (1954).

20. *Bolling v. Sharpe*, 347 U.S. 497 (1954). See also *Hirabayashi v. United States*, 320 U.S. 81 (1943).

in the national capital. It is proper to say in this instance that the due process clause of the Fifth Amendment *does* address the problem of equality despite its words. Sometimes, even when the words of a constitutional provision are clear, the Supreme Court must pay attention instead to "the felt necessities of the time," as Justice Holmes famously described the common law process.[21]

Original Intent and Purpose

In 1985, Attorney General Edwin Meese called for a style of constitutional interpretation derived from the original understandings of the framers of the Constitution.[22] "Originalism" has become a rallying cry for conservative critics of the judiciary, but as an approach to constitutional interpretation it is deeply problematic. Searching for the actual intent of the framers of the original Constitution (or of its later amendments) proves just as frustrating as searching for legislative intent. Just like legislators advocating for statutes they have drafted, constitutional framers make arguments in debate that they don't fully believe in order to win support. Others do not express what they do believe in order to avoid offending, so the records of debates over the Constitution can be deeply misleading. The painful process of negotiation and accommodation that produced the Constitution in 1787 left many questions unresolved. Most confounding of all, the framers could have had no intent in relation to the new facts that have surfaced since their work concluded.[23]

Originalists have turned from an "intent" to an "original meaning" approach, in which the words of the Constitution are understood not in terms of specific intentions of the framers but in light of common usage at the time of the founding. This refinement does not resolve the fundamental problem that constitutional language is usually so general and abstract that it cannot provide a straightforward answer to the questions that arise in constitutional litigation. But even where original meaning could provide such an answer, the Court has sometimes ignored it. Indeed, the Court has on occasion even ignored the clear *purpose* behind provisions in the

21. *Bolling v. Sharpe* was a key precedent in the case described at the outset of this book, *United States v. Windsor*, in which the Supreme Court considered whether the Defense of Marriage Act violated the due process clause of the Fifth Amendment.

22. Edwin Meese III, "The Attorney General's View of the Supreme Court: Toward a Jurisprudence of Original Intention," *Public Administration Review* 45 (1985): 701–704.

23. For further elaboration, see Lief Carter, *Contemporary Constitutional Lawmaking: The Supreme Court and the Art of Politics* (Elmsford, NY: Pergamon Press, 1985), 52–55. For a thorough review of the intellectual history of the founding period, see Jack N. Rakove, *Original Meanings* (New York: Alfred A. Knopf, 1996).

Constitution, for example, when it expanded the right to counsel in criminal cases. The Sixth Amendment states, "In all criminal prosecutions, the accused shall enjoy the right . . . to have the assistance of counsel for his defense." The framers who drafted the Sixth Amendment merely sought to alter the common law rule that prevented an accused felon from bringing an advocate to court. The amendment makes no reference to the problem that a defendant may be too poor to hire a lawyer. Yet in 1938, the Court held that these words required the federal government to provide lawyers for the poor, and the Court has since expanded the right to protect those accused of felonies and misdemeanors in state and local courts.[24]

And consider again the mortgage moratorium laws of the Great Depression. If we examine the purpose of the contract clause from the framers' viewpoint, we discover that they feared excessive democracy. They worried that popularly elected legislators would enact the "selfish" interests of the masses. The masses contain more debtors than creditors, and it was precisely in economically difficult times that the framers most feared that debtors, empowered to vote, would put irresistible pressure on legislators to ease their debts. Hence the Court in *Home Building and Loan* rejected more than constitutional words and more than the specific intent of some individual framers: It arguably rejected the historical purpose of the provision. But the Court did so wisely because it understood that postponing mortgage foreclosures could benefit creditors and debtors alike, an economic understanding not available to the framers in the late eighteenth century.

H. Jefferson Powell has shown two reasons why the leading figures of the founding period would have rejected the idea that their own actual hopes and expectations of the Constitution would dictate legal conclusions in the future. First, at common law, the reading of texts such as wills and contracts rejected considering the actual intentions of the parties in favor of giving words their "reasonable," "grammatical," or "popular" meaning. But even more fundamentally, the framers, the vast majority of whom were members of the Protestant tradition, believed that texts ought to speak for themselves, unmediated by church or scholarly authority. They believed that all people should be free to interpret biblical texts for themselves and that complex scholarly interpretations—interpretations imposed by experts such as officials within the Catholic Church—had no presumptive authority.

---

24. *Johnson v. Zerbst*, 304 U.S. 458 (1938); *Gideon v. Wainwright*, 372 U.S. 335 (1963); *Argersinger v. Hamlin*, 407 U.S. 25 (1972). For a persuasive defense of this shift, see Anthony Lewis's classic, *Gideon's Trumpet* (New York: Random House, 1964).

Powell notes that George Washington required in his will the non-legal arbitration of any ambiguity in administering its provisions precisely so that in a hearing to resolve a dispute over it, the decision maker could consider testimony about Washington's actual intent in the matter, testimony that would have been held inadmissible under common law. Participants in Philadelphia, though, did not make much of an effort to document their intentions in drafting the Constitution. (This may be why the *Federalist Papers*, a series of commentaries designed to build support for the Constitution, are cited by judges and scholars as evidence of intent even though the papers are in fact works of political rhetoric that purposefully obscure the circumstances behind the drafting of some constitutional provisions.) James Madison believed that usage and the lessons learned from political practice should override any "abstract opinion of the text." Thus, although James Madison had thought the First Bank of the United States was unconstitutional, as president he signed a bill chartering the Second Bank of the United States because the people had approved of the bank and it had worked.[25] In summary, there is every reason to believe that the framers saw their creation very much as playwright Tom Stoppard, in one of the epigraphs to this chapter, sees his plays. Their texts are mere words on paper until they come alive on stage—in the case of the framers, on the many stages in which politics plays out.

In the framers' approach we see the beginnings of America's major contribution to Western philosophy—pragmatism.[26] Despite the way it is sometimes used in everyday discourse, *pragmatism* does not refer to an unprincipled, selfish attempt to "do whatever it takes to win." Pragmatism holds that our attitudes and choices should follow primarily from the lessons experience teaches us about what works in concrete situations, not from abstract rules or theories. The "radicalism of the American revolution," as Gordon Wood calls it, succeeded in implanting a democracy that made a pragmatic move away from the values and beliefs of the framers inevitable. Wood quotes a political leader of the generation that followed the framers:

25. H. Jefferson Powell, "The Original Understanding of Original Intent," *Harvard Law Review* 98 (1985): 885–948. Compare Richard Kay, "Adherence to the Original Intentions in Constitutional Adjudication: Three Objections and Responses," *Northwestern University Law Review* 82 (1987): 226–292.

26. For a wonderful intellectual history of the origins of pragmatism in the United States, see Louis Menand, *The Metaphysical Club* (New York: Farrar, Straus, and Giroux, 2001).

"We cannot rely on the views of the founding fathers anymore," Martin Van Buren told the New York convention in 1820. "We have to rely on our own experience, not on what they said or thought." "They had many fears," said Van Buren, "fears of democracy, that American experience had not borne out."[27]

So in constitutional law, just as in statutory law, intent is a muddled concept. We have argued in favor of a purpose-oriented approach to statutory interpretation, acknowledging that it often leaves some discretion to judges to pick among competing purposes. But in constitutional law, even when the historical purpose behind a clause is relatively clear, judges sometimes ignore it.

Stare (In)decisis

In 1940, the Supreme Court held that a public school could require all children—including Jehovah's Witnesses, whose religious convictions forbade it—to salute the flag each day. In 1943, the Court overruled itself and held the opposite.[28] In 1946, the Court refused to require state legislatures to make electoral districts roughly equal in population, but in 1962, the Court ruled that the Constitution requires just that.[29] In 1986 the Supreme Court declared that laws against sodomy were constitutional; in 2003 the Court found that such laws violate the Fourteenth Amendment.[30]

While the justices sometimes make stare decisis a primary rationale for their decisions,[31] they have also from time to time recognized reasons to ignore precedents in constitutional law. After all, no legislature sits mainly to update constitutional policy in light of new conditions. It is not simply that the Court should correct its own mistakes—that is always wise policy, as we have argued in the previous chapter. It is also the case that wise policy at one time is not necessarily wise policy at another. If we take seriously the idea that the Constitution is law and so ought to have teeth, then the courts must do the updating. As Justice William O. Douglas once said:

27. Gordon Wood, *The Radicalism of the American Revolution* (New York: Alfred A. Knopf, 1992), 368–369.

28. *Minersville School District v. Gobitis*, 310 U.S. 586 (1940), and *West Virginia State Board of Education v. Barnette*, 319 U.S. 624 (1943).

29. *Colegrove v. Green*, 328 U.S. 549 (1946), and *Baker v. Carr*, 369 U.S. 186 (1962).

30. *Bowers v. Hardwick*, 478 U.S. 186 (1986), and *Lawrence v. Texas*, 539 U.S. 558 (2003).

31. One such instance was *Planned Parenthood v. Casey*, as discussed in chapter 2.

The place of *stare decisis* in constitutional law is . . . tenuous. A judge looking at a constitutional decision may have compulsions to revere past history and accept what was once written. But he remembers above all else that it is the Constitution which he swore to support and defend, not the gloss which his predecessors may have put on it. So he comes to formulate his own views, rejecting some earlier ones as false and embracing others. He cannot do otherwise unless he lets men long dead and unaware of the problems of the age in which he lives do his thinking for him.[32]

Of course, people rely on constitutional decisions. Teachers before the 1943 decision believed they could require all students—regardless of their individual beliefs—to salute the flag. State judges in 1963 did not believe they had to appoint counsel in all felonies. The Texas police officers who arrested John Lawrence in 2003 believed that laws against sodomy were constitutionally valid. The point is that constitutional values may be important enough to override reliance on past policy.

Judicial Review and Democratic Theory

If neither the conventions of legal justification nor the backstop of legislative correction of judicial decisions limits the Supreme Court's power and discretion, then what does? This question has preoccupied constitutional scholarship for more than a century. The great constitutional theorist Alexander Bickel coined the phrase "the countermajoritarian difficulty" to summarize the problem: how could a democracy empower unelected judges to make decisions about many of the nation's most important controversies, sometimes against the wishes of the majority of the people?[33]

This issue surfaced in the debates before the 2000 presidential election. When George W. Bush was asked what kind of judges he would pick for the Supreme Court, he contended that, unlike his opponent, he would appoint competent judges who would not seek to use their position to "write social policy":

I believe that the judges ought not to take the place of the legislative branch of government, that they're appointed for life and that they

32. William O. Douglas, "Stare Decisis," *Columbia Law Review* 49, no. 6 (1949): 735–758, 736, echoing Justice Vanderbilt's dissent in *Fox v. Snow*, discussed in chapter 3.

33. Alexander Bickel, *The Least Dangerous Branch: The Supreme Court at the Bar of Politics*, 2nd ed. (New Haven, CT: Yale University Press, 1986), 16.

ought to look at the Constitution as sacred. They . . . shouldn't misuse their bench. I don't believe in liberal activist judges.[34]

We have argued that in constitutional law, as in statutory and common law, judges cannot help but make social policy. Another problem with Bush's position, though, is that it's not clear that judges can avoid being "activists," whether of the conservative, liberal, or moderate varieties. This is because activism has several dimensions, and a decision that is inactivist on one dimension may be activist on others. Professor Bradley C. Canon suggests six such dimensions:

1. Majoritarianism: Does the decision nullify an act of an elected legis-lature?
2. Interpretive stability: Does the decision overrule prior court prece-dent?
3. Interpretive fidelity: Does the decision contradict the manifest intent of the framers?
4. Substance: Does the decision make new basic policy for the society (as, for example, *Brown v. Board of Education* began a new policy of school desegregation)?
5. Specificity: Does the decision require people to follow specific, court-created rules?
6. Availability of political alternatives: Are other political institutions equally able and willing to formulate effective policy in the area the decision touches?[35]

In this light, consider *Planned Parenthood v. Casey*, the Supreme Court's 1992 decision reaffirming the right to an abortion, which we discussed in chapter 2. By striking down part of a Pennsylvania law restricting abor-tions, the Supreme Court overturned the policy choice of an elected legis-lature (though not necessarily the policy choice of the majority of Amer-icans) and so according to Canon's dimensions 1 and 6 was being activist. But notice that if the Supreme Court had decided in favor of Pennsylvania,

34. "The 2000 Campaign: Transcript of Debate between Vice President Gore and Governor Bush," *New York Times*, October 4, 2000. History has hardly treated the Con-stitution as "sacred." Movements to amend it began practically at its adoption and have continued ever since. See John R. Vile, *Re-Framers: 170 Eccentric, Visionary, and Patri-otic Proposals to Rewrite the U.S. Constitution* (Santa Barbara, CA: ABC-CLIO, 2014).

35. Bradley C. Canon, "A Framework for the Analysis of Judicial Activism," in *Su-preme Court Activism and Restraint*, ed. Stephen Halpern and Charles Lamb (Lexington, MA: Lexington Books, 1982), chap. 15.

it also would have been activist, this time according to dimension 2 and perhaps 4 (since the Court would be approving a new policy regarding abortion). Moreover, the decision the Court did make in *Casey* seems to be "nonactivist" according to dimension 5 (since the Court did not announce a detailed set of rules for abortion regulation) and to dimension 3 (since it's doubtful that any of the framers had any intent about the constitutionality of abortion, much less a "manifest" one).

As this example suggests, activism is a much more complex concept than politicians such as George W. Bush typically acknowledge. And yet Bush's comments do point to an oft-voiced concern about the Supreme Court's role in American democracy. That concern is emphasized when we realize that the Court has (rightly, we have argued) at times ignored the clear words of the Constitution, the clear intent of the framers, and the clear historical purposes of constitutional provisions. How can we keep unelected judges from misusing their power to interpret the Constitution?

Theories of Judicial Self-Restraint

Academic legal sleuths have been on the case for more than a century now. They seek a theory of constitutional justification that would constrain the justices and thus resolve the countermajoritarian difficulty. Their concern is not merely "academic," for the Supreme Court has time and time again misused its power. In the late nineteenth and early twentieth centuries, for example, the Supreme Court tried to proclaim itself the final arbiter of social and economic policy. It actively thwarted economic and social reforms at all levels of government, holding that most forms of economic regulation were illegitimate.

So in *United States v. E.C. Knight* (1895), the Court aggressively reduced national power over commerce by defining the commerce power (contrary to precedents going back to Chief Justice John Marshall) to cover only the physical movement of goods among the states.[36] In 1905, in *Lochner v. New York*, the Court struck down statutory protections against harsh working conditions in bakeries by creating, under the Fourteenth Amendment's due process clause, a constitutional right to individuals' freedom to make any contracts they choose, subject only to the "reasonable" exercise of the state's police power. The Court decided what was reasonable.[37] In 1918, Congress forbade the shipment in interstate commerce of goods made with

---

36. *United States v. E.C. Knight*, 156 U.S. 1 (1895).
37. *Lochner v. New York*, 198 U.S. 45 (1905).

child labor. Although the statute was designed to fall within the limits on Congress's commerce power set forth in *E.C. Knight,* the Court struck the law down, reasoning that there was nothing inherently harmful about the goods themselves being shipped.[38]

The Court was operating under a philosophy in which any regulation that had the effect of redistributing income or power from one group to another was automatically suspect.[39] Thus, Justice David Brewer in 1893 told the New York Bar Association that strengthening the judiciary was necessary to protect the country from the greedy masses who were demanding redistribution:

> I am firmly persuaded that the salvation of the Nation, the permanence of government of and by the people, rests upon the independence and vigor of the judiciary. To stay the waves of popular feeling, to restrain the greedy hand of the many from filching from the few that which they have honestly acquired . . . [40]

This claim to unlimited judicial power, and the political controversy it created, prompted a search for theories that would constrain the judiciary in its interpretation of the Constitution.

The first of these theories, authored in 1893 by James B. Thayer of the Harvard Law School, attempted to reaffirm the representative nature of American constitutional government. All acts of elected bodies, he argued, should carry a heavy presumption of constitutionality. The courts may properly overturn legislation only on a showing that the legislature has made a very clear mistake.[41]

Thayer's thesis proved unsatisfactory for two reasons. First, like the golden rule of statutory interpretation, it contained no standards for determining what counted as a clear mistake. From the perspective of Justice Brewer (and Justice Field, who thought the income tax marked the beginning of a war waged by the poor against the rich), economic regulation was a clear mistake. Thayer's position left to courts the responsibility for doing the extralegal analysis necessary to decide what counts as a clear mistake:

38. *Hammer v. Dagenhart,* 247 U.S. 251 (1918).

39. Howard Gillman, *The Constitution Besieged: The Rise and Demise of Lochner Era Police Powers Jurisprudence* (Durham, NC: Duke University Press, 1993).

40. Justice David J. Brewer, "The Movement of Coercion," speech given at the New York State Bar Association, January 17, 1893, available at the website of the Minnesota Legal History Project.

41. James B. Thayer, "The Origin and Scope of the American Doctrine of Constitutional Law," *Harvard Law Review* 7 (1893): 129–156.

"The ultimate arbiter of what is rational and permissible is indeed always the courts, so far as litigated cases bring the question before them."[42]

Second, if Thayer's theory did nudge the Court toward his position, the Court would then lack power to protect violations of civil liberties. Yet before the final collapse of the Court's economic activism in 1937, it had begun to move into the civil liberties area. In 1931, in *Near v. Minnesota*, the Court struck down a Minnesota law permitting prior censorship of the press.[43] In a 1932 case, *Powell v. Alabama*, it reversed the death sentences of eight black defendants sentenced to death after a one-day trial in Scottsboro, Alabama, in which they, plus a twelve-year-old defendant who escaped the death sentence, were denied adequate representation of counsel.[44]

The synthesis of the two extremes—the theory that justified judicial abstinence from evaluating the rationality of economic policy without curtailing its power to protect civil liberties—appeared quietly (and in the most obscure legalese possible) in the fourth footnote to a 1938 case in which the Court upheld congressional authority to regulate the ingredients in milk products processed for interstate commerce. This now-famous "*Carolene* footnote four" reads:

> There may be narrower scope for operation of the presumption of constitutionality when legislation appears on its face to be within a specific prohibition of the Constitution, such as those of the first ten amendments, which are deemed equally specific when held to be embraced within the Fourteenth. . . .
>
> It is unnecessary to consider now whether legislation which restricts those political processes which can ordinarily be expected to bring about a repeal of undesirable legislation, is to be subjected to more exacting judicial scrutiny under the general prohibitions of the Fourteenth Amendment than are most other types of legislation. . . .
>
> Nor need we inquire whether similar considerations enter into the review of statutes directed at particular religious . . . or national . . . or racial minorities . . . whether prejudice against discrete and insular minorities may be a special condition, which tends seriously to curtail the operation of those political processes ordinarily to be relied upon to protect minorities, and which may call for a correspondingly more searching judicial inquiry.[45]

42. Ibid., 152.
43. *Near v. Minnesota*, 283 U.S. 697 (1931).
44. *Powell v. Alabama*, 287 U.S. 45 (1932).
45. *United States v. Carolene Products Co.*, 304 U.S. 144, 152–153 (1938).

The first paragraph justified cases such as *Near*, because the First Amendment guarantees a free press, and *Powell*, because the Fifth and Sixth Amendments guarantee a fair trial. In such cases, the Court deemed that the Fourteenth Amendment's due process clause applied these federal restrictions to state and local governmental actions.

The note's second paragraph explained why the Court need not intervene in economic policy: fights over allocation of economic resources—like the debate over the working conditions in bakeries in *Lochner*—are usually waged by well-organized groups on various sides of the issue. The political compromises among those interests may not equate with a professional economist's definition of rationality, but they are legally acceptable because all sides participate in the process, and especially when the presumably less powerful interest—here, bakery workers—prevail. But if the electoral machinery that generates robust political competition itself breaks down, the Court may intervene, for example, as in the reapportionment cases.[46]

The footnote's third paragraph suggests that even when the machinery of electoral politics works properly, prejudice against racial, religious, or other minorities may prevent them from being heard. The Court's leadership regarding racial segregation took place at a time when blacks in the Deep South were systematically denied the chance to organize and vote. These racist policies arguably violated all three parts of the *Carolene* footnote's approach to the Constitution.

In 1980, John Hart Ely and Jesse Choper developed the details of these theories.[47] To the three *Carolene Products* points, Choper added a fourth: the Court should avoid upsetting democratic choices about the balance of power between national and local government. The fact that state and local parties and elections select the members of Congress and that reelection depends on satisfying local demands ensures a rough competitive balance of state and local power without help from the Supreme Court.

Many more scholarly theories of the Court's role have emerged since 1937. Herbert Wechsler, for example, advocated that the Court decide cases only on the basis of "neutral principles," rules that future courts can apply in cases with very different partisan or political alignments. For example, a principle protecting those who demonstrate for racial justice must be artic-

46. *Baker v. Carr*, 369 U.S. 186 (1962), and see *Reynolds v. Sims*, 377 U.S. 533 (1964).
47. John Hart Ely, *Democracy and Distrust: A Theory of Judicial Review* (Cambridge, MA: Harvard University Press, 1980); and Jesse Choper, *Judicial Review and the National Political Process: A Functional Reconsideration of the Role of the Supreme Court* (Chicago: University of Chicago Press, 1980).

ulated in such a way as to protect demonstrating members of the American Nazi Party.[48]

Wechsler, Choper, and Ely joined many other constitutional theorists who sought in the post-*Brown* years to find the proper place for judicial review in democratic theory. But despite their scholarly elegance, none of their proposed solutions satisfactorily resolved the countermajoritarian difficulty. That requires some mechanism that actually limits the constitutional power of the Supreme Court, not merely an academic theory about how the Court might best limit itself.

In practice, after all, the Court has never consistently followed any such theory. Consider the Court's decision in *Griswold v. Connecticut*, in which the Court struck down state laws prohibiting the distribution of contraceptives. The "right of privacy" created by the Court to justify the result is hardly a "specific prohibition" in the Bill of Rights, and the people it protects—women and men both—are as far from an insular and discrete minority as we could imagine.[49] The Court's extension of the principle of privacy in the abortion cases beginning with *Roe*—including the right to sexual privacy of single females—might seem to practice Wechsler's neutral principles concept, but for the fact that the Court also ruled that the Constitution permits government to deny funds for abortion to the indigent who are otherwise qualified to receive them.[50] Indeed, Justice Stone, the coauthor of *Carolene Products*' footnote four, voted (perhaps for Bickelian reasons) against allowing the Court to intervene in legislative reapportionment, in direct contradiction to his footnote's second paragraph.[51]

We have already seen that a precedent does not dictate how a judge applies it. (If it did, a case that cited the precedent would usually not reach the appellate courts in the first place, as the two conflicting parties would be able to predict how the appellate judge would rule and thus forgo the expenses of further litigation.) Just as fact freedom allows different judges to apply the same precedents in opposite ways, so each constitutional theory does not dictate or constrain. The history of judicial review, starting with *Marbury v. Madison*,[52] more resembles a tool bench, where the judge decides how the case ought to come out and then chooses whatever tool seems handiest to get the job done. All abstract theories about the Supreme

48. Herbert Wechsler, "Toward Neutral Principles of Constitutional Law," *Harvard Law Review* 73 (1959): 1–35.
49. *Griswold v. Connecticut*, 381 U.S. 479 (1965).
50. *Roe v. Wade*, 410 U.S. 113 (1973), but see *Harris v. McRae*, 448 U.S. 297 (1980).
51. *Colegrove v. Green*, 328 U.S. 549 (1946).
52. *Marbury v. Madison*, 5 U.S. 87 (1803).

Court's role fail to answer our question. But perhaps the political role of the Supreme Court makes theoretical consistency both impossible and unnecessary. We explore that possibility next.

Political Constraints on the Court

Grand theories of constitutional lawmaking of the sort we have just reviewed dominated the academic discussion of constitutional law for decades. The main problem with these grand theories is that in practice, Supreme Court justices neither care much about them nor make decisions consistent with them.[53] Political scientists have instead looked for constraints on the Supreme Court in the practical operation of politics itself.

This resolution of the constitutional paradox was expressed most pithily in 1901 by Finley Peter Dunne's satirical character Mr. Dooley: "th' supreme coort follows th' iliction returns."[54] *Martin* Shapiro, a leading figure in political jurisprudence, put it this way:

> No regime is likely to allow significant political power to be wielded by an isolated judicial corps free of political restraints. To the extent that courts make law, judges will be incorporated into the governing coalition, the ruling elite, responsible representatives of the people, or however else the political regime may be expressed.[55]

Subject to a few historical exceptions, particularly the Court's dogmatic opposition to economic regulation during the early New Deal, the theory holds that the Court rarely strays far enough from dominant popular opinion to worry about checking it through legal doctrine or theories of judicial review.[56] This approach combines historical observations of instances in which presidential selections of justices have steered the Court onto more popular courses with analyses of the structural and procedural characteristics of the Court's work that make it politically responsive. The rest of this section weaves the important threads of this perspective together.

First, most constitutional decisions do not invalidate the work of popularly elected legislators. Judicial review frequently sets aside the actions—a

53. See generally Lief Carter, *Contemporary Constitutional Lawmaking.* Also see Mark Graber, "Constitutional Politics and Constitutional Theory: A Misunderstood and Neglected Relationship," *Law and Social Inquiry* 27 (2002): 309–338.

54. *Mr. Dooley's Opinions* (New York: R. H. Russell, 1901), 26.

55. Martin Shapiro, *Courts: A Comparative Political Analysis* (Chicago: University of Chicago Press, 1981), 34.

56. See Robert Dahl, "Decision-Making in a Democracy: The Supreme Court as National Policy Maker," *Journal of Public Law* 6 (1957): 279–295, at 294.

police search and seizure of criminal evidence, for example, or regulations created by a federal agency—of nonelected administrative personnel who, like judges, are only indirectly affected by electoral politics. Where the work of elected representatives *is* concerned, the Court has found constitutional defects in only a tiny fraction of all statutes passed by Congress since World War II. In nearly all of these instances, the Court has invalidated not an entire statutory scheme or policy but only an offending clause or provision.[57] The most activist of court decisions touch only a tiny fraction of the "democratic" work of Congress.

Furthermore, the work of Congress does not necessarily reflect "majority will" because many matters of governance are so complex, technical, and/or dull that the public is not informed or passionate enough to have such a will. The benefit of elections in the daily operation of politics comes from the fact that elected politicians need to listen to interest groups and individual citizens because they seek as many votes from as many different sources as possible. The legal process has a different but equally effective method for forcing judges to listen: anyone can file a lawsuit about anything, and a judge must hear that suit, at least long enough to determine whether it is bogus.

Historically, the president fills a vacancy on the Supreme Court on average slightly less often than once every two years. The system of presidential appointment usually means that changes in the composition of the Court track the outcome of national elections, admittedly in a very rough way, and thus of public opinion. Barack Obama's two appointees, Elena Kagan and Sonia Sotomayor, have tended to vote with the liberal bloc on the Court; George W. Bush's two appointees, Samuel Alito and Chief Justice John Roberts, clearly reflected Bush's conservative philosophy. President Nixon pledged to restore "law and order" to country, so it was unsurprising that his appointees stalled the expansion of the liberal Warren Court's protection of the rights of the accused.[58] In part because of this electoral connection, Supreme Court decisions often line up fairly closely with public opinion. For example, Justices O'Connor, Souter, and Kennedy voted to follow the *Roe v. Wade* abortion precedent in 1992, at a time when popular opinion seemed to favor just that result.

---

57. Through the year 2014, the Supreme Court had over the course of its history invalidated, in whole or part, 177 acts of Congress, but far more state (955) and local (122) laws. *Constitution of the United States of America: Analysis, and Interpretation, Centennial Edition* (Washington, DC: Government Printing Office, 2014), 2287–2579.

58. Kevin J. McMahon, *Nixon's Court: His Challenge to Judicial Liberalism and its Political Consequences* (Chicago IL: University of Chicago Press, 2011).

Constitutional decisions possess all the characteristics of the common law tradition. No one decision permanently sets the course of law. The process is a thoroughly incremental one in which, case by case, new facts and new arguments repeatedly come before the courts, and the law can be adjusted to new facts and conditions. A judicial commitment to protecting liberties does not require the courts to articulate a complete theory of equal protection or due process.[59]

For the most part, the Court has avoided creating legal doctrine that appears to "take sides" along popular partisan lines. Decisions defending the freedom of civil rights activists to organize and demonstrate also protect antiabortion activists. The Court, though it had four appointees from the Truman administration, nonetheless ruled in 1952 that President Truman's attempt to avert a work stoppage by seizing the nation's steel mills was illegal. In 1974 the Court, loaded with Nixon appointees, denied President Nixon's claim of executive privilege in the Watergate crisis.

The main thrust of the Madisonian constitutional scheme works to prevent too much power from accumulating in one place. The dispersion of power takes place more through the sharing than the separating of power. Different institutions must compromise because none can act effectively without cooperating with the others. Perhaps, therefore, the indeterminacy of constitutional theory is a blessing in disguise, a measure of the success of Madison's vision.[60]

These indisputable characteristics of American politics may help us to answer the challenge posed by Bickel's countermajoritarian difficulty. American government is not constructed to be purely majoritarian, but to be a system of separated institutions sharing power. The courts are typically the least majoritarian of these institutions, but they do not usually fall very far out of line with the dominant political opinions of the time. As Alexander Hamilton said in defending the federal judicial structure in Federalist No. 78, the judiciary is the "least dangerous branch" because it has the power of neither "purse nor sword." That is, it has neither the staff nor the budget to implement its own decisions, so it must rely on others,

---

59. Felix Cohen, "Transcendental Nonsense and the Functional Approach," *Columbia Law Review* 35 (1935): 809–849. See also Martin Shapiro, "Stability and Change in Judicial Decision Making: Incrementalism or Stare Decisis?" *Law in Transition Quarterly* 2 (1964): 134–157. And see Janet S. Lindgren, "Beyond Cases: Reconsidering Judicial Review," *Wisconsin Law Review* (1983): 583–638.

60. See Walter Murphy, James Fleming, Sotirios Barber, and Stephen Macedo, *American Constitutional Interpretation*, 3rd ed. (Mineola, NY: Foundation Press, 2003), chaps. 1–4, especially pp. 79–89.

especially the other branches of government, to put its rulings into effect.[61] No wonder the Court rarely takes on the branch most connected to the people, Congress, in a major dispute.

Taken together, these facts about the role of courts within American government answer the democracy question that Bickel and others have posed. But do all these facts provide an acceptable substitute for persuasive legal justification? Do they obviate the need for good legal reasoning when the Court engages in judicial review?

Two lines of reasoning indicate that they do not. First, while there is no cause for alarm about the Supreme Court's political role, the political constraints on the Court just described don't provide guides for wise constitutional interpretation. Good legal reasoning generates outcomes that losers in specific cases, like losers in good games, find fair and trustworthy. Courts can't say, "You lose because we're Democrats and you are a Republican!" The legal "game" is different from, say, the legislative game, where such partisanship is legitimate. For the losing litigant, the knowledge that the numbers might change in a year or two, when the president appoints more sympathetic justices, seems beside the point.

Second, the argument that the Court is democratic because it "follows the election returns" is hardly reassuring. The Constitution in part seeks to protect individuals from what Alexis de Tocqueville called "the tyranny of the majority."[62] If the judiciary tracks public opinion too closely, it will not reliably provide this protection. The unpopular speaker or member of a scorned minority may thrive only if the courts are *not* politically responsive. That, after all, is the thrust of *Carolene Products'* footnote four. If we must sustain the belief that the Constitution is a central source of political structure and communal values—if we need to believe in it—then conventional political jurisprudence does not itself get us where we want to go.

Beyond Theory

In recent years legal scholars have largely abandoned the attempt to find a grand theoretical solution to the problem of judicial review.[63] Instead, they have sought to make constitutional discourse both more realistic and more

---

61. *The Federalist Papers* (New York: Mentor, 1961), 464–472. For a provocative study of the limits of the judiciary in implementing its rulings, see Gerald Rosenberg, *The Hollow Hope: Can Courts Bring about Social Change? (Chicago: University of Chicago Press, 2008); see also Hall, The Nature of Supreme Court Power.*

62. Alexis de Tocqueville, *Democracy in America*, trans. George Lawrence, ed. J. P. Mayer (New York: Harper and Row, 1969), 250.

63. With one exception: They continue to squabble over originalism.

principled. One group of scholars has attempted to validate and reinvigorate discussion about constitutional issues outside the judiciary, "popular constitutionalism," arguing that courts must share responsibility with the people for resolving difficult legal issues.[64] Another group has urged judges to write "minimalist decisions," opinions that don't sweep too far beyond the facts of the case, so as to facilitate learning from later cases that arise and from dialogue with the other branches of government.[65] Both perspectives remind us that courts are enmeshed in a larger system of separated powers, which challenges the notion that courts by themselves can protect individual freedoms. Recent constitutional scholarship focuses not on finding the "right answer" to difficult constitutional issues but on improving the process by which judges arrive at their judgments. This focus reflects the constitutional aspiration to form "a more perfect union." "We the people," being imperfect, will never fully achieve a "perfect union," but it is essential that we not abandon our effort to combine the lessons of the past with our experience in the present to define what is politically good.

We present our theory about how judges should justify their decisions in all areas of law, constitutional law included, in the next chapter (and in appendix B). For now our contention is that a preoccupation with doctrine may do more harm than good. The judge or scholar who insists on a doctrinally elegant legal framework for a case such as "originalism" or "neutral principles" or the political theory embedded in the *Carolene* footnote may shut herself off from the cares and aspirations of the litigants themselves. The people whose lives the courts shape will not likely have theoretical elegance at the top of their list of priorities. Perhaps this is what Justice Harry Blackmun meant in a 1983 interview:

> Maybe I'm oversensitive . . . [b]ut these are very personal cases. We're dealing with people—the life, liberty, and property of people. And because I grew up in poor surroundings, I know there's another world out there we sometimes forget about.[66]

64. Mark Tushnet, *Taking the Constitution away from the Courts* (Princeton, NJ: Princeton University Press, 2000); Larry D. Kramer, *The People Themselves: Popular Constitutionalism and Judicial Review* (New York: Oxford University Press, 2005); and George Thomas, *The Madisonian Constitution* (Baltimore: Johns Hopkins University Press, 2008).

65. Cass R. Sunstein, *One Case at a Time: Judicial Minimalism on the Supreme Court* (Cambridge, MA: Harvard University Press, 2001).

66. John Jenkins, "A Candid Talk with Justice Blackmun," *New York Times Magazine*, February 20, 1983, 23–24. And recall New Mexico Judge Bosson's sympathetic apology to the losers in *Elane Photography v. Willock*, discussed in note 5.

ILLUSTRATIVE CASE

Alonzo King was arrested after he allegedly assaulted several people with a shotgun. During the booking process, officials used a buccal (cheek) swab to obtain a DNA sample from his mouth. Several months later, officials determined that King's sample matched the DNA from an unsolved rape case. King was promptly arrested and indicted for rape. After King's motion to suppress the DNA evidence was denied, he was convicted and sentenced to life in prison. The Maryland Court of Appeals overturned the conviction on the grounds that the buccal swab was a constitutionally unreasonable search under the Fourth Amendment and as applied to state law by the Fourteenth Amendment. Maryland appealed to the Supreme Court of the United States. The Supreme Court by a 5–4 vote reinstated King's conviction.

Maryland v. King
U.S. Supreme Court
569 U.S. ___ (2013)

JUSTICE KENNEDY delivered the opinion of the Court.

. . . The advent of DNA technology is one of the most significant scientific advancements of our era. The full potential for use of genetic markers in medicine and science is still being explored, but the utility of DNA identification in the criminal justice system is already undisputed. Since the first use of forensic DNA analysis to catch a rapist and murderer in England in 1986, law enforcement, the defense bar, and the courts have acknowledged DNA testing's "unparalleled ability both to exonerate the wrongly convicted and to identify the guilty. It has the potential to significantly improve both the criminal justice system and police investigative practices." . . .

[U]sing a buccal swab on the inner tissues of a person's cheek in order to obtain DNA samples is a search. Virtually any "intrusion into the human body," *Schmerber v. California* (1966), will work an invasion of "'cherished personal security' that is subject to constitutional scrutiny." The Court has applied the Fourth Amendment to police efforts to draw blood, scraping an arrestee's fingernails to obtain trace evidence, and even to "a [B]reathalyzer test, which generally requires the production of alveolar or 'deep lung' breath for chemical analysis."

A buccal swab is a far more gentle process than a venipuncture to draw blood. It involves but a light touch on the inside of the cheek; and although it can be deemed a search within the body of the arrestee, it requires no "surgical intrusions beneath the skin." The fact that an intrusion is negligible is of central relevance to determining reasonableness, although it is still a search as the law defines that term.

"As the text of the Fourth Amendment indicates, the ultimate measure of the constitutionality of a governmental search is 'reasonableness.'" In giving content to the inquiry whether an intrusion is reasonable, the Court has preferred "some quantum of individualized suspicion . . . [as] a prerequisite to a constitutional search or seizure. But the Fourth Amendment imposes no irreducible requirement of such suspicion." . . .

The Maryland DNA Collection Act provides that, in order to obtain a DNA sample, all arrestees charged with serious crimes must furnish the sample on a buccal swab applied, as noted, to the inside of the cheeks. The arrestee is already in valid police custody for a serious offense supported by probable cause. The DNA collection is not subject to the judgment of officers whose perspective might be "colored by their primary involvement in 'the often competitive enterprise of ferreting out crime.'" As noted by this Court in a different but still instructive context involving blood testing, "[b]oth the circumstances justifying toxicological testing and the permissible limits of such intrusions are defined narrowly and specifically in the regulations that authorize them. . . . Indeed, in light of the standardized nature of the tests and the minimal discretion vested in those charged with administering the program, there are virtually no facts for a neutral magistrate to evaluate." . . .

The legitimate government interest served by the Maryland DNA Collection Act is one that is well established: the need for law enforcement officers in a safe and accurate way to process and identify the persons and possessions they must take into custody. It is beyond dispute that "probable cause provides legal justification for arresting a person suspected of crime, and for a brief period of detention to take the administrative steps incident to arrest." Also uncontested is the "right on the part of the Government, always recognized under English and American law, to search the person of the accused when legally arrested." . . . Even in that context, the Court has been clear that individual suspicion is not necessary, because "[t]he constitutionality of a search incident to an arrest does not depend on whether there is any indication that the person arrested possesses weapons or evidence. The fact of a lawful arrest, standing alone, authorizes a search." . . .

First, "[i]n every criminal case, it is known and must be known who has been arrested and who is being tried. . . . Disguises used while committing a crime may be supplemented or replaced by changed names, and even changed physical features." An "arrestee may be carrying a false ID or lie about his identity," and "criminal history records . . . can be inaccurate or incomplete." A suspect's criminal history is a critical part of his identity that of-ficers should know when processing him for detention. . . . Police already seek this crucial identifying information. They use routine and accepted means as varied as comparing the suspect's booking photograph to sketch artists' depictions of persons of interest, showing his mugshot to potential witnesses, and of course making a computerized comparison of the arrestee's finger-prints against electronic databases of known criminals and unsolved crimes. In this respect the only difference between DNA analysis and the accepted use of fingerprint databases is the unparalleled accuracy DNA provides. . . .

Second, law enforcement officers bear a responsibility for ensuring that the custody of an arrestee does not create inordinate "risks for facility staff, for the existing detainee population, and for a new detainee." DNA identi-fication can provide untainted information to those charged with detaining suspects and detaining the property of any felon. For these purposes officers must know the type of person whom they are detaining, and DNA allows them to make critical choices about how to proceed. . . .

Third, looking forward to future stages of criminal prosecution, "the Government has a substantial interest in ensuring that persons accused of crimes are available for trials." A person who is arrested for one offense but knows that he has yet to answer for some past crime may be more inclined to flee the instant charges, lest continued contact with the criminal justice system expose one or more other serious offenses. . . .

Fourth, an arrestee's past conduct is essential to an assessment of the danger he poses to the public, and this will inform a court's determination whether the individual should be released on bail. . . .

Finally, in the interests of justice, the identification of an arrestee as the perpetrator of some heinous crime may have the salutary effect of freeing a person wrongfully imprisoned for the same offense. . . .

DNA identification represents an important advance in the techniques used by law enforcement to serve legitimate police concerns for as long as there have been arrests, concerns the courts have acknowledged and ap-proved for more than a century. Law enforcement agencies routinely have used scientific advancements in their standard procedures for the identifica-tion of arrestees. . . . Perhaps the most direct historical analogue to the DNA technology used to identify respondent is the familiar practice of fingerprint-ing arrestees. From the advent of this technique, courts had no trouble de-termining that fingerprinting was a natural part of "the administrative steps incident to arrest." In the seminal case of *United States v. Kelly*, 55 F.2d 67 (2nd Cir. 1932), Judge Augustus Hand wrote that routine fingerprinting did not violate the Fourth Amendment precisely because it fit within the accepted means of processing an arrestee into custody:

> Finger printing seems to be no more than an extension of methods of identification long used in dealing with persons under arrest for real or supposed violations of the criminal laws. It is known to be a very certain means devised by modern science to reach the desired end, and has become especially important in a time when increased population and vast aggregations of people in urban centers have rendered the notoriety of the individual in the community no longer a ready means of identification.

. . . DNA identification is an advanced technique superior to fingerprinting in many ways, so much so that to insist on fingerprints as the norm would make little sense to either the forensic expert or a layperson. The additional intrusion upon the arrestee's privacy beyond that associated with fingerprinting is not significant and DNA is a markedly more accurate form of identifying arrestees. A suspect who has changed his facial features to evade photographic identification or even one who has undertaken the more arduous task of altering his fingerprints cannot escape the revealing power of his DNA. . . .

In this critical respect, the search here at issue differs from the sort of programmatic searches of either the public at large or a particular class of regulated but otherwise law-abiding citizens that the Court has previously labeled as "'special needs'" searches. When the police stop a motorist at a checkpoint, or test a political candidate for illegal narcotics, they intrude upon substantial expectations of privacy. So the Court has insisted on some purpose other than "to detect evidence of ordinary criminal wrongdoing" to justify these searches in the absence of individualized suspicion. Once an individual has been arrested on probable cause for a dangerous offense that may require detention before trial, however, his or her expectations of privacy and freedom from police scrutiny are reduced. . . .

In addition the processing of respondent's DNA . . . did not intrude on respondent's privacy in a way that would make his DNA identification unconstitutional. . . . It is undisputed that law enforcement officers analyze DNA for the sole purpose of generating a unique identifying number against which future samples may be matched. . . . If in the future police analyze samples to determine, for instance, an arrestee's predisposition for a particular disease or other hereditary factors not relevant to identity, that case would present additional privacy concerns not present here. . . .

When officers make an arrest supported by probable cause to hold for a serious offense and they bring the suspect to the station to be detained in custody, taking and analyzing a cheek swab of the arrestee's DNA is, like fingerprinting and photographing, a legitimate police booking procedure that is reasonable under the Fourth Amendment.

JUSTICE SCALIA, with whom JUSTICE GINSBURG, JUSTICE SOTOMAYOR, and JUS-TICE KAGAN join, dissenting.

The Fourth Amendment forbids searching a person for evidence of a crime when there is no basis for believing the person is guilty of the crime or is in possession of incriminating evidence. That prohibition is categorical and without exception; it lies at the very heart of the Fourth Amendment. Whenever this Court has allowed a suspicionless search, it has insisted upon a justifying motive apart from the investigation of crime.

It is obvious that no such noninvestigative motive exists in this case. The Court's assertion that DNA is being taken, not to solve crimes, but to *identify* those in the State's custody, taxes the credulity of the credulous. And the Court's comparison of Maryland's DNA searches to other techniques, such as fingerprinting, can seem apt only to those who know no more than today's opinion has chosen to tell them about how those DNA searches actually work.

At the time of the Founding, Americans despised the British use of so-called "general warrants"—warrants not grounded upon a sworn oath of a specific infraction by a particular individual, and thus not limited in scope and application. The first Virginia Constitution declared that "general warrants, whereby any officer or messenger may be commanded to search suspected places without evidence of a fact committed," or to search a person "whose offence is not particularly described and supported by evidence," "are griev-ous and oppressive, and ought not be granted." . . . As ratified, the Fourth Amendment's Warrant Clause forbids a warrant to "issue" except "upon prob-able cause," and requires that it be "particula[r]" (which is to say, *individu-alized*) to "the place to be searched, and the persons or things to be seized." And we have held that, even when a warrant is not constitutionally necessary, the Fourth Amendment's general prohibition of "unreasonable" searches im-ports the same requirement of individualized suspicion.

Although there is a "closely guarded category of constitutionally permis-sible suspicionless searches," that has never included searches designed to serve "the normal need for law enforcement. . . ." Even the common name for suspicionless searches—"special needs" searches—itself reflects that they must be justified, *always*, by concerns "other than crime detection." We have approved random drug tests of railroad employees, yes—but only because the Government's need to "regulat[e] the conduct of railroad employees to ensure safety" is distinct from "normal law enforcement." . . . To put it another way, both the legitimacy of the Court's method and the correctness of its outcome hinge entirely on the truth of a single proposition: that the primary purpose of these DNA searches is something other than simply discovering evidence of criminal wrongdoing. As I detail below, that proposition is wrong.

The Court alludes at several points to the fact that King was an arrestee, and arrestees may be validly searched incident to their arrest. But the Court does not really *rest* on this principle, and for good reason: The objects of a search incident to arrest must be either (1) weapons or evidence that might easily be destroyed, or (2) evidence relevant to the crime of arrest. Neither is the object of the [DNA] search at issue here. . . . The Court hastens to clarify that it does not mean to approve invasive surgery on arrestees or warrantless searches of their homes. That the Court feels the need to disclaim these consequences is as damning a criticism of its suspicionless-search regime as any I can muster. . . .

[T]he Court elaborates at length the ways that the search here served the special purpose of "identifying" King. But that seems to me quite wrong—unless what one means by "identifying" someone is "searching for evidence that he has committed crimes unrelated to the crime of his arrest." At points the Court does appear to use "identifying" in that peculiar sense—claiming, for example, that knowing "an arrestee's past conduct is essential to an assessment of the danger he poses." If identifying someone means finding out what unsolved crimes he has committed, then identification is indistinguishable from the ordinary law-enforcement aims that have never been thought to justify a suspicionless search. . . .

King was arrested on April 10, 2009, on charges unrelated to the case before us. That same day, April 10, the police searched him and seized the DNA evidence at issue here. . . . King's DNA sample was not received by the Maryland State Police's Forensic Sciences Division until April 23, 2009—two weeks after his arrest. It sat in that office, ripening in a storage area, until the custodians got around to mailing it to a lab for testing on June 25, 2009—two months after it was received, and nearly three since King's arrest. After it was mailed, the data from the lab tests were not available for several more weeks, until July 13, 2009, which is when the test results were entered into Maryland's DNA database, *together with information identifying the person from whom the sample was taken*. Meanwhile, bail had been set, King had engaged in discovery, and he had requested a speedy trial—presumably not a trial of John Doe. It was not until August 4, 2009—four months after King's arrest—that the forwarded sample transmitted (*without* identifying information) from the Maryland DNA database to the Federal Bureau of Investigation's national database was matched with a sample taken from the scene of an unrelated crime years earlier. . . .

[I]f anything was "identified" at the moment that the DNA database returned a match, it was not King—his identity was already known. . . . Rather, what the August 4 match "identified" was *the previously-taken sample from the earlier crime*. That sample was genuinely mysterious to Maryland; the State knew that it had probably been left by the victim's attacker, but nothing else. King was not identified by his association with the sample; rather, the sample was identified by its association with King. The Court effectively destroys its own "identification" theory when it acknowledges that the object of this search was "to see what [was] already known about [King]." King was who he was, and volumes of his biography could not make him any more or any less King. No minimally competent speaker of English would say, upon noticing a known arrestee's similarity "to a wanted poster of a previously unidentified suspect," that the *arrestee* had thereby been identified. It was the previously unidentified suspect who had been identified—just as, here, it was the previously unidentified rapist.

That taking DNA samples from arrestees has nothing to do with identifying them is confirmed not just by actual practice (which the Court ignores) but by the enabling statute itself (which the Court also ignores). The Maryland Act at issue has a section helpfully entitled "Purpose of collecting and testing DNA samples." . . . That provision lists five purposes for which DNA samples may be tested. By this point, it will not surprise the reader to learn that the Court's imagined purpose is not among them. . . . "[I]t is safe to say that if the Court's identification theory is not wrong, there is no such thing as error." . . .

The Court asserts that the taking of fingerprints was "constitutional for generations prior to the introduction" of the FBI's rapid computer-matching system. This bold statement is bereft of citation to authority because there is none for it. The "great expansion in fingerprinting came before the modern era of Fourth Amendment jurisprudence," and so we were never asked to decide the legitimacy of the practice. As fingerprint databases expanded from convicted criminals, to arrestees, to civil servants, to immigrants, to everyone with a driver's license, Americans simply "became accustomed to having our fingerprints on file in some government database." But it is wrong to suggest that this was uncontroversial at the time, or that this Court blessed universal fingerprinting for "generations" before it was possible to use it effectively for identification. . . .

Today, it can fairly be said that fingerprints really are used to identify people—so well, in fact, that there would be no need for the expense of a separate, wholly redundant DNA confirmation of the same information. What DNA adds—what makes it a valuable weapon in the law-enforcement arsenal—is the ability to solve unsolved crimes, by matching old crime-scene evidence against the profiles of people whose identities are already known. That is what was going on when King's DNA was taken, and we should not disguise the fact. Solving unsolved crimes is a noble objective, but it occupies a lower place in the American pantheon of noble objectives than the protection of our people from suspicionless law-enforcement searches. The Fourth Amendment must prevail.

The Court disguises the vast (and scary) scope of its holding by promising a limitation it cannot deliver. The Court repeatedly says that DNA testing, and entry into a national DNA registry, will not befall thee and me, dear reader, but only those arrested for "serious offense[s]." . . . I cannot imagine what principle could possibly justify this limitation, and the Court does not attempt to suggest any. If one believes that DNA will "identify" someone arrested for assault, he must believe that it will "identify" someone arrested for a traffic offense. This Court does not base its judgments on senseless distinctions. At the end of the day, *logic will out*. When there comes before us the taking of DNA from an arrestee for a traffic violation, the Court will predictably (and quite rightly) say, "We can find no significant difference between this case and *King*." Make no mistake about it: As an entirely predictable consequence of today's decision, your DNA can be taken and entered into a national DNA database if you are ever arrested, rightly or wrongly, and for whatever reason. . . .

The most regrettable aspect of the suspicionless search that occurred here is that it proved to be quite unnecessary. All parties concede that it would have been entirely permissible, as far as the Fourth Amendment is concerned, for Maryland to take a sample of King's DNA as a consequence of his conviction for second-degree assault. So the ironic result of the Court's error is this: The only arrestees to whom the outcome here will ever make a difference are those who *have been acquitted* of the crime of arrest (so that their DNA could not have been taken upon conviction). In other words, this Act manages to burden uniquely the sole group for whom the Fourth Amendment's protections ought to be most jealously guarded: people who are innocent of the State's accusations. . . .

Today's judgment will, to be sure, have the beneficial effect of solving more crimes; then again, so would the taking of DNA samples from anyone who flies on an airplane (surely the Transportation Security Administration needs to know the "identity" of the flying public), applies for a driver's license, or attends a public school. Perhaps the construction of such a genetic panopticon is wise. But I doubt that the proud men who wrote the charter of our liberties would have been so eager to open their mouths for royal inspection. . . .

I therefore dissent. . . .

QUESTIONS ABOUT THE CASE

1. Does the taking of an arrested person's fingerprints differ significantly from taking that person's DNA in a swab? If so, how and why? In this regard, bear in mind that if Mr. King had been convicted of assault with a shotgun, the Constitution would then have clearly permitted taking his DNA, so presumably authorities would eventually have linked Mr. King to the original rape.

2. What reasons does Maryland give to justify taking DNA swabs from arrested persons who have not yet been found guilty of the crime for which they were arrested? Does the case fact that King's DNA results were not returned for months, coupled with the social background fact that DNA identification takes time, undermine Justice Kennedy's argument that obtaining the DNA sample in Mr. King's case was reasonable? If not, why not?

3. What of the argument that arresting officers need the DNA information to reduce risks to themselves or others from the arrestee? Is this consistent with the many weeks between the taking of the sample and the results returned from the lab?[67]

4. By now it should be more than obvious that we find that Scalia practiced good legal reasoning in *King* and Kennedy did not. To what extent does Scalia's commitment to the original understanding of the meaning of the text of the Fourth Amendment determine his result? Does not Scalia's approach in fact support an approach to the Constitution that takes full account of new developments, technological and otherwise, in society, developments that

---

67. In a passage from his opinion omitted above, Scalia wrote:

Surely, then—*surely*—the State of Maryland got cracking on those grave risks immediately, by rushing to identify King with his DNA as soon as possible. . . . Nothing could be further from the truth. Maryland officials did not even begin the process of testing King's DNA that day. Or, actually, the next day. Or the day after that. And that was for a simple reason: Maryland law forbids them to do so. A "DNA sample collected from an individual charged with a crime . . . *may not* be tested or placed in the statewide DNA data base system prior to the first scheduled arraignment date." Md. Pub. Saf. Code Ann. § 2–504(d)(1).

Maryland v. King, 569 U.S. ___ (2013), p. 6.

the framers, or anyone else at the time, could not possibly have understood the words of the Constitution to cover? How can taking account of such developments be squared with a commitment to originalism? Or does Scalia's argument, like the result in *Home Building and Loan*, achieve the purposes behind the Constitution's actual words: protecting creditors then and protecting against police-state practices now?

5. Justice Scalia has become a household name in good part because he makes strong and public statements about issues of legal reasoning that form the very core of this book. For example, in a book review published in 2005, Justice Scalia considered the popular outcry that he acknowledged would follow if the Court only applied the Constitution as reasonable people would have understood its text when it was written. Courts would refuse to protect people claiming the right to make reproductive choices for themselves, for example, because the text of the Constitution makes no explicit law on these subjects. Wrote Scalia: "That is precisely the answer they should have received: The federal Constitution says nothing on these subjects, which are therefore left to be governed by state law."[68] We hope this book has made plain by now why we believe that no form of originalism can persuasively resolve disputes over constitutional interpretation, but Justice Scalia nevertheless poses important questions for you to ponder. Do you find plausible Justice Scalia's fear that if judges are not bound by original meaning, nothing else will bind them? Does Justice Scalia convince you that he practices what he preaches consistently? What do you make of the fact that Scalia, a devout Roman Catholic, often reaches results that support conservative Catholic teachings? Does this matter if his legal reasoning is persuasive, as in this illustrative case? Why or why not? (Does it matter that the Court currently has six Catholic members, making it highly unrepresentative of the United States on this score?)

6. What do you make of Scalia's sometimes blunt, sarcastic, and folksy rhetoric? Do his references to things like "dear reader" demean the honor of the law? We know that only a tiny fraction of the population actually reads judicial opinions, but does Scalia, by writing in this style, appeal to nonlawyer readers? Might a judge who writes this way be more likely to create trustworthy opinions and results than do judges who think only technically and analytically?

68. Antonin Scalia, "Law & Language," *First Things*, November 2005. In 2015, John Strand's play *The Originalist* premiered at Arena Stage, in Washington, DC. The play pits in debate the conservative Scalia against a self-described "flaming liberal" law clerk. Both agree that Scalia is "a monster" to some and "a hero" to others. By implication the play raises again the question of whether either liberal or conservative ideologies, as opposed to a devotion to the craft of good legal reasoning itself, should play a significant role in legal interpretation.

Or does Scalia's sarcastic dismissal of his fellow justices' conclusions (and of the winning litigant's position) undermine respect for the legal system?

7. Readers who enjoy examining newsworthy cases like *Maryland v. King* may benefit from applying the four elements of legal reasoning to other recent U.S. Supreme Court decisions in the headlines. We particularly recommend a closer examination of three such cases that conservatives praised but liberals criticized. Does your application of the elements of legal reasoning to these cases, or to any politically controversial cases this book describes, lead you to trust outcomes that differ from how you would judge these cases using only your personal social and political beliefs?

- *McCullen v. Coakley* (2014): Massachusetts's Reproductive Health Care Facilities Act makes it a crime to knowingly stand on a "public way or sidewalk" within thirty-five feet of an entrance or driveway to any "reproductive health care facility," defined as "a place, other than within or upon the grounds of a hospital, where abortions are offered or performed." The Court overturned this statute.

- *McCutcheon v. Federal Elections Commission* (2014): Inspired by the Court's controversial 2010 decision *Citizens United v. Federal Election Commission*, Shaun McCutcheon, an Alabama businessman, sued when he was denied his wish to contribute, in 2012, to various conservative causes, more than his legally allowed $177,000 aggregate limit for the year. The Republican National Committee joined him in his lawsuit, which argued that the law violated the First Amendment. They won.

- *Shelby County v. Holder* (2013): Here, the Supreme Court by a 5–4 vote struck down Section 5 of the 1965 Voting Rights Act. The provision required states with a history of state-sponsored segregation to demonstrate to the U.S. Justice Department that their voting laws and policies did not discriminate against racial minorities. Congress had reauthorized Section 5 in 2006 by large majorities, and George W. Bush had signed the legislation. Keep in mind that both the Fourteenth Amendment, which bars states from denying equal protection of the laws, and the Fifteenth Amendment, which outlaws state attempts to deny the right to vote on the basis of race or color, specifically authorize Congress to enact legislation enforcing these prohibitions.

CHAPTER 6

Law and Politics

The ultimate goal is to break down the sense that legal argument is autonomous from moral, economic and political discourse.

—DUNCAN KENNEDY

When judges make law and scholars propose rules of law, they necessarily rely on their vision of society as it is and as it ought to be. If law is to be made well, those visions must be accurate and attractive.

—MARK TUSHNET

Fair fɛər[:] beautiful; pleasing. . . . [Gothic] *fagr* fitting.
—*The Oxford Dictionary of English Etymology* (1966)

The Rule of Law

On the night of July 31, 2001, Roy Moore, the elected chief justice of the Alabama Supreme Court, had a 5,280-pound granite monument placed in the rotunda of the state's Judicial Building in Montgomery. Chief Justice Moore did so without the knowledge or consent of the other eight justices on the Court. The monument depicted a book, presumably the Holy Bible, open to two pages on which the stonemason had carved the King James translation of the Ten Commandments. A private evangelical group, Coral Ridge Ministries, paid the costs of the project. Within days, Stephen Glassroth, a Jewish attorney practicing in Montgomery, sued to have the monument removed.

In the summer of 2003, after Moore lost both at trial and on appeal,

federal district court judge Myron Thompson commanded Moore to remove the display.[1] Refusal would subject the state of Alabama to a fine of
$5,000 a day for contempt of court. The federal courts cited precedents
that, under the establishment clause of the First Amendment, prohibited
public schools from posting the Ten Commandments in classrooms and
prohibited courthouses from displaying the Ten Commandments unless
accompanied by other secular historical examples of the sources of American law. Moore had specifically refused one request to place in the Judicial Building's rotunda a plaque containing the words of Martin Luther
King Jr.'s "I Have a Dream" speech and another request to put an atheist
symbol there. On August 26, the eight remaining justices of the Alabama
Supreme Court, who by then had voted to suspend Moore from his office
for refusing to comply with the court order to remove the monument,
hired a moving company in Georgia (no Alabama company would take
the job) and moved "Roy's Rock" from the rotunda to a courthouse area
not open to the public.

In an essay in the *Wall Street Journal*, titled "In God I Trust," Chief Justice Moore wrote, "Today, I argue for the rule of law, and against any unilateral declaration of a judge to ban the acknowledgment of God in the public
sector." His defense of the display included the following legal arguments:[2]

- The Constitution of the State of Alabama specifically invokes "the
  favor and guidance of Almighty God."
- As the state's chief justice, Moore wrote, "I am entrusted with the
  sacred duty to uphold the state's constitution. I have taken an oath
  before God and man to do such, and I will not waver from that commitment."
- In preventing Moore from complying with his sacred duty, the federal court has "violated the rule of law."
- The founding fathers were greatly influenced by William Blackstone,
  who stated that judges have no power to make laws, only interpret
  them: "No judge has the authority to impose his will on the people
  of a state."
- If the federal courts had ordered "the churches of my state to be
  burned to the ground," Moore said, the Alabama courts would rightly
  refuse to enforce the order, and the same principle applies here.

1. *Glassroth v. Moore*, 299 F. Supp. 2d 1290 (N.D. Ala. 2002).
2. Roy Moore, "In God I Trust," *Wall Street Journal*, August 25, 2003.

- The "separation of church and state" in the First Amendment of the U.S. Constitution endorses "the legitimate jurisdictional separation between church and state," not the "separation of God and state."
- Literally read, the First Amendment's language—"Congress shall make no law respecting an establishment of religion"—obviously does not apply here, since Congress had not made a law requiring a display of the Ten Commandments in courthouses.

Moore concluded:

Not only does Judge Thompson put himself above the law, but above God, as well. I say enough is enough. We must "dare to defend our rights," as Alabama's state motto declares. No judge or man can dictate what we believe or in whom we believe. The Ninth and Tenth Amendments are not a part of the Constitution simply to make the Bill of Rights a round number. The Ninth Amendment secured our right as a people. The 10th guaranteed our right as a sovereign state. Those are the rules of law.[3]

At the core of Moore's bold political action, which made front-page stories around the country, lies a political debate about the issues you have studied so far in this book. In a nutshell, that debate and this book ask, what is the rule of law? We could, of course, analyze the Roy Moore story as just another political power struggle, another case of ambition countering ambition, as James Madison put it in *The Federalist Papers*.[4] Moore claimed that the people of Alabama had elected him to his judicial post. He, having taken an oath to defend the Alabama constitution, was just doing his job. The federal court judges, appointed to their posts for life, represent a different, national constituency; therefore, they reached a different conclusion. Perhaps because William Pryor, Alabama's attorney general,

---

3. Ibid. The Ninth Amendment reads, "The enumeration in the Constitution, of certain rights, shall not be construed to deny or disparage others retained by the people." The Tenth reads, "The powers not delegated to the United States by the Constitution, nor prohibited by it to the States, are reserved to the States respectively, or to the people."

4. Writing in defense of the separation of legislative, judicial, and executive powers from one another in the U.S. Constitution, Madison wrote, "Ambition must be made to counteract ambition" so that no one faction could gain tyrannical control over government. "Federalist Papers #51," in *The Federalist Papers*, ed. Isaac Kramnick (New York: Penguin, 1987), 319.

agreed that the federal court order was valid and had to be enforced, federal power outmuscled Moore in this struggle.[5]

This book suggests another way to frame the Roy Moore story. Recall our basic definition of law: law is a language used to prevent or resolve conflicts using rules made by the state as a starting point. We call this language "legal reasoning." Legal reasoning, when done well, helps reassure communities that judges resolve disputes with integrity. A good justification, in harmonizing the elements of the case at hand, reminds us that fairness and beauty are close cousins. They work in "accurate and attractive" ways, as the epigraph to this chapter by Mark Tushnet puts it. Legal materials contain too many sources of generality, vagueness, and ambiguity—as many ways of combining legal rules and the facts of individual cases as there are combinations of visually distinctive pills—to generate singularly objective correct answers to legal questions. Nevertheless, just as musical amateurs can tell better performances of Beethoven's Fifth Symphony or of Adele's "Rolling in the Deep" from worse ones, so can nonlawyers tell fair—that is, harmonized or "beautiful," "pleasing" and "fitting"—legal justifications from less attractive ones.

A well-reasoned appellate opinion integrates or harmonizes in a persuasive way the case facts, rules of law, social background facts, and shared values that are relevant to a dispute. We examine these four elements of legal reasoning as they apply to Moore's argument later in this chapter. First, though, we return to the analysis in chapter 1 of the critical importance of judicial impartiality. There, we made the following argument: Judicial impartiality plays a major role in maintaining peaceful and progressive politi-

5. After Moore's removal from the bench, he campaigned twice, unsuccessfully, for the governorship of Alabama, but in 2012 he was elected once again as chief justice of the Alabama Supreme Court. In 2015 Moore was involved in a controversy with remarkable parallels to the Ten Commandments case, this time concerning a federal district court judge's ruling that Alabama laws against same-sex marriage were unconstitutional. Moore wrote a memo ("State of Alabama—Judicial System: Administrative Order of the Chief Justice of the Supreme Court") ordering state probate judges not to follow the ruling, noting that the Alabama Constitution specifically restricted marriage to opposite-sex couples. In public statements Moore claimed that no federal court had the power to order a state to change its policies regarding marriage. Kent Faulk, "Alabama Supreme Court First in Nation to Defy Federal Court Gay Marriage Order," *Alabama. com,* March 6, 2015. Later in 2015, when the Supreme Court, in *Obergefell v. Hodges* 576 U.S. ___, ruled that laws prohibiting same-sex marriage were unconstutional, Moore made public speeches in which he argued the decision "destroyed the institution of God" and reflected Satanic influence. An ethics complaint filed against Moore charged that he had urged state officials to defy the Court's ruling. Casey Toner, "Alabama Supreme Court Chief Justice Roy Moore: Same-Sex Marriage Ruling 'Destroyed the Institution of God,'" *Alabama.com,* July 12, 2015.

cal regimes. It does so because the existence of a neutral third-party judge, a triadic process of conflict resolution as we have called it, keeps conflicts from turning into two-against-one power struggles. The presence of a third-party referee allows the loser of a conflict to accept the loss without feeling wronged or worse, humiliated, and hell-bent on revenge. Judges, then, have the job of keeping communities peaceful and trustworthy, two of the core tasks of politics.

Communities and the Rule of Law

Did you notice a remarkable feature of Roy Moore's argument for placing the Ten Commandments in the Alabama courthouse? Moore insisted that he was merely following the rule of law. The rule of law is so central to American political culture that political activists across the spectrum invoke it. It is fundamental because it is how communities with classically liberal political cultures justify the use of governmental power.

Communities are groups of people who seek to work and play cooperatively and productively together. Communities come in all sizes, from families and teams and clusters of "good neighbors" to states and nations that are communities of strangers. Sometimes, and particularly in small groups with long histories, cooperation comes easily. People know the customs that bind one another. They trust one another not to cheat, and so they trust the economic and social trades they make with one another. But as communities get larger, some people must rule others.[6] Someone must use power to coerce those who have not cooperated either to become cooperative or to get out of the group. Here, formal political institutions emerge—leaders with weapons, codes of rules, and courts to enforce them.

Liberal political systems try to minimize the harm that rulers do to the ruled by imposing on the powerful the obligation to justify their use of power based on community norms and understandings. We have an expectation, for example, that presidents will not simply make decisions but also explain and justify their decisions to the public, through speeches, press conferences, and writings.

Here enters legal reasoning, which is also a kind of explanation and justification. Our political system generates an immense quantity of le-

---

6. Anarchists, among others, dispute this claim. See Jimmy Casas Klausen and James Martel, *How Not to Be Governed: Readings and Interpretations from a Critical Anarchist Left* (Lanham, MD: Lexington Books, 2011).

gal texts—statutes, regulations, constitutional provisions, and the prior judicial opinions that we call *precedents*. These texts represent attempts to give communities rules by which their members can live together. Yet inevitably, from time to time these attempts fail, and social cooperation falters. Every appellate case covered in this book illustrates such a failure. Mr. Francioso and Mr. Repouille wanted to become U.S. citizens, but a U.S. attorney tried to stop them; Edith Windsor believed she was entitled to be treated just like any other widow, but the IRS disagreed. Roy Moore insisted that the Fourteenth Amendment does not prevent him from placing the Ten Commandments in his courthouse, but some Alabama residents disagreed. When conflicts such as these arise, the parties may call on judges to resolve the dispute. And because we insist on justification in our legal culture, we do not simply permit judges to exercise their power by declaring their decisions. They must justify what they have done.

The judge's resolution of the conflict uses the legal texts as a starting point but not, as we have shown, the endpoint. This is partly because words are ambiguous, and in a diverse society, people can understand them differently. But this is also because in law, as in life, no set of rules can cover every possible situation. To understand this point better, consider an analogy that literary theorist Stanley Fish makes to the game of basketball:

> Suppose you were a basketball coach and taught someone how to shoot baskets and how to dribble the ball, but had imparted these skills without reference to the playing of an actual basketball game. Now you decide to insert your student into a game, and you equip him with some rules. You say to him, for instance, "Take only good shots." "What," he asks reasonably enough, "is a good shot?" "Well," you reply, "a good shot is an 'open shot,' a shot taken when you are close to the basket (so that the chances of success are good) and when your view is not obstructed by the harassing efforts of opposing players." Everything goes well until the last few seconds of the game; your team is behind by a single point; the novice player gets the ball in heavy traffic and holds it as the final buzzer rings. You run up to him and say, "Why didn't you shoot?" and he answers, "It wasn't a good shot." Clearly, the rule must be amended, and accordingly you tell him that if time is running out, and your team is behind, and you have the ball, you should take the shot even if it isn't a good one, because it will then *be* a good one in the sense of being the best shot in the circumstances. (Notice how both the

meaning of the rule and the entities it covers are changing shape as this "education" proceeds.) Now suppose there is another game, and the same situation develops. This time the player takes the shot, which under the circumstances is a very difficult one; he misses, and once again the final buzzer rings. You run up to him and say, "Didn't you see that John (a teammate) had gone 'back door' and was perfectly positioned under the basket for an easy shot?" and he answers "But you said . . ." Now obviously it would be possible once again to amend the rule, and just as obviously there would be no real end to the sequence and number of emendations that would be necessary. Of course, there will eventually come a time when the novice player (like the novice judge) will no longer have to ask questions; but it will not be because the rules have finally been made sufficiently explicit to cover all cases, but because explicitness will have been rendered unnecessary by a kind of knowledge that informs rules rather than follows from them.[7]

Legislatures, constitution makers, and judges who set precedents are each in the position of Fish's basketball coach, unable to anticipate every possible dispute that may arise under the rules they propound. That's why, as we have argued, judges must look beyond the words of legal texts in order to implement the law wisely. And that's also why judges must justify their decisions rather than simply announcing them.

Judges justify their decisions in the language of legal reasoning. This book argues that when a judicial opinion creates a plausible fit among the four elements of legal reasoning, the judge has met the obligation to use his or her power in the way American political culture expects. By implication, we have argued as well that when judges harmonize the four elements—the facts of cases, the official legal texts, social background facts about the world in which we live, and norms widely shared in our polity—they *necessarily* create an image of a viable community. In the remainder of this chapter we explain why you should believe this.

Impartiality and Trust

Governing a large community, a group of total strangers who happen to live, often by the millions, in one city, state, or nation, is a difficult business.

---

7. Stanley Fish, *"Fish v. Fiss," Stanford Law Review* 36 (1984): 1325–1347, at 1329–1330.

It is more difficult than, say, running McDonald's or the Seattle Symphony, for several reasons:

- The government's rules speak to the public, to the community, to everyone, in a way that McDonald's rules (or for that matter, the pope's rules) do not.
- The community is the greatest source of disruption and uncertainty in our lives because it exposes us to the work of strangers that we, individually, have no power to control. The community is the place where people's psychological need for confidence in structure is greatest, for it is the one place that binds everyone. The rules that the *government* makes and enforces must maintain confidence that social structures hold—confidence that even strangers can share values.
- People need to maintain this confidence even when they cannot express precisely the right limit or value by which to judge a concrete situation.

The judicial process and legal reasoning therefore help preserve the confidence that the community can reconcile rules, facts of disputes, social conditions, and ethics. Our confidence does not rest entirely or immediately on the quality of legal reasoning, but the language of legal justification is one important means by which those who govern can reassure us that our communal life is "accurate and attractive." Unlike other social processes in and out of government, courts must make *some* decision— reach some closure on the problems litigants bring to them. Like game umpires and referees, they cannot just walk away and refuse to decide. Regardless of the ultimate wisdom of the solution, we need to believe that our community contains forums in which decision and action replace indecision and drift. In this book, we have criticized many conventional practices, habits, and assumptions in legal reasoning precisely because good legal reasoning is so vital to the flourishing of communities. Reason in law must, as Duncan Kennedy put it in another epigraph for this chapter, "break down the sense that legal argument is autonomous from moral, economic and political discourse," or it will ultimately destroy our confidence in community.

The legal process, in the face of the infinite complexity and uncertainty of the world, must contain a method of applying the abstractions of law to human affairs that people accept. This does not require finding the perfect solution. It is sufficient if the process reaches acceptable reconciliations of facts, social conditions, laws, and ethical values. For this process to succeed, judges must speak for the community—not for their profession or their personal religious or ideological beliefs, or to ensure that the side with which they identify wins. Therefore, we consider next the qualities of a good judge.

A Psychological Sidebar

Imagine you are mired in a dispute in which your fortunes are at stake. What sort of person would you want to judge your case? Which qualities of mind and character would lead you to trust the judge? Conversely, which attributes would you find unnerving? We suspect, for example, that Roy Moore's behavior as chief justice of Alabama might make those who did not share his particular form of Christianity uncomfortable were he to rule over their disputes. Why?

Consider these different personality types:

- Open minded and skeptical versus righteous and certain
- Even tempered and steady versus emotional and impulsive
- Attentive and focused versus easily distracted
- Disciplined and hard working versus fun loving and lazy

Humans have observed and dramatized differences in personality for millennia. From classical Greek mythology forward, literature has celebrated archetypes that distinguish rational and even-tempered characters from emotional and impulsive ones. The Greek pantheon, for example, describes Apollo, the god of music and the arts, archery, medicine, and knowledge, as radically different from Dionysus, the god of wine, religious rituals, ecstasy, and theater.[8] The world of classical opera offers us the hotheaded Carmen and, in *Der Rosenkavalier*, the detached and reflective Marschallin. Mark Twain contrasts the crafty Tom Sawyer with the more undisciplined Huckleberry Finn. And *Through the Looking Glass* offers several remarkably mercurial characters, including Humpty Dumpty, who insists he can make words mean whatever he wants, and the White Queen, who boasts she sometimes "believe[s] six impossible things before breakfast"!

---

8. In Thucydides's account of the "Mytelenian debate," concerning whether Athens should enslave and kill all residents of a town that had defied them, he describes Cleon as scornful of those who wish to slow down and have an extended debate over the matter. Diodotus, defending both the wisdom of debate and the lives of the Mytelenians, replies: "I think the two things most opposed to good counsel are haste and passion; haste usually goes hand in hand with folly, passion with coarseness and narrowness of mind." Diodotus's arguments carried the day. *History of the Peloponnesian War*, book 3, 3.42 [1].

Most readers, we are confident, would prefer Apollo to Dionysus as a judge in their case—and panic at the sight of Humpty Dumpty or the White Queen on the bench. Litigants want judges who are open minded and do not jump to conclusions based on biases and prejudices, who will coolly take all the arguments and facts into account before ruling. And if they lose a case, litigants want the kind of judge who will patiently explain the reasons for the decision rather than mock and scorn their side. So, how to find judges with such dispositions and avoid those who are impetuous, emotional, prejudiced, and righteous? How to recruit judges who are judicious rather than "judgmental"?

Psychological research suggests that the quest for a judge with the ideal personality type may be pointless: depending on the circumstances, each of us can be impulsive or reasoning, judgmental or open minded, attentive or easily distracted. To be human is to have the capacity for both Apollonian and Dionysian—and, at times, Humpty-Dumptyish—behavior. One influential line of research, for example, describes people as operating in two modes, an automatic "fast" mode that enables us to perform many tasks almost effortlessly, including quite complicated maneuvers like driving, as well as a "slow" mode in which we more carefully reason through our choices.[9] The fast mode, like the bad judge, impulsively jumps to conclusions based on limited information.

The Nobel Prize–winning psychologist Daniel Kahneman describes this mode as a "lazy controller" that guides behavior by finding familiar patterns in the barest bits of data and drawing quick conclusions based on those patterns. The lazy controller then moves on to the next task, neglecting to check the accuracy of its work.[10] Because it is so lazy and automatic, the fast mode occasionally generates profound errors of judgment. Social psychologists, for example, have shown how implicit bias against racial minorities leads people to unconsciously discriminate and so perpetuate social inequalities.[11] Yet despite its limitations, the fast mode is the one in which humans mostly operate. This can be a good thing when survival

9. For a review and defense of "dual processing" theories, see Jonathan St. B. T. Evans and Keith E. Stanovich, "Dual Process Theories of Higher Cognition: Advancing the Debate," *Perspectives on Psychological Science* 8 (2013): 223–241.

10. Kahneman's fascinating book *Thinking, Fast and Slow* offers many examples of how humans get tripped up by the fast mode (New York: Farrar, Straus, and Giroux, 2011).

11. Irene C. Blair, Nilanjana DasGupta, and Jack Glaser, "Implicit Attitudes," in *APA Handbook of Personality and Social Psychology*, vol. 1, *Attitudes and Social Cognition*, ed. M. Mikulincer and P. R. Shaver (Washington, DC: American Psychology Association, 2014), 665–691.

depends on quickly steering around an obstacle (or lions and tigers and bears, as our ancestors did).

You might imagine that the fast mode is reserved for such emergencies, or for mundane tasks like shoveling the snow or washing the dishes. According to the psychologist Jonathan Haidt, though, people's fundamental judgments about right and wrong start not from the considered reflection of the slow mode, but with the intuitions and sentiments that arise in the fast mode. To see this, consider the following scenario of Haidt's. Has the individual in the story done anything morally wrong?

> A man goes to the supermarket once a week and buys a chicken. But before cooking the chicken, he has sexual intercourse with it. Then he cooks it and eats it.[12]

What was your immediate response? Did you summon your deepest ethical principles, apply them to the story, draw a preliminary conclusion, consider counterarguments, then render a final verdict? More likely, your first thought was revulsion, an overriding sense that the man's conduct was out of bounds in some way. It was only after this first thought that, perhaps prompted by the context of reading a book on reasoning, you slowed down to think about how you could make sense of your judgment. Haidt and his colleagues performed experiments in which they asked people to make moral judgments about a series of similarly brief scenarios—not all, we should add, as viscerally repellent. They found that people often made strong judgments about the scenarios but struggled to defend those judgments when questioned about them, a phenomenon he labels "moral dumbfounding." Often they would justify their conclusions by inventing facts not in the scenario ("a neighbor could see it and be disgusted"). Their struggle to explain themselves did not, though, lead them to change their minds about their judgments. His subjects, Haidt says, "were working quite hard at reasoning, but it was not reasoning in search of truth; it was reasoning in support of their emotional reactions."[13]

Haidt's point is not to denigrate moral instincts; indeed, he points out that without such an intuitive moral sense we would be adrift, calculating each day the pros and cons of such choices as to whether to murder our parents or drive our car into a crowd. His contention, though, is that our in-

---

12. Jonathan Haidt, *The Righteous Mind: Why Good People Are Divided by Politics and Religion* (New York: Vintage Books, 2013), 4.

13. Ibid., 29.

stincts, our gut feelings, drive our moral judgments. He pictures the brain as having within it an elephant, who chooses through intuition and emotion, and a rider, who reasons through choices. It is "rider," not "driver," for a reason—the elephant is mainly doing the choosing about where to go.[14] The rider's main job is to be a spokesperson for the elephant, to come up with a reasoned rationale for whatever it has done and wherever it wants to do.[15]

This seems a dismal portrait of human judgment, especially for those aspiring to impartiality in law—to say nothing of those seated before a judge. It gets to the heart of a fear about judges, that they will rule on the basis of prejudices and biases rather than good legal reasoning. Social institutions, however, are built in part to mitigate the frailties of human nature. Because humans are prone to overconfidence about their intuitions, and tend to act as lawyers for their gut feelings, social institutions that value truth seeking create mechanisms that force people to defend their conclusions before others.[16] In American appellate law, whatever the method by which judges arrive at their decisions, they must justify their choices in published opinions. Moreover, the vast majority of American appellate judges rule as part of panels, which forces judges of different worldviews and experiences to reckon with each other's gut instincts.[17] If appellate judges cannot, through their legal reasoning, convince others of the soundness of their conclusions, they can be overruled or discounted.[18] Judges report that they often encounter cases in which their initial impulse "wouldn't write." The writing

14. Haidt has been criticized for his claim that one must "talk to the elephant" to change a person's mind about a moral judgment. For an argument that riders are more powerful and elephants more trainable than Haidt suggests, see Tziporah Kasachkoff and Herbert D. Saltzstein, "Reasoning and Moral Decision-Making: A Critique of the Social Intuitionist Model," *European Journal of Developmental Science* 2 (2008): 287–302.

15. As Benjamin Franklin wrote, "So convenient a thing to be a reasonable creature, since it enables one to find or make a reason for every thing one has a mind to do." See *The Autobiography of Benjamin Franklin: Poor Richard's Almanac and Other Papers* (New York: A. L. Burt Co., 1900).

16. In the sciences, for example, researchers who seek to publish their results in journals must describe in tedious detail the methods by which they reached their conclusions—and subject their explanation to review by anonymous colleagues.

17. Political scientists have found that appellate judges assigned to panels with judges of different party backgrounds appear to work harder to justify their conclusions by writing more detailed opinions than do judges on panels with ideological soul mates. See Frank Cross and Emerson Tiller, "A Modest Proposal for Improving American Justice," *Columbia Law Review* 99 (1999): 215–234.

18. For a powerful and subtle examination of how judges are both constrained and enabled to create new law by their fellow judges, see Malcolm M. Feeley and Edward L. Rubin, *Judicial Policy Making and the Modern State* (New York: Cambridge University Press, 1998), 204–233.

process itself showed them that they couldn't convincingly justify their instinctive choice to the legal community, and so they had to reconsider what their instincts told them was the right decision. By being forced to justify their conclusions to others, judges can internalize the slow mechanisms of reasoning through their decisions, fighting back against the human tendency to jump to conclusions.[19]

Indeed, there is reason to believe that those trained in a particular expertise like law may be able to reshape their gut instincts, their fast mode, and so tame and steer their elephants.[20] (It is not an accident that fields of expertise are often described as "disciplines.") Studies of experts such as chess masters, nurses in intensive care units, and firefighters show that they can develop gut instincts, fast modes, that are quick, unbiased, and accurate. In those fields the consequences of misjudgment are powerful and immediately visible; for judges and lawyers they are not so clear, and so we cannot say that judges develop "accurate" instincts in quite the same way. But because they are so immersed in the language of law and legal reasoning, judges and lawyers may be able to develop decision-making styles quite different from those of nonlawyers, approaching disputes with a disciplined, logical thinking process that leads them away from jumping to conclusions. Appendix B, which describes how judges justified their conclusions about a particularly difficult case, illustrates this disciplined reasoning style, and contrasts it with the dramatically opposed tendencies of elected representatives and political activists.

Rather than searching, then, for judges with ideal personalities, communities should consider how legal institutions and the legal profession can tame the human tendency in all of us to leap to conclusions based on the bits of a case that seem particularly compelling, and so nourish the human capacity for reasoned, impartial judgment.

Impartial Judgment

But what exactly does it mean to be "impartial"? If judges, even those immersed in the slow habits of mind associated with legal reasoning, inevitably bring to the bench a lifetime of experiences and worldviews, and if,

19. For a somewhat discouraging study of the extent to which legal training affects legal reasoning, see Eileen Braman, *Law, Politics and Perception: How Policy Preferences Influence Legal Reasoning* (Charlottesville: University of Virginia Press, 2009). On the psychology of judging more generally, see David Klein and Gregory Mitchell, eds., *The Psychology of Judicial Decision Making* (New York: Oxford University Press, 2010).

20. Daniel Kahneman and Gary Klein, "Conditions for Intuitive Expertise: A Failure to Disagree," *American Psychologist* 64 (2009): 515–526.

as we noted near the outset of chapter 2, generations of political scientists have demonstrated that those experiences and worldviews help shape their decision making, how can anyone be an impartial judge?

Imagine yourself in each of these three situations:

1. A midsummer afternoon in Wrigley Field. The Cubs versus the Cardinals. You are calling balls and strikes behind home plate.
2. The production set for Fox television's *American Idol*. You are judging who will be the winner for the year.
3. Eight thirty in the evening, in the home of your young family. The children are squabbling. They appeal to you for judgment:

    LAURIE: Daddy, Robbie bit me!

    ROBBIE: I did not!

    LAURIE: You did too! Look! Tooth marks!

    ROBBIE: But Dad! Laurie took my dime!

    LAURIE: I took your dime 'cause you stepped on my doll and broke it.

    ROBBIE: But it was an accident, dum-dum.

    LAURIE: I am not a dum-dum, you fathead!

Each of these situations calls for judgment. Each judge makes decisions that affect the claims of others and decides before an audience that has some expectations about how the judge should decide. Without necessarily determining what the judge should conclude, the audience knows what the judge should look at and will test the judgment against these expectations. Even a child seeking justice from a parent does so.

To judge is to decide the claims of others using criteria that arise out of the expectations of the relevant audience. We shall see shortly where this definition leads in law. For the moment, consider what these three nonlegal judging situations do and do not have in common.

First and most important, notice that the three are not equally reasoned. Reasoning—the slow mode in which humans think beyond simply matching what they see to predetermined patterns or categories—influences the umpire calling balls and strikes only indirectly, in the creation of the strike zone. The umpire for the most part is in the fast mode, judging whether the pitch he or she observes falls within the predetermined categories of ball or strike. The parent and the talent judge, however, must think beyond predetermined categories. Parents cannot, for example, escape from making some calculation about the effects of their decision on their children, or at least on their own sanity.

This is because rules do not equally affect all three situations. On the one hand, the umpire works with an elaborate set of written rules about baseball, most of which he commits to memory. The fast mode works well here because the umpire's job is usually just to apply the rules to the facts. In baseball, time is of the essence, which is why its rules are so elaborate. Additionally, baseball allows for precise rules because, as in most sports, we can pinpoint what matters to us in time and space. On the other hand, we cannot define singing talent so precisely. Television talent-show judges exercise more discretion because their rules do not so precisely tell them what to seek.[21] Finally, the squabbling children may invoke no family rule at all. The family may have no regulation forbidding or punishing Robbie's toothy assault on his sister and his lie, and no conventions governing Laurie's theft or the children's gratuitous exchange of insults. But even in the absence of a family rule, the children need their parents to pass judgment. As a result, these three kinds of judges have different opportunities to make rules for the future. The parent can explicitly respond to the squabble by announcing what is right and wrong and declaring his official policy for the future. Such a setting of limits may be precisely what the children hope the parent, as judge, will do. But talent-show judges may do so only informally and umpires hardly at all, given the audience's expectations of their roles.

The job of judging, then, does not always, as it does in appellate law, involve the application of rules or the slow process of reasoning through the rules. We will turn to the unique properties of reasoning through rules later, but first we must pin down that quality inherent in all judging: impartiality.

Impartiality is not a mysterious concept. The *Merriam Webster Dictionary* defines *partial* as "relating to a part rather than the whole; not general or total." To decide *impartially*, then, one must postpone the final decision until all the relevant information has been gathered. Such suspensions of judgment restrain the very human impulse to jump to conclusions based on whatever first strikes the judge as most compelling. It means that the information—the placement of the pitch, the talent contestant's perfor-

---

21. There is another interesting difference: with rare exceptions, such as when she calls the game on account of rain or ejects an ornery manager or player, the umpire has minimal control over who wins. But the judges of the singing contest *declare* the winner. This differential effect on the outcome explains why we have only one home-plate umpire but several judges in singing contests and on the vast majority of appellate courts. (Notice that when umpires do make discretionary calls, they are more likely to consult other umpires than when they call routine events like balls and strikes.)

mance, and the children's actual behavior—rather than a personal affection or preference for one party determines the result.[22]

While "impartiality" is not itself a difficult concept—we have all judged and been judged in our lives—it is often difficult for audiences to satisfy themselves that judges actually decide impartially. Because in every case judges create losers, judges are always at risk of creating community discontent; a backlash is always possible. The judge's only long-range security, therefore, is to care about and try as best she can *to fulfill the expectations of judgment that the audience imposes.*

So, to judge is to be judged. The argument assumes, of course, that audiences can, in fact, distinguish their expectations of the process of decision from their hopes that one side—their side!—will win. We authors are convinced that people can do so, though we rely more on our experiences as sports fans, employees, teachers, and family members than we do on psychological experiments. Teams can lose championships, employees can receive poor assignments, students can receive disappointing grades, and children can be ordered to wash the dishes, all without doubting that the judges have decided impartially.

Professor Robert Cover thus wrote:

> The critical dimension of the rule of law is not the degree of specificity with which an actor is constrained, but the very fact that the actor must look outside his own will for criteria of judgment. There is a difference—intelligible to most pre-adolescents—between the directions "Do what you want" and "Do what you think is right or just."[23]

22. Empirical research on how jurors in trials think builds on a very similar definition of impartiality. These studies document the frequency with which jurors close their minds and refuse to admit new facts, sometimes long before a trial ends—they are unable to restrain their elephants, jumping to conclusions based on a few facts. Effective trial lawyers know how to keep minds open: they tell stories. Jurors then have rival frameworks for anticipating what facts are missing. A jury trial is often a contest between two competing narratives, two stories. See Neil Vidmar and Valerie Hans, *American Juries: The Verdict* (New York: Prometheus, 2007).

23. Robert Cover, book review of R. Berger's *Government by Judiciary*, *New Republic*, January 14, 1978, 27. Two essays in which judges vigorously defended the impartiality of the appellate courts are Harry T. Edwards's "Public Misperceptions Concerning the Politics of Judging," *Colorado Law Review* 56 (1985): 619–646, and Patricia Wald's "Thoughts on Decisionmaking," *West Virginia Law Review* 87 (1984): 1–12. And see the Australian film *Breaker Morant*, directed by Bruce Beresford, a powerful essay on the politicization of the judicial process.

To "look outside his own will for criteria of judgment"—if we have any single key to legal judgment, it is here.

To judge is to decide the claims of others before an audience. The judgmental decision need not be reasoned, as the umpire's calling of pitches reveals. But judgmental decisions must be impartial, which means in the end that, in order to appear impartial, they must conform to audience expectations of the process of decision. By whatever means they have in fact reached their conclusions, fast or slow, rider or elephant, judges must reassure their audience that they have considered all the factors the audience believes relevant to their decision.

In law, as in all contexts in which judging takes place, the audience can never know for sure why judges decided as they did. It cannot see inside a judge's head. That is why the legal audience is so concerned with the way appellate judges justify their decisions, because it is the only visible evidence of their impartiality.

What criteria will a legal audience use to assess the impartiality of an appellate judge? To answer that question, we must determine what the legal audience expects of the appellate process. We gave our answer to this question in chapter 1: we believe that the audience for law expects the process to harmonize case facts, legal rules, social background facts, and shared values. This is the test of judicial impartiality, and hence of reason in law. When judges justify the result they reach in a case, they must attempt to convince readers that the result does *not* depend on their emotional reactions to disputes or to their religious, ideological, or other loyalties. In appellate law judges do this by accurately characterizing the facts in the case, by not relying on false assumptions and conclusions about social conditions, by plausibly reading the rules in context, and by articulating values that the community of readers considers relevant to the dispute. The result need not please everyone, but that is not the point. Judges cannot and need not discover one right solution that everyone somehow believes best. They convince us of their impartiality as long as they convince us that they have described these four elements coherently and in good faith. We expect law judges, unlike umpires, to engage in *reasoned* judgment when they do so.

Let us here anticipate a problem that often bothers alert readers at this stage of the argument: Only an infinitesimal number of people in a community read its courts' appellate opinions. How can we argue, then, that judges must build and maintain trust and impartiality by performing for an audience that is by definition very large and almost totally ignorant of the very performances we're talking about? Doesn't history show us that the actual political reaction to controversial cases depends on whose ox was gored?

We have three responses to this troublesome problem. First and foremost, judges must try to persuade the parties, and particularly the losers, that the results are impartial. But these parties do come from, and share understandings of facts and values in common with, the larger audience. In writing for "the people," judges will more likely write persuasively for the parties when they avoid obscure legalese and write opinions that nonlawyers can understand. This is why we find Justice Scalia's opinion in *Maryland v. King* more satisfying than Justice Kennedy's. Scalia speaks not only to Mr. King but to all people rightly apprehensive that the DNA taken from arrestees will be used against them. Second, the words of the most prominent cases over time tend to get out. Anthony Lewis's now-classic book *Gideon's Trumpet* did much to explain and justify the reasoning behind extending constitutional protections to the accused.[24] Conversely, *Roe v. Wade*, the Court's landmark abortion decision, which was widely criticized for its unconvincing reasoning, might have forestalled so much of the subsequent litigation had it constructed a clearer and more coherent statement of what the right of privacy did and did not entail and why. When judges write decisions in these landmark cases, they know that the audience goes far beyond the parties and lawyers in the dispute.

Finally, social practices like judging either flourish or decay from within.[25] When judges treasure the craft of legal reasoning and celebrate those who do it excellently, the practice of judging is strengthened, and other forms of ordering, based on partisanship or favoritism, are displaced. When the craft of good legal reasoning is diminished, cynicism grows, morale suffers, and other forms of ordering gain sway. These effects diffuse from the judges to the lawyers who follow their cues, and from the lawyers to members of the public who consult them. So although much of the work of good legal reasoning is indirect, and its effects hard to demonstrate, we believe it powerful all the same.

24. Anthony Lewis, *Gideon's Trumpet* (New York: Random House, 1964).

25. This crucial point about legal reasoning is made by William Popkin in *Evolution of the Judicial Opinion: Institutional and Individual Styles* (New York: New York University Press, 2007), 173. On the importance of cultivating excellence in social practices, see Alasdair Macintyre, *After Virtue: A Study in Moral Theory* (South Bend, IN: University of Notre Dame Press, 1981), 175–189.

Applying the Theory

Let us now apply our theory of legal reasoning to some of the judicial opinions this book has applauded and some it has criticized.[26]

Consider first *Prochnow*, the case concerning blood testing and paternity. We are tempted to condemn the judge's opinion for flying in the face of science: the Court reached a result that we all know couldn't be true. If so, we would simply criticize the opinion for its failure to harmonize in its reasoning the social background facts in the case. But the difficulties with the *Prochnow* opinion go deeper. If the opinion means to tell us that juries and trial judges should be free to speculate on whether God or nature or some hidden force temporarily suspended the laws of science, the opinion should have addressed that claim head on. Such a principle would revolutionize our entire notion of how law works, for if a verdict based on speculations about God's will can stand, a judge or jury can find anything it wants, and no judge would or could ever overturn a trial verdict for being inconsistent with the weight of the evidence.

We have seen another less supernatural and more plausible explanation for the *Prochnow* result. Perhaps the legislature favored fatherhood so strongly that it authorized juries and judges to disregard science for the sake of allowing children to grow up with fathers. It might have done this in part to protect children who would otherwise be labeled "illegitimate"—a real disadvantage at the time of the case. But if that was the basis on which the Court acted, it should have said so, partly to give the legislature a chance to react in the case that the Court had misread the statute, and partly to explain why, if the statutory purpose was to protect children, the legislature had authorized blood tests in the first place. The majority opinion read the statute mechanically and legalistically, that is, without attention to the other three elements in legal reasoning. It said that the words of the statute make the tests admissible but not conclusive; therefore, the law allows judges and juries to disregard the tests.

Instead, the Court could have harmonized all four elements by saying, "We know all about science, and we know the blood tests in this case are incompatible. We admit that no evidence in the trial contradicted the blood tests, but we read the purpose of this law to favor paternity and we believe

26. You will notice that we have not "spoiled" the ending of several of the cases we have described in this book—for example, the Obamacare statutory interpretation case, *King v. Burwell*, or two of the cases with which this book began, *United States v. Windsor* and the case of the conjoined twins. We invite interested readers to look these cases up and assess for themselves the quality of the legal reasoning used to justify the judges' decisions.

this value is widely shared in the community." That reasoning would give us a coherent vision of the community that we can discuss and seek to sustain or change. Instead, the majority implies that we live in a confusing and unknowable world in which anything can happen, one in which we can't trust science or God or the conventional trial court methods of fact-finding.

The legal reasoning of *Repouille v. United States,* the second of the two citizenship cases paired at the end of chapter 2, also fails. Here a clear precedent stated law that seemed to apply directly to the case. The first citizenship case, *Francioso,* decided by the same judge just one month earlier, said that the naturalization decision should rest on judgments about the person seeking naturalization and should evaluate the person's life and the particularities of the moral decisions the applicant has made. Yet in *Repouille,* Learned Hand contradicted himself, moving away from the facts of the applicant's life and resting his decision instead on the morality of euthanasia in the abstract. The reasoning in *Repouille* leads us to believe that law doesn't matter. It increases our mistrust, perhaps not in Learned Hand, but in the justice of the decision.

We argue not that *Prochnow* and *Repouille* "came out wrong," but that the opinions in these cases were not well reasoned. A different opinion could have persuasively justified the result each case reached, but the opinions we read fail to do so. They are incoherent. They only confuse lawyers who must advise future clients with similar cases—confuse and thereby perhaps encourage litigation when law should instead encourage cooperation. Worse, they leave lay readers, including the losers in these two cases, with the suspicion that those with power over them have lied to them.

You should, we hope, be able to see in each of the cases that this book has criticized one or more of the four elements that were not harmonized. For example, the evidence introduced in trial about baseball in *Toolson* made a strong case that baseball was a business in interstate commerce that monopolized the sport. Why does the Court ignore those facts? In *Lochner,* the bakers' working conditions case, the Court majority ignored the social background evidence that baking was particularly unhealthy. *Repouille* ignores a legal rule created by that judge's own precedent. The majority in *Fox v. Snow* ignored the ethical value of carrying out the hopes of those who write wills, and so on.

We should, of course, turn this analysis on the cases these pages have applauded. For example, *Hynes,* the diving board case, harmonizes (1) the fact in Harvey's case that the wire might have killed him had he been a swimmer lawfully using the river and the fact that the railroad had not maintained the wires and poles; (2) the social background fact that property boundaries become increasingly hard to see and remember as life becomes more complex, urban, and interconnected; (3) a plausible reading of the thrust of the *Hoffman* and *Beck* precedents; (4) the deeply ethical value that law should promote cooperation—that the law of tort ought to encourage the railroad, a powerful economic entity, to prevent the dangerous wires it owns, and that only it legally controls, from injuring others.

Finally, let us apply the four elements of good legal reasoning so as to test Roy Moore's claim that he, not the federal courts, honors the rule of law. The case is so rich that discussion could go on for many pages. Here are just a few ways to question whether he has harmonized the four elements of legal reasoning.

THE LEGAL RULES

The legal issue in this case was, on its surface, very simple. Judge Moore was under a federal court order to remove the monument. While we might say that a private citizen has some kind of "right" to disobey a court order and accept punishment for contempt of court, it is legally difficult to argue that a sitting judge has a right to disobey a court order. But why does a *federal* trial judge's order, in this case Judge Thompson's order, bind the chief justice of a *state* court?

Before the Civil War, much of Moore's legal argument would have seemed to many people entirely valid. The First Amendment forbids the establishment of religion by Congress, not the states ("*Congress* shall make no law"). Indeed, though Americans in some sense fought the Civil War over slavery, the war, more broadly, resolved the question of whether the federal government has the power to enforce its reading of law over and against that of the states. Union victory in the Civil War generated the Thirteenth, Fourteenth, and Fifteenth Amendments. These legal additions to "the supreme Law of the Land" enacted powerful constraints on state legal authority and power. The Fourteenth Amendment, for example, commands: "[N]or shall any State deprive any person of life, liberty, or property without due process of law; nor deny to any person within its jurisdiction the equal protection of the laws."

Starting in the early twentieth century, the Supreme Court began using this language to protect persons against state violations of the rights guaranteed to them by the original Bill of Rights, including the First Amendment. Thus, in the 1947 case *Everson v. Board of Education*, Justice Black wrote for the Court: "Neither a state nor the Federal Government can, openly or secretly, participate in the affairs of any religious organizations

or groups and *vice versa.*[27] Since that time, the federal courts have interpreted the establishment clause so as to unambiguously prohibit religious
displays such as Moore's.[28] In 1993, the Eleventh Circuit reaffirmed a trial
judge's order to remove a display of the Ten Commandments, created with
private funds, from the superior court in Cobb County, Georgia, unless the
display was part of a historical display of secular as well as sacred sources of
American law.[29] Judge Moore invoked the Ninth and Tenth Amendments
to support his case. You can judge for yourself whether the words of these
amendments plausibly support Moore's case.[30] You should also consider
that the post–Civil War amendments, particularly the Fourteenth, presumably amended the Ninth and Tenth amendments along with the rest of the
Constitution.

THE FACTS OF THE CASE

Case law has regularly permitted publicly funded and maintained museums and cemeteries to contain religious imagery along with other non-
religious images. The Court, though sharply divided, has also upheld the
display of Christmas nativity scenes on public property as long as they
were part of a general holiday display of reindeer, plastic Santas, and other
popular symbols of the season.[31] Indeed, it would make no sense for a
public museum to exclude works on religious themes as part of an art collection or a historically continuous depiction of the evolution of artistic
themes and styles, precisely because religion and artistic expression are
closely connected. And cases, including the Cobb County case, make it
very clear that courts may display the Ten Commandments in such a historical context. This, of course, is what Roy Moore expressly refused to
do.[32] In fact, the only way to explain his express refusal would be to take

27. *Everson v. Board of Education,* 330 U.S. 1 (1947).

28. Two years after Moore's suspension, the Supreme Court decided a pair of cases
involving government buildings and the Ten Commandments. In *McCreary v. ACLU,*
545 U.S. 844 (2005), the Court declared unconstitutional a recently installed courthouse
exhibit of documents titled *The Foundations of American Law and Government,* which
included the Ten Commandments. In *Van Orden v. Perry,* 545 U.S. 677 (2005), the Court
ruled that a monument inscribed with the Ten Commandments that had stood on the
Texas State Capitol grounds since the 1960s was constitutional; the monument was one
of three dozen historical markers and displays on the grounds.

29. *Harvey v. Cobb County,* 811 F. Supp. 669 (1993).

30. See note 2, *supra,* for the text of those amendments.

31. *Lynch v. Donnelly,* 465 U.S. 668 (1984), is the "plastic Santa" case.

32. "Roy's Rock" did have, inscribed on its sides, quotations from other political
sources that supported, he claimed, his theocratic view of the state. These included the
motto "In God we trust" and the phrase "under God" from the Pledge of Allegiance. Sev-

him at his word. He wanted his court and his state follow religious law, which is precisely what federal precedents, from *Everson* forward, consistently forbid. Moore also cites the Alabama constitution's invocation of the "favor and guidance of Almighty God." Thus, the case facts on the record indicate that Moore's purpose was to promote the idea that God, and not the laws on the books, must guide the decisions of the Alabama courts.

SOCIAL BACKGROUND FACTS

One of the intriguing facts about the Ten Commandments as a biblical text is that there is no single agreed-upon translation of the Decalogue into English. Different faiths have different translations. Roy Moore used the King James Version, an Anglican work perceived, at least when King James promulgated it, as hostile to Roman Catholicism. Hence Roy Moore's message expresses not just the generic religious message of, say, the legally permissible motto "In God we trust," but a particular sect's translation of that message, one inconsistent with other translations, both Christian and Jewish.

Consider another social background fact about the place of courts in society. Is not a courthouse *about* the business of following rules—legal "commandments"—in the way that a museum, say, is not? To believers such as Roy Moore, the Ten Commandments are most certainly law. Does not a display of the Decalogue *in a courthouse* send a message to this effect: "The law we will follow in this building is not the law of the state but of some higher power"? If Alabama law and the Ten Commandments somehow did not conflict with each other, this problem might not seem so severe, but in fact, they do. Alabama law, for example, does not require businesses to "keep the Sabbath holy" by ceasing commerce on that day. Wouldn't a claim to follow religious law as opposed to state law make it impossible to do law at all, at least by our definition, because law would no longer "resolve conflicts using rules made by the state as a starting point"?

Finally, having studied legal reasoning, are you willing to say that William Blackstone, the legal thinker Moore cited in defending himself, is wrong as a matter of fact when he argues that judges only interpret but do

---

eral months after he installed the monument, he installed two plaques, about seventy-five feet removed from the monument and on the side wall behind columns. One plaque quoted the Bill of Rights. The other quoted from Martin Luther King Jr.'s "Letter from Birmingham Jail" and from the works of Frederick Douglass, both of which endorsed the importance of divine moral law.

not make law? Might we at least say that lawmaking and law interpreting are, in the actual behavior of judges, two sides of the same coin?

WIDESPREAD SOCIAL VALUES

Judging by the prayer gatherings outside the Alabama courthouse as this Ten Commandments drama played out,[33] the social values of many Alabamians, and presumably of Christian fundamentalists around the country, supported Moore. Alabama voters elected him to the Alabama Supreme Court because he campaigned to bring the Ten Commandments back into Alabama public life. Does this support for the value of a theocratic government resurrect Moore's argument?

No. Good legal reasoning requires a judge to harmonize together all four elements. No matter how sincerely he held it, Judge Moore did not harmonize fundamentalist values, widely shared though they are in Alabama, with the other three elements, and it is not clear how anyone could do so. Moreover, other values, also deeply woven into American legal and political culture, seem far more relevant. These include tolerance for religious diversity and equality before the law. Can we say that a display of one Christian sect's translation of the Decalogue displayed in a courthouse reassures members of, say, the Jewish or Muslim or Baha'i faiths—not to mention atheists—that they will receive equal treatment before the law?

Alert readers may well challenge this analysis. We seem to claim that Roy Moore was legally wrong. But how can we say Moore is wrong if legal reasoning does not generate "correct" answers in the first place? First of all, we do not argue that Moore is in some objective sense wrong. We suggest only that the legal argument he in fact made is atrociously bad. His argument boils down to the assertion, like that of Alice's queen, that "the law is whatever I feel it ought to be," and so it does not square with any accepted meaning of the rule of law. As we saw when critiquing the *Prochnow* case, the invocation of God as ultimate authority for a legal decision makes law itself impossible. Perhaps we can trust Moore's sincerity as a Christian, although it's possible that Moore was merely using this cause to advance his own political career. But his argument does not enable us to trust him as a sitting and impartial judge.

Could Moore have defended his position in a well-reasoned way and

33. The *New York Times* described the crowd as "wearing their beliefs on their backs, with T-shirts reading 'Jesus is the Standard' and 'Satan is a nerd'. . . . All day they blew ram's horns, shook Bibles, passed out cans of Coke, and knelt on the courthouse steps under a punishing sun." Jeffrey Gettleman, "Monument Is out of Sight, but Not out of Mind," *New York Times*, August 28, 2003.

stayed within the rule of law? Of course. Such an argument might have
two parts. First, Moore would have admitted that no body of existing precedents supports the placement of this monument, standing alone, in the
courthouse. But he would then invoke a value deeply ingrained in our political traditions, that political freedom confers on people the right, perhaps
even the duty, to engage in peaceful civil disobedience when they think the
law is wrong. He might even have cited Martin Luther King Jr.'s practice
of that very value in Alabama. Second, he would argue that the Supreme
Court's cases applying the establishment clause to the states are themselves
badly reasoned. The establishment clause is part of the First Amendment,
and because the First Amendment forbids only Congress, not Alabama,
from establishing religion, Moore's opponents must rely on the due process
clause of the Fourteenth Amendment, which has long been held by the
Court to require states not to establish religion. But how, he might argue,
does his monument "deprive any person of life, liberty, or property" under the Fourteenth Amendment? He would defend his action in terms of
the need to bring a test case to the Supreme Court and thereby invite the
Court to revise a constitutional mistake, the extension of the Fourteenth
Amendment to disputes about religious displays.

The Court's decisions in the religion cases, including its interpretation of the Fourteenth Amendment, are rooted in part in the belief that
religion and the state both flourish when they are put at some distance
from each other. Strong historical evidence suggests that fanaticism in all
its forms, including religious fanaticism, has too often fueled the fires of
hatred that ignite human atrocities. The founding fathers well knew the
horrors of the religious wars of Europe and of the Spanish Inquisition.
The Holocaust only continued a pattern of Jewish persecution dating back
more than a thousand years. As we write, the terrorist group ISIS has
sworn to attack its enemies because they blaspheme what ISIS believes to
be the one true religion. Israelis and Palestinians skirmish endlessly over
what is to them holy space. If the human race hopes to minimize such
atrocities and maximize peaceful cooperation, it must find ways to keep
at bay the emotional Dionysian element in all of us and to embrace more
rational Apollonian institutions like the rule of law that we described at
this chapter's beginning.

But for all its social, political, and historical persuasiveness, this argument for strong separation of church and state is not *legal* but prudential.
Moore's hypothetical defense, couched in terms of the traditions of civil
disobedience and of the possibility that the Supreme Court's establishment
jurisprudence misinterprets the Constitution, would come much closer

to honoring the rule of law than did the argument he actually made. Even this better-reasoned argument, though, does not justify Moore's deliberate refusal to obey the court order to remove the monument after he lost on appeal.

Ultimately, then, it does not and should not matter whether judges' decisions are in some sense shaped and conditioned—even predetermined—by their political philosophies, ideological visions of the good society, or what they ate for breakfast.[34] What Roy Moore personally believes or feels should not matter to us in the slightest. We should care only that judges justify their results by using the elements of legal reasoning—facts, rules, and shared values—rather than bald assertions of personal belief and feeling. When Justice Scalia, during an interview with CBS's *60 Minutes*, defended the Supreme Court's decision in *Bush v. Gore* primarily by saying, "Get over it. It's so old by now," he gives his own opinion, but he did not, on that occasion, talk legal talk.[35]

With the following illustrative case we end this chapter. Unlike the cases that end the preceding chapters, this one is hypothetical. However, in solving its problems, you will find yourself using many of the tools of good legal reasoning that apply to real-life cases. You will find as you delve deeper into it that focusing only on your own moral views about right and wrong will distract you from analyzing wisely how to resolve this legal reasoning challenge.

But must we conclude that, except for the role played by widely shared social values in good legal reasoning, law has no morality of its own? In one of the twentieth century's great works of legal theory, Harvard's Lon Fuller insisted that law does have its own morality. In his book *The Morality of Law*, he wrote:

> If I were asked . . . to discern one central indisputable principle of what may be called substantive natural law . . . I would find it in the injunction: Open up, maintain and preserve the integrity of the channels of communication.[36]

34. Critics of legal realism have for years mocked it by claiming that it characterizes law as the product of "what the judge ate for breakfast." A recent study, however, turned this taunt around, finding that Israeli judges were more likely to grant parole to prisoners immediately after their food breaks. Shai Danziger, Jonathan Levav, and Liora Avnaim-Pesso, "Extraneous Factors in Judicial Decisions," *Proceedings of the National Academy of Sciences* 108 (2011): 6889–6892.

35. "Justice Scalia on the Record," *60 Minutes*, CBS News, April 27, 2008.

36. Lon Fuller, *The Morality of Law* (New Haven, CT: Yale University Press, 1964), 186.

"Open up, maintain and preserve the integrity of the channels of communication"—in a nutshell, this is precisely what reason, done intelligently and impartially in law, strives to achieve.

ILLUSTRATIVE CASE

Professor Sanford Levinson of the University of Texas School of Law presents his students with the following problem at the beginning of their study of constitutional law.[37] We urge you to use Levinson's "adulterer's hypothetical" to further explore the many facets of legal reasoning that we've discussed in this book. How would you answer the questions he asks directly and also implies? Hints: Be wary of jumping to quick conclusions here, as you might have done when you first encountered Jonathan Haidt's man who uses a chicken carcass for sexual pleasure. This chapter has proposed that persuasive legal justifications entail a trust that the judge has decided "in good faith." How do the concepts of faith, and good faith, play out in your response to Levinson's questions? Thinking about these concepts may lead you away from your initial gut reactions to these cases and toward more soundly reasoned conclusions.

"On Interpretation: The Adultery Clause of the Ten Commandments"

In 1970 a number of concerned citizens, worried about what they regarded as the corruption of American life, met to consider what could be done. During the course of the discussion, one of the speakers electrified the audience with the following comments:

> The cure for our ills is a return to old-time religion, and the best single guide remains the Ten Commandments. Whenever I am perplexed as to what I ought to do, I turn to the Commandments for the answer, and I am never disappointed. Sometimes I don't immediately like what I discover, but then I think more about the problem and realize how limited my perspective is compared to that of the framer of those great words. Indeed, all that is necessary is for everyone to obey the Ten Commandments, and our problems will all be solved.*

---

37. Sanford Levinson, "On Interpretation: The Adultery Clause of the Ten Commandments," *Southern California Law Review* 58 (1985): 719–725.

Within several hours the following plan was devised: As part of the effort to encourage a return to the "old-time religion" of the Ten Commandments, a number of young people would be asked to take an oath on their eighteenth birthday to "obey, protect, support, and defend the Ten Commandments" in all of their actions. If the person complied with the oath for seventeen years, he or she would receive an award of $10,000 on his or her thirty-fifth birthday.

The Foundation for the Ten Commandments was funded by the members of the 1970 convention, plus the proceeds of a national campaign for contributions. The speaker quoted above contributed $20 million, and an additional $30 million was collected—$15 million from the convention and $15 million from the national campaign. The interest generated by the $50 million is approximately $6 million per year. Each year since 1970, 500 persons have taken the oath. *You* are appointed sole trustee of the Foundation, and your most important duty is to determine whether the oath-takers have complied with their vows and are thus entitled to the $10,000.

It is now 1987, and the first set of claimants comes before you:

(1) Claimant *A* is a married male. Although freely admitting that he has had sexual intercourse with a number of women other than his wife during their marriage, he brings to your attention the fact that "adultery," at the time of Biblical Israel, referred only to the voluntary intercourse of a married woman with a man other than her husband. He specifically notes the following passage from the article *Adultery*, I JEWISH ENCYCLOPEDIA 314:

> The extramarital intercourse of a married man is not *per se* a crime in biblical or later Jewish law. This distinction stems from the economic aspect of Israelite marriage: The wife as the husband's possession . . . , and adultery constituted a violation of the husband's exclusive right to her; the wife, as the husband's possession, had no such right to him.

A has taken great care to make sure that all his sexual partners were unmarried, and thus he claims to have been faithful to the original understanding of the Ten Commandments. However we might define "adultery" today, he argues, is irrelevant. His oath was to comply with the Ten Commandments; he claims to have done so. (It is stipulated that *A*, like all the other claimants, has complied with all the other commandments; the only question involves compliance with the commandment against adultery.)

Upon further questioning, you discover that no line-by-line explication of the Ten Commandments was proffered in 1970 at the time that *A* took the oath. But, says *A*, whenever a question arose in his mind as to what the

Ten Commandments required of him, he made conscientious attempts to research the particular issue. He initially shared your (presumed) surprise at the results of his research, but further study indicated that all authorities agreed with the scholars who wrote the *Jewish Encyclopedia* regarding the original understanding of the Commandment.

(2) Claimant *B* is *A*'s wife, who admits that she has had extramarital relationships with other men. She notes, though, that these affairs were entered into with the consent of her husband. In response to the fact that she undoubtedly violated the ancient understanding of "adultery," she states that that understanding is fatally outdated:

(a) It is unfair to distinguish between the sexual rights of males and females. That the Israelites were outrageously sexist is no warrant for your maintaining the discrimination.

(b) Moreover, the reason for the differentiation, as already noted, was the perception of the wife as property. That notion is a repugnant one that has been properly repudiated by all rational thinkers, including all major branches of the Judeo-Christian religious tradition historically linked to the Ten Commandments.

(c) She further argues that, insofar as the modern prohibition of adultery is defensible, it rests on the ideal of discouraging deceit and the betrayal of promises of sexual fidelity. But these admittedly negative factors are not present in her case because she had scrupulously informed her husband and received his consent, as required by their marriage contract outlining the terms of their "open marriage."

(It turns out, incidentally, that *A* had failed to inform his wife of at least one of his sexual encounters. Though he freely admits that this constitutes a breach of the contract he had made with *B*, he nevertheless returns to his basic argument about original understanding, which makes consent irrelevant.)

(3) *C*, a male (is this relevant?), is the participant in a bigamous marriage. *C* has had no sexual encounters beyond his two wives. (He also points out that bigamy was clearly tolerated in both pre- and post-Sinai Israel and indeed was accepted within the Yemenite community of Jews well into the twentieth century. It is also accepted in a variety of world cultures.)

(4) *D*, a practicing Christian, admits that he has often lusted after women other than his wife. (Indeed, he confesses as well that it was only after much contemplation that he decided not to sexually consummate a relationship with a coworker whom he thinks he "may love" and with whom he has held hands.) You are familiar with Christ's words, *Matthew* 5:28: "Whosoever looketh on a woman to lust after, he hath committed adultery with her al-

ready in his heart." (Would it matter to you if *D* were the wife, who had lusted after other men?)

(5) Finally, claimant *E* has never even lusted after another woman since his marriage on the same day he took his oath. He does admit, however, to occasional lustful fantasies about his wife, *G*, a Catholic, and is shocked when informed of Pope John Paul II's statement that "adultery in your heart is committed not only when you look with concupiscence at a woman who is not your wife, but also if you look in the same manner at your wife." The Pope's rationale apparently is that all lust, even that directed toward a spouse, dehumanizes and reduces the other person "to an erotic object."

Which, if any, of the claimants should get the $10,000? (Remember, *all* can receive the money if you determine that they have fulfilled their oaths.) What is your duty as trustee in determining your answer to this question? . . .

---

*Cf. Statement of President Ronald Reagan, Press Conference, February 21, 1985, reprinted in the *New York Times*, February 22, 1985: "I've found that the Bible contains an answer to just about everything and every problem that confronts us, and I wonder sometimes why we won't recognize that one Book could solve a lot of problems for us." [Note in original.]

APPENDIX A

Introduction to Legal Procedure and Terminology

Here is a relatively short but complete judicial opinion. This "case of the stolen airplane" makes a brief appearance in chapter 1 and plays a more important role in chapter 4. This appendix uses the case to define and illustrate most of the more common terms of judicial organization and procedure.

The Case

McBoyle v. United States
U.S. Supreme Court
283 U.S. 25 (1931)

Mr. Justice Holmes delivered the opinion of the Court.

The petitioner was convicted of transporting from Ottawa, Illinois, to Guymon, Oklahoma, an airplane that he knew to have been stolen, and was sentenced to serve three years' imprisonment and to pay a fine of $2,000. The judgment was affirmed by the Circuit Court of Appeals for the Tenth Circuit. A writ of *certiorari* was granted by this Court on the question whether the National Motor Vehicle Theft Act applies to aircraft. Act of October 29, 1919, c. 89, 41 Stat. 324, U.S. Code, title 18, § 408. That Act provides: "Sec. 2. That when used in this Act: (a) The term 'motor vehicle' shall include an automobile, automobile truck, automobile wagon, motor cycle, or any other self-propelled vehicle not designed for running on rails ... Sec. 3. That whoever shall transport or cause to be transported in interstate or foreign commerce a motor vehicle, knowing the same to have been stolen, shall be punished by a fine of not more than $5,000, or by imprisonment of not more than five years, or both."

Section 2 defines the motor vehicles of which the transportation in interstate commerce is punished in Section 3. The question is the meaning of the
word "vehicle" in the phrase "any other self-propelled vehicle not designed
for running on rails." No doubt etymologically it is possible to use the word to
signify a conveyance working on land, water, or air, and sometimes legislation
extends the use in that direction, e.g., land and air, water being separately
provided for, in the Tariff Act, September 21, 1922, c. 356, § 401 (b), 42 Stat.
858, 948. But in everyday speech "vehicle" calls up the picture of a thing moving on land. Thus in Rev. St. § 4, intended, the Government suggests, rather
to enlarge than to restrict the definition, vehicle includes every contrivance
capable of being used "as a means of transportation on land." And this is
repeated, expressly excluding aircraft, in the Tariff Act, June 17, 1930, c. 497,
§ 401 (b), 46 Stat. 590, 708. So here, the phrase under discussion calls up
the popular picture. For after including automobile truck, automobile wagon,
and motor cycle, the words "any other self-propelled vehicle not designed
for running on rails" still indicate that a vehicle in the popular sense, that is
a vehicle running on land, is the theme. It is a vehicle that runs, not something, not commonly called a vehicle, that flies. Airplanes were well known
in 1919 when this statute was passed, but it is admitted that they were not
mentioned in the reports or in the debates in Congress. It is impossible to
read words that so carefully enumerate the different forms of motor vehicles
and have no reference of any kind to aircraft, as including airplanes under a
term that usage more and more precisely confines to a different class. The
counsel for the petitioner have shown that the phraseology of the statute as
to motor vehicles follows that of earlier statutes of Connecticut, Delaware,
Ohio, Michigan, and Missouri, not to mention the late Regulations of Traffic
for the District of Columbia, title 6, c. 9, § 242, none of which can be supposed
to leave the earth.

Although it is not likely that a criminal will carefully consider the text of the
law before he murders or steals, it is reasonable that a fair warning should
be given to the world in language that the common world will understand, of
what the law intends to do if a certain line is passed. To make the warning fair,
so far as possible the line should be clear. When a rule of conduct is laid down
in words that evoke in the common mind only the picture of vehicles moving
on land, the statute should not be extended to aircraft simply because it may
seem to us that a similar policy applies, or upon the speculation that if the
legislature had thought of it, very likely broader words would have been used.
United States v. Bhagat Singh Thind, 261 U.S. 204, 209, 43 S. Ct. 338.

Judgment reversed.

Legal Terms

McBoyle v. United States was the result of an appeal brought by Mr. Mc-Boyle after his criminal conviction in a lower court. When a person feels disappointed by the result a court reaches in a lawsuit in which he or she is a *party*, he or she may (unless the highest court has already heard the case) *appeal* to a higher court. In an appeal the *appellant* (the party taking up the appeal) argues that the lower-court judge interpreted and applied the law of the case erroneously. Appeals do not reopen the facts of the case or consider new testimony or evidence. Appeals are limited to questions about whether the lower court reasoned well about the legal issues in the case. In *McBoyle*, the appellant (Mr. McBoyle) argued successfully that the lower courts wrongly interpreted the National Motor Vehicle Theft Act to include airplanes. Thus, in this case the *appellee*, the U.S. government, lost in the "court of last resort."

In this and all cases, the initial *plaintiff* (in this case the United States) must prove it has a *cause of action*.[1] That is, the plaintiff must find some official legal text somewhere that says that what the initial *defendant* (Mc-Boyle) did was legally wrong. A cause of action clearly exists in this case, since McBoyle obviously helped transport something stolen. But not all harms are legal causes of action. If a professor wears an offensively ugly necktie to class and a student sues him for the pain he suffers at having to stare at rank ugliness for fifty minutes, the student will lose because no legal text makes such an offense *actionable*. If an official legal text made recovery actionable for the tort of having to look at ugly neckties, then the plaintiff might recover money *damages* from the professor or might win a court *injunction* in which a court would order him never to wear such a tie again.

A cause of action existed in *McBoyle* because the plaintiff, in this case

---

1. Readers beginning the trek toward mastery of basic legal terminology should know that the threshold legal question is never "Can I sue?" Suing or appealing is simply a matter of filling out the right forms and delivering them to the right office in the right courthouse. One can, for example, file a complaint in court against a neighbor for keeping ferrets or not mowing the lawn. To bar someone physically from filing a lawsuit at a clerk's office would amount to the tort of false imprisonment, and maybe the crime of kidnapping. So the real question is this: "On which grounds will a court throw out a lawsuit or an appeal?" Thus, for example, the Republican majority in the House of Representatives raised some eyebrows twice in 2014, first when it sued President Obama for illegally implementing the Patient Protection and Affordable Care Act, and second when it threatened to sue Obama over his executive order exempting about five million immigrants from immediate deportation. Such lawsuits may be "political theater," as some Democrats called them, but the legal system allows them regardless of their ultimate merits. See Jeremy W. Peters, "House Votes to Sue Obama for Overstepping Powers," *New York Times,* July 30, 2014.

the United States government, could claim that the defendant, Mr. Mc-Boyle, violated a legal rule enacted by Congress: the National Motor Vehicle Theft Act. No statutes, common law cases, or bureaucratic regulations protect against the hurt we call embarrassment, so embarrassment does not constitute a legal cause of action. There are, however, common law rules of negligence. If a professor wears a combination of pants, jacket, and necktie that causes a student to have a severe seizure, and if that student then explains to the professor the problem and asks him not to wear that combination again, and if the professor then forgets and causes a second seizure requiring medical attention, the rules of negligence, described in chapter 3, might give the student a cause of action.

The legal system normally classifies legal actions as either *civil* or *criminal*. As long as we don't think about it too much, we think we know the difference: In a criminal case like McBoyle's a governmental official, a *prosecutor*, has the responsibility for filing complaints for violations of laws that authorize the judge to impose a punishment—usually a fine, imprisonment, or both—on behalf of the polity. *McBoyle* is a criminal case, prosecuted by a U.S. attorney working for the U.S. Department of Justice, because the National Motor Vehicle Theft Act prescribes a punishment for those convicted under it.

In a civil case, in contrast, the plaintiff seeks a judicial decision that will satisfy him or her personally. Civil remedies usually consist either of a court award of money damages to compensate for harm already done or of a court order commanding the defendant to stop doing (or threatening to do) something injurious.

In practice these distinctions between civil and criminal actions blur at their edges. Units of government, acting as civil plaintiffs, may file lawsuits to enforce policies that benefit the entire country. The U.S. government does so when it files civil antitrust actions. A private citizen may file and win a lawsuit in which the judge imposes "punitive damages" on defendants, which, like criminal penalties, are aimed at punishing bad conduct. Punitive damages can far exceed the dollar expense that the injured plaintiff actually paid out; when they are excessive, appellate courts often reduce them

Occasionally in public debate there is talk about "decriminalizing" some form of behavior. To decriminalize something does not automatically legalize it. Jurisdictions that decriminalize marijuana use merely reduce the penalty to the equivalent of a parking ticket. This prevents prosecutors from seeking criminal penalties for possession of small amounts of marijuana. But civil lawsuits over marijuana use remain possible, so that, for example, a person injured in an accident could still bring a personal injury claim against a "stoned" driver. When a legal issue is civil rather than criminal, the rules of evidence change significantly. For example, in the civil trial brought against football star O. J. Simpson for wrongful death by the heirs of Ronald Goldman and Nicole Brown, Mr. Simpson could not, as he did in his criminal trial, refuse to testify.

The kind of rule on which a lawsuit is based very much shapes the *evidence* that the parties introduce in trial. We can, for example, imagine that when the owner of the airplane McBoyle transported got it back, he found that it needed $1,000 of repairs. The owner of the plane might file a civil suit against McBoyle seeking to recover damages from him to pay for the repairs and for the damage the owner suffered by not having use of his vehicle. At this imaginary trial, McBoyle's lawyers might try to introduce evidence that the airplane needed the repairs before McBoyle transported it. In the actual criminal case, however, the facts at issue and the evidence presented are completely different. The evidentiary questions at this trial might wrestle with whether McBoyle knew the plane was stolen. In the actual criminal trial, McBoyle denied any involvement, but the trial court found that he had hired a Mr. Lacey to steal the airplane directly from the manufacturer and fly it to Oklahoma. The jury found that McBoyle paid Lacey more than $300 to do so.[2]

The four elements of legal reasoning introduced in chapter 1 include two kinds of facts about which lawyers and judges may reason. One set of facts we may call the facts of the dispute at issue between the parties. These are events and observations that the people in the lawsuit must either prove or disprove through their evidence to prevail at trial. Thus, the United States government had to prove that McBoyle knew the plane he transported was indeed stolen. These facts are settled one way or the other by the *trier of fact*: either a jury or a judge sitting without a jury. (Jury trials are longer and more costly than "bench trials." The large majority of lawsuits filed are in fact settled by negotiation without any trial, and most trial court proceedings take place without juries.)

A second kind of fact (which we have called "social background facts") also influences legal reasoning. In *McBoyle*, the Court, including the trial judge, must interpret the word *vehicle* in this statute so as to decide whether it covers airplanes. Here are questions about some social background facts relevant to this dispute: How common were airplanes when Congress passed the statute in 1919? Did congressional debates discuss and reject

2. See *McBoyle v. United States*, 43 F.2d 273 (1930).

the idea of including the word *airplanes* in the statute? What social problem prompted busy Congress members to pass the National Motor Vehicle Theft Act? Every state, including both Illinois and Oklahoma, had laws prohibiting theft. Why was a national law about stealing and transporting motor vehicles necessary in 1919?

Notice that, unlike the facts at issue between the parties, these social background issues have no direct connection with the parties at all. They do not have to be proved at trial. Sometimes lawyers at trial will address them, but just as often these factual issues will arise only on appeal, where the lawyers will argue them orally or in their written briefs. Furthermore, judges are free to research such issues on their own or through their clerks with no help from the parties before them, and then base their legal conclusions on them. Often the social background facts appear only implicitly in the opinion. They are the judge's hunches about the way the world works that we can only infer from what the judge does say. Every appellate opinion reviewed in these pages rests in part on such explicit or implicit hunch assertions.

In addition to the requirement of a cause of action, litigants must meet a number of other procedural requirements before courts will decide their case "on the merits." For our purposes we may divide these procedures into requirements for *jurisdiction* and *justiciability*.

"Jurisdiction" prescribes the legal authority of a court to decide the case at all. More specifically, a court must have (a) *jurisdiction over the subject matter* and (b) *jurisdiction over the person* before it can decide. Neither of these requirements is terribly mysterious. Subject matter jurisdiction refers to the fact that all courts are set up by statutes that authorize the court to decide some kinds of legal issues but not others. A local traffic court has jurisdiction to hear only a small subset of cases: traffic violations. State probate courts hear issues about the wills and estates of the deceased. The federal court system has a variety of specialized courts, such as the U.S. Tax Court and the U.S. Court of International Trade. In both federal and state judicial systems, some courts have statutory authority to hear a broad scope of cases. These are called *courts of general jurisdiction*.[3] In the federal

---

3. The U.S. Supreme Court has subject matter jurisdiction, according to Article III of the Constitution, to sit as a trial court when one state sues another state. In 2014 Nebraska and Oklahoma filed one such suit against Colorado, claiming that Colorado's legalization of marijuana has been so poorly managed that it interfered with their ability to block the distribution and consumption of marijuana in their own states. Jack Healy, "Nebraska and Oklahoma Sue Colorado over Marijuana Law," *New York Times*, December 18, 2014.

system, U.S. district courts, and at the state level, *superior courts* (as they are called in most states), serve as the trial courts in which most serious lawsuits begin. The U.S. District Court for the Western District of Oklahoma is such a court, and it therefore had subject matter jurisdiction to try the criminal case against McBoyle.

Jurisdiction over the person refers to the fact that before a court can impose judgments on people, the court's agents must first catch them and serve them with the papers notifying them that they are named as defendants in a lawsuit. The agents who *serve process* on defendants—sheriffs in the states and U.S. marshals in the federal system—have authority to find people and serve notice on them only within the geographic territory the court governs.[4] A sheriff working for a court in Georgia cannot serve someone who lives in Alabama unless the sheriff can catch the person in (or attach land that person owns to) Georgia. This jurisdiction over the person is sometimes called *territorial jurisdiction.*

McBoyle's case raises an interesting problem of jurisdiction over the person. Federal law requires that defendants be tried in the district where the crime was committed. McBoyle claimed that because he never flew the airplane, or left Illinois for that matter, he could not have committed a crime in the Western District of Oklahoma, Mr. Lacey's destination. The U.S. Court of Appeals for the Tenth Circuit rejected that argument, saying that the crime ran with the airplane, and that the crime was committed in Oklahoma, even if McBoyle wasn't in Oklahoma at the time.

Most courts in the United States possess authority to decide what the U.S. Constitution (in Article III) calls "cases" and "controversies." Over the years this phrase has been interpreted to mean a genuinely adversarial contest in which plaintiff and defendant desire truly different outcomes. Judges cannot initiate lawsuits. They can initiate "contempt of court" pro-

4. In November 2006, a collection of civil rights groups filed a lawsuit in Karlsruhe, Germany, against former secretary of defense Donald Rumsfeld and eleven other members of the Bush administration, charging them with war crimes committed against detainees in military prisons in Guantánamo and elsewhere. German law gives its courts "universal jurisdiction," empowering them to prosecute anyone for crimes committed anywhere in the world; hence, the German courts had subject matter jurisdiction. They did not, however, have jurisdiction over the persons of these named defendants unless they were physically served in Germany itself. The lawsuit was thus primarily a political statement. Mark Landler, "12 Detained Sue Rumsfeld in Germany, Citing Abuse," *New York Times,* November 15, 2006. The Bush administration claimed that American courts lacked jurisdiction over the person to hear challenges to treatment of detainees in Guantánamo, since Guantánamo is legally part of Cuba, but the Supreme Court in 2004 rejected the argument on the basis that the United States had "complete jurisdiction and control" over the Guantánamo base. *Rasul v. Bush,* 542 U.S. 466 (2004).

ceedings against parties who flout any direct judicial command, and this power to fine or jail people gives judges the practical power to keep order and enforce rulings, but judges for the most part respond to and rule on the initiatives that litigants take.

Rules of *justiciability* ensure that judges decide true adversary contests. These rules serve three functions: (1) to avoid wasting judicial time and resources on minor matters, (2) to improve the quality of information that reaches them by hearing different points of view, and (3) to justify refusing to decide politically delicate cases that might damage the courts' political popularity.

Thus, courts generally refuse to hear *moot* cases, cases in which the harm the plaintiff tried to prevent never happened or, for whatever reason, cannot happen in the future. Plaintiffs must have *standing*, which means that the plaintiff must be among those directly injured (or directly threatened) by the defendant's actions. The standing requirement, for example, has shaped the course of litigation over same-sex marriage. In Oregon a federal judge denied standing to the National Organization for Marriage to participate as defendants in a lawsuit challenging Oregon's ban on same-sex marriage. The judge ruled that the group could not show that any of its members would be personally injured by the legalization of same-sex marriage.[5] Similarly, the Supreme Court ruled in *Hollingsworth v. Perry* that the sponsors of a California ballot measure prohibiting same-sex marriage, Proposition 8, lacked standing to appeal a federal court ruling striking down the law.[6] *Exhaustion* requires that plaintiffs exploit their primary opportunities for settling a case, especially through bureaucratic channels, before going to court. *Ripeness* is a requirement that prevents plaintiffs from pursuing issues that do not currently threaten them and that might never occur in the future. A late 2014 headline raised a ripeness issue. A group of atheists was considering suing Maryland and six other states whose constitutions require those seeking public office to swear their allegiance to God. But the U.S. Supreme Court unanimously struck down such requirements in 1961, and states had not enforced the provisions since, so a lawsuit challenging them might well have been dismissed on the grounds that it was not ripe until someone actually blocked an atheist from public office.[7]

5. Kirk Johnson, "Judge Blocks Motion to Defend Oregon Marriage Ban," *New York Times*, May 15, 2014.

6. *Hollingsworth v. Perry*, 570 U.S. ___ (2013).

7. Laurie Goodstein, "In Seven States, Atheists Fight for Removal of Belief Rule," *New York Times*, December 6, 2014.

No justiciability problems arose in *McBoyle*. McBoyle's case reached the U.S. Supreme Court in this fashion: The trial court found McBoyle guilty. (In criminal cases the trial court expresses its *disposition* in terms of guilt and innocence. Civil dispositions find the defendant liable or not liable.) McBoyle appealed, and the Court of Appeals, ruling on both the jurisdictional claim and the statutory interpretation claim, *affirmed* (upheld) the trial court's decisions on these two matters of law. McBoyle appealed again, and the U.S. Supreme Court *reversed*, although as chapter 4 shows, Justice Holmes's reasoning turns out on closer inspection to be shallow and incomplete.

A Theory of Law in Politics

THE CASE OF TERRI SCHIAVO

It is usually more important that a rule of law be settled, than that it be settled right.

—JUSTICE LOUIS D. BRANDEIS

In our country are evangelists and zealots of many different political, economic and religious persuasions whose fanatical conviction is that all thought is divinely classified into two kinds—that which is their own and that which is false and dangerous.

—JUSTICE ROBERT H. JACKSON

The spirit of liberty is the spirit which is not too sure that it is right.

—JUDGE LEARNED HAND

[Caesar:] And so, to the end of history, murder shall breed murder, always in the name of right and honor and peace, until the gods are tired of blood and create a race that can understand.

—GEORGE BERNARD SHAW, *Caesar and Cleopatra*

This appendix explains in detail the theoretical framework that underlies this book's description of legal reasoning and the role it plays in good government. What follows belongs in an appendix for several reasons, the simplest being that there is nothing here that a reader needs to know in order to understand the basics of the common law legal process or to learn how to tell good legal reasoning from bad.

The second reason is that we use this appendix to provide a more abstract and theoretical perspective on the political nature of legal reasoning than the one outlined in the text. As political scientists we are convinced that the institutions and cultural practices that together constitute the rule of law describe an important, recent, and still-evolving component of wise and effective human governance. We have described well-reasoned dispute resolution as a device for peacefully resolving conflicts that threaten to spiral out of control and so divide communities. In this appendix we compare legal reasoning to another way in which humans try to resolve their differences: electoral and legislative democracy. We do this through the prism of the remarkable case of Terri Schiavo, who suffered cardiac arrest and massive brain damage in 1990 but whose life was prolonged artificially until 2005 as lawyers and politicians battled over whether she would wish to be kept alive in that condition. We compare how the controversy over her life was addressed, first by elected politicians, interest groups, and bloggers, and then by judges and lawyers.

We do not claim that the Schiavo story illustrates universal differences among electoral, legislative, and legal politics. It is an extreme case, marked by angry and at times outrageous political rhetoric and an array of lawsuits that seemed to drag on forever. We certainly don't believe that electoral and legislative politics are always shallow and ignorant, or that litigation and court decisions are always thoughtful and wise. Elected politicians, deliberating together, can make innovative and even courageous social policy: Congress's enactment of the Civil Rights Act of 1964 and the Voting Rights Act of 1965 changed the politics of racial justice in ways the courts could not have achieved. Conversely, as we have shown time and again in this book, judges often make poorly reasoned decisions. It is tempting, in an age of cynicism about electoral and legislative politics, to denigrate legislators and celebrate judges as heroes. We do not mean to do that here. We do believe, however, that there are important differences between electoral, legislative and legal politics—and that Terri Schiavo's case, because it is an extreme one, demonstrates these contrasting tendencies with special drama and clarity.

We first sketch a generic description of politics and governance, with special attention to how political systems have evolved to reduce the too-common frequency with which humans behave brutally toward other humans. We suggest that historically evolving forms of governance have moved for centuries toward the goal of reducing the frequency of human atrocities. As we have argued throughout this book, the process of resolving disputes in court can be likened to a sport or game. The common law legal system, because it is an adversarial system, is such a game; like good games, it resolves conflicts short of human brutality. Electoral politics in a democracy is also a competitive game. We therefore describe what we take to be the elements of good games.[1] We then analyze the ways in which American legal politics succeeded, while American electoral and legislative politics failed, to stage "a good game" in the Schiavo case.

Politics and Death

Politics at its core trades in force and coercion. It is what both human tribes and many "groupish" species of animals do to keep their members sufficiently under control and cooperative enough for the group to gather food, make shelters, and defend against external enemies.[2] Political authorities use physical force via muscle and weapons to threaten individuals into behaving, and they punish them when they don't.[3] *Politics* can be used, then, to describe how people try to make other people do things that these others presumably don't want to do and would not selfishly do if left to their own devices. In addition to physical force, people use their money and information in order to coerce and blackmail others to behave. But since group leaders cannot be everywhere at once threatening and beating up all selfish shirkers and rebels, and because coercion provokes resentment and the urge to fight back, leaders find it more effective to coerce by invoking their "authority."

Here rules, though not "the rule of law," enter the picture. Authority— "Shut up and do what I say *because* I have the right to say so!"—in practice communicates by rules. "I govern by divine right!" said the kings and queens of old, and say some fanatical religious leaders today. "I embody God on Earth, and as God's agent, I command you to obey God's rules. God authorizes me to kill or imprison you, or take away your fortune, if you don't." Leaders employ abstract rules and invoke them in as higher powers that command obedience. Moses coming down to deliver the Ten Commandments from the mountain describes the instantiation of political authority by divine rule perfectly. This story is a "twofer," since it describes

---

1. Lief Carter has explored in more detail the analogy between law and politics on the one hand, and organized sports and games on the other, that we describe here. See his "Law and Politics as Play," *Chicago-Kent Law Review* 83 (2008): 1333–1386.

2. Leaders of higher primate groups such as chimpanzees illustrate this dynamic. See Frans de Waal, *Chimpanzee Politics: Power and Sex among Apes* (Baltimore: Johns Hopkins University Press, 1982).

3. Politics also involves much symbolism, the celebrations around icons, flags, deities, sports mascots and icons, and the like, often involving singing, dancing, chanting, and marching together, which makes people want to belong to a group and sacrifice their personal interests for the sake of group survival. See William H. McNeill, *Keeping Together in Time* (Cambridge, MA: Harvard University Press, 1995).

both ten substantive and authoritative tribal rules and at the same time gives Moses the personal authority to get (not always successfully) his tribe to work together. But of course since in actual human practice, "guys in the sky" do not physically hand down laws from above, humans have to invent the rules and find ways to make them stick. Both electoral democracy and state-run authoritarian capitalism as seen in nations such as China are just the latest systems in which people make rules and attempt to induce peaceful acquiescence from their subjects.

But now, to extend another metaphor from the book of Genesis, sin, in the form of human brutality and violence, raises its ugly head. Warfare against "the other," raping women and slaughtering children and enslaving those not killed in battle, committing genocide and holocaust, engaging in wanton mass killings—these are the worst things that the human species does. And rule by authority alone does not routinely stop the killing; it can even encourage it.

With the exception of our closest genetic cousins, chimpanzees, very few animal species behave this way. Something in human culture and organization—particularly since the transition from hunter-gatherer communities to complex agrarian and eventually urban cultures starting about eight thousand years ago—seems somehow to correlate with human brutality. Even the most cursory scan of human history provides an appalling number and variety of human atrocities. Think of the Crusades, or the holocausts of Hitler and Pol Pot, or the slaughter of Native Americans by invading Christian Europeans, or more recently, the seemingly endless battles between Israelis and Palestinians, the Lord's Resistance Army in Uganda, Boko Haram in Nigeria, the broadcast beheadings of "infidels" by the Islamic State, and the slaughter of schoolchildren by the Taliban in Pakistan.[4] There is a pattern to these atrocities that seems tightly linked to a sense of righteousness, to the committed belief, as Justice Jackson's epigraph to this appendix suggests, that "I and my tribe have the one and only right way to do things. Those who don't conform must be eliminated." In fact, ruling through authority, whether of God or of some impersonal ideology, as in the case of atheistic Soviet and Maoist communism, inevitably creates a sense of righteousness that enables people to kill in the name of defending that authority.

Existential human fear underlies this all-too-familiar pattern of brutality and violence. Symbols and customs and practices unite groups into the

---

4. See, for example, the *New York Times* headline from December 17, 2014: "Taliban Besiege Pakistan School, Leaving 145 Dead."

tribes that in turn cooperate to gather food and make shelter and "provide for the common defense," as the preamble to the Constitution puts it. Both individual survival and tribal existence—hence the adjective *existential*—depend on maintaining the commitment to these symbols. Atrocities are the behaviors that humans do when they believe that the things that keep them alive—their symbols, their turf, their children and hence their own genes—are threatened, and humiliation can trigger a self-protecting but brutal response. It so recently did when two Muslim believers, angered by crude depictions of Muhammad in a French satirical magazine, *Charlie Hebdo*, attacked the magazine's office and slaughtered some of its staff. It is how, as Shaw's epigraph to this appendix suggests, "murder shall breed murder, always in the name of right and honor and peace."[5]

On an increasingly populated and interdependent planet, where humans have the technological means to exterminate themselves, humans had better find a way to short-circuit this cycle of righteousness, humiliation, and brutality. We need to search the horizon for patterns in which people in passionate and high-stakes conflict with one another nevertheless resolve conflict peacefully. So the question becomes whether we can find some forms of human governance that resolve conflicts peacefully yet consistently with a world of infinite realities and infinite potential disagreements about them. We are looking for ways of governing that satisfy the basic human existential need for security without calling on the traditional authoritarian forms of social control—rule by singular, universal, and hence often "holy" law—that can trigger that cycle of righteousness, humiliation, and brutality.

Politics and Life

We find what we are looking for, a form of conflict resolution and governance that avoids the brutality cycle, in the modern practice of organized competitive games. Electoral democracies and the adversarial legal process have both evolved into games, as have the basic features of economic production and exchange through regulated market competition. Perhaps these modern institutions have evolved this way through some subconscious human evolutionary recognition that the survival of the species depends on reducing mass violence. Perhaps they have evolved more con-

---

5. Of course, clever and rational political leaders go to war for selfish gain, perhaps of treasure and territory, but the successful leader will convince the "boots on the ground" who risk their lives in battle that they are fighting for a righteous cause: "Onward, Christian soldiers / marching as to war," as the old hymn puts it.

sciously, the way we saw in chapter 3, when players of soccer created rules that made their game less violent. For whatever reasons, the incidence of human violence is indeed trending down worldwide.[6] By games we mean organized competitions played under certain conditions that we call "rules and regulations." We will describe these conditions shortly, but we emphasize here that this book's frequent comparison of judging to sports refereeing was not just a metaphor or a heuristic tool.[7] Both sports refereeing and legal judging are examples of how human beings have learned to organize conflict resolution through the rule of law. The rule of law, in other words, is the phrase we use to describe the conditions that allow good—and by *good* we mean "peaceful"—competition to happen. For traditionalists, the rule of law consists in the "right" substantive rules and policies by which people ought to live. But we have seen that no such objectively right abstract rules can have meaning apart from the distinctive facts of concrete cases. Indeed, all conflicts in electoral politics at some level are tussles to determine which substantive rules, rules about such things as morality and justice, ought rightly to govern.

Elements of Good Games

We argue here that the rule of law encompasses those things humans have learned to do to govern themselves peacefully. It avoids invoking holy absolutes whose violation guarantees humiliation and can trigger violent responses. Since vastly more people play games, or at least understand the basic rules and practices of games, than closely follow conventional politics and law, the best way to understand the elements of the rule of law is through the lens of sports and games. But these elements can equally apply to the competitions of law and of politics. So, what are these elements and how do they short-circuit the brutality cycle?

UNCERTAINTY, CONTINGENCY, AND
THE ACCEPTANCE OF LOSING

Religious and ideological fundamentalists cannot accept loss because their framework for organizing their worlds contains no viewpoint from which, unlike Learned Hand in our epigraph, they can see how they might not be

---

6. See Stephen Pinker, *The Better Angels of Our Nature: Why Violence Has Declined* (New York: Vintage Books; London: Penguin Books, 2011).

7. Keith J. Bybee employs a quite different comparison, to the practice of courtesy and politeness, in his fascinating book *All Judges Are Political Except When They Are Not: Acceptable Hypocrisies and the Rule of Law* (Palo Alto, CA: Stanford University Press, 2010).

right. But the fun and excitement of games happen *because* their outcomes are uncertain and depend on the contingencies that arise in the striving by both sides to win. Those who enter into games know that they may lose, and that the risk of losing is the price they pay for the satisfaction of playing with a chance to win. In many games, such as marathon races, most of the contestants lose, but they accept losing and do not strike out angrily to "get even."

EQUALITY

Losers in games more easily accept their loss when they know that they could have won today and, when they didn't, still have the resources to win another day.[8] A one-sided game—a rout or a foregone conclusion—is no game at all. To give each side a realistic chance to win, good games seek to ensure that the players and teams have relatively equal access to resources and talent. The word *equal* derives from the Latin *aequalis*, meaning "level," and the level playing field is the heart of the concept of political equality: No individuals shall, by virtue of things that they cannot control, such as their race, ethnicity, gender, and sexual orientation, be denied the resources to give them a chance to "win" in the game of life. It is the value that underlies the ruling in *Gideon v. Wainwright* that indigent felons should be assigned a state-funded attorney so that they have a chance to prove their innocence in the game of a legal trial.

PRECISION OF RULES

Rules and their means of enforcement must be clear enough to the players that the game does not decay into a fight over what the rules mean.

UNQUESTIONED AUTHORITY OF REFEREES

For the same reason that the rules should be as precise as possible, players must accept the finality of the decisions of referees or the game will collapse.

REFEREE IMPARTIALITY AND THE PERCEPTION OF FAIRNESS

Game fans who believe that "the fix is in" or that the referees for whatever reason have predetermined (i.e., "prejudged" or "prejudiced") the game's outcome in favor of the opponent will quickly leave, if they do not riot outright.

8. Tom R. Tyler, *Why People Obey the Law* (Princeton, NJ: Princeton University Press, 2006).

TRANSPARENCY

Games take place in clearly framed spaces and in bounded times. To trust its outcome, participants and fans alike must believe that they have seen what actually happened. Former NBA basketball player and U.S. senator Bill Bradley once praised basketball, saying, "People come and see and know that what they see is real."[9] When spectators believe that games are secretly "rigged" behind the scenes, the game loses credibility its and, eventually, its fans.

DECEPTION

Competitive games are amoral in all respects. Anything goes unless a rule prohibits it and a player gets caught violating it. Games capitalize on the human tendency to better oneself by deceiving others, but in doing so, they remove the temptation for players to act "righteously," to defend an action by claiming that it was morally correct and thus restarting the righteousness cycle.[10]

MINIMIZATION OF CHANCE

Games of pure chance, like games of dice, may be pleasant pastimes, but they hardly count as good games. Except where a coin flip helps promote game equality, as in designating which football team can choose how to start a game, good games minimize the impact of chance elements and maximize the role of skill and strategy.

Collectively, these elements of good games influence the psychology of players and fans in profound ways. The deep desire to win in a good game encourages players to pay attention to their mistakes and improve their skills rather than blame an "enemy" for the loss. Good play requires curiosity. This curiosity—about the conditions on the field, the skills of the opponent, the fairness of the referees—is driven not by abstract theories and by religious or ideological ideals but by the realities of competition. This curiosity also inevitably humanizes the opponent. Daniel Kahneman's

9. Bill Bradley, *Life on the Run* (New York: Vintage Books, 1976), 111.

10. Compare Tony Blair, who as British prime minister defended his support of the 2003 invasion of Iraq: "Hand on heart, I did what I thought was right. . . . I did what I thought was right for our country." Quoted in Anne Applebaum, "The Riddle That Is Blair," *Washington Post*, May 15, 2007. Lief Carter's "Law and Politics as Play" explores how the theoretical infinity of possibilities that the real world presents, for example in the vast number of recognizably distinguishable pills, makes naive the belief to a certainty that something is ultimately righteous.

research found that each opponent in a conventional conflict believes that the other side acts out of malice and hostile motives.[11] But winning in a good game requires opposing players to live in the same world, for one player to "want what I want" and to "need to know me as much as I need to know him." The curiosity that players must develop about "the other" *in order to win* displaces ethnocentrism, xenophobia, moral superiority, and other righteous impulses that normally lead to hatred, the desire for revenge, and brutal violence. It is why, after a good game, winners and losers routinely shake hands and often hug one another.

On a more practical level, playing a game requires players to avoid relying on prayer and magical thinking instead of skill for victory, agreeing with the opponent about what the rules of the game are, sticking to the subject (as in "Keep your eyes on the ball!"), and thinking and acting as rationally as is humanly possible. Indeed, these features of good games may be the best invention we humans have yet devised to induce us think rationally and overcome the tendency to jump to fast, opinionated, and moralistic conclusions as chapter 6 described. Many billions of people— anyone who has played or followed an internationally popular game like soccer—already know what we have described intuitively, and this intuitive knowledge undergirds the rule of law. We will now draw on these elements of good games and their psychological consequences to evaluate how the following case fared in the world of electoral and legislative politics and then in law.

The Case of Terri Schiavo

The Undisputed Facts[12]
Theresa Marie "Terri" Schindler was born into a Catholic family in 1963. She married Michael Schiavo in November 1984. On February 25, 1990, she suffered cardiac arrest and collapsed. Before her heart restarted, the loss of oxygen to her brain caused brain damage that left her completely unresponsive for ten weeks. In June of that year, a court appointed Michael Schiavo as Terri's legal guardian. Terri's parents, the Schindlers, did not object to his appointment or to transferring her to a hospital for rehabil-

---

11. Daniel Kahneman and Jonathan Renshon, "Why Hawks Win," *Foreign Policy*, January–February 2007, 34–38.

12. This factual summary is based on the extensive coverage of the Schiavo case provided by *The Jurist*, published by the University of Pittsburgh law school. The word **Schiavo** yields more than five million hits on Google.

itation. Later that year, Michael and the Schindlers, with whom he was living, moved Terri to the Schindler home. Caring for Terri, however, was overwhelming, and three weeks later they moved her to a facility.

In November 1990 Michael took Terri to California for an experimental procedure, the implant of a "thalamic stimulator" in her brain. She showed no significant change, and the following January, Terri was moved to the Mediplex rehabilitation center in Brandon, Florida, to receive twenty-four-hour care. In July 1991 she was transferred to the Sable Palms skilled-care facility, where for the next three years she received continuing neuro-logical testing, as well as regular and aggressive speech and occupational therapy. These treatments produced no significant improvement in her condition.

In May 1992 Michael moved out of the Schindlers' home. In August Terri was awarded $250,000 in an out-of-court medical malpractice settlement with one of her physicians. In another malpractice lawsuit, in November 1992, a jury awarded approximately $750,000 to a trust specifically for Terri's ongoing medical care. The jury also awarded about $300,000, after medical expenses, to Michael, for loss of consortium.

In February 1993 Michael and the Schindlers had a falling out. The Schindlers then tried to have Michael legally removed as Terri's legal guardian. The Court appointed a guardian for the purposes of this action. He reported in 1994 that Michael had acted appropriately and attentively toward Terri, and the Schindlers' motion was denied.

In 1998 Michael Schiavo, Terri's husband and legal guardian, petitioned the courts to allow removal of the gastric feeding tube that helped keep her alive. Her parents opposed this petition. The Court appointed a second guardian ad litem. Drawing on the guardian ad litem's report, a court found that Terri had made "credible and reliable" statements to her husband and several other relatives that she wouldn't want to be kept "on a machine" with no hope of recovery.

On January 24, 2000, a full trial commenced on the issues, presided over by Judge George Greer of Florida's Sixth Judicial Circuit Court for Pinellas and Pasco Counties. On February 11, 2000, Judge Greer ruled that Terri would have chosen to have the feeding tube removed, and he therefore ordered its removal. His ruling is reprinted later in this appendix.

In 2002 the Schindlers challenged the medical diagnosis that Terri remained in a "persistent vegetative state." Four neurologists and one ra-diologist examined Terri. The Schindlers recorded six hours of videos of Schiavo. CAT scans and electroencephalograms (EEGs) were submitted in evidence, but the courts again found that Schiavo was in a persistent vegetative state with no realistic hope for recovery and would have wanted, in those circumstances, to discontinue life support.

At this point, the chronology becomes so clogged with legal and political moves, by the Schindlers, the Florida legislature, Florida's then governor Jeb Bush, and eventually the U.S. Congress and President George W. Bush, that a complete description would take many pages. Before Terri died on March 31, 2005, the Schiavo case included innumerable motions, petitions, and hearings in the Florida courts; fourteen appeals; five suits in federal district court; Florida legislation (so-called Terri's Law) that was struck down by the Florida Supreme Court; a subpoena by a U.S. congressional committee in an attempt to qualify Schiavo for "witness protection"; federal legislation (known as the Palm Sunday Compromise); and four refusals by the U.S. Supreme Court to hear the case. Schiavo's feeding tube was removed a third and final time on March 18, 2005, and she died thirteen days later. An autopsy performed after her death found that Schiavo had a severely atrophied brain, less than half the normal weight. The autopsy thus confirmed the medical evidence before Judge Greer that her brain was irreversibly damaged.

The Electoral and Legislative Frame

Before you read the following materials, we emphasize that we do not canvass all the political maneuvering and public commentary on Schiavo's case.[13] As you will see if you do a Google search for the names of actors and issues involved in the case, there is a seemingly endless supply of speeches, blog posts, and other materials about it. We have chosen from this vast supply a few representative examples of the kind of rhetoric that the political system tends to generate about controversial public issues. Again, our point is merely to show how strikingly this way of talking and analyzing differs from the procedures and ways of talking within the legal system.

13. Thus we forgo comment on the claim that one of the doctors who insisted that Schiavo could be rehabilitated was once nominated for a Nobel Prize. Opponents of Michael Schiavo indeed made the claim, but the doctor in question was "nominated" only in the sense that his congressman had written a letter to the Nobel committee nominating him. In fact, the Nobel committee accepts nominations only from those whom it invites to nominate, and the congressman in question had never been invited to nominate. If you had written a letter nominating Osama bin Laden for the Nobel Peace Prize, bin Laden could not thereby honestly have claimed to be a Nobel Prize nominee.

July 21, 2003

The Honorable Jeb Bush
Governor of Florida
Re: Terri Schiavo case

Dear Governor Bush,
I am the director of a Catholic organization, Women for Faith &
Family, representing about 50,000 women who affirm Catholic
teachings. I have just become aware of the case of Terri Schindler
Schiavo http://www.terrisfight.org, and of her parents' effort to
obtain guardianship from her husband, Michael Schiavo, in order
to care for her. Mr. Schiavo is attempting to have her feeding tube
removed to cause her death.

I have reviewed the information and watched the video clips on
the web site, and am convinced that she is not in the so-called "persistent vegetative state." She is obviously responsive, and, though
impaired, capable of meaningful interaction with those who love
her and care for her. She is not "terminally ill" or dying, so removal
of the feeding tube that sustains her cannot be considered morally
permissible. She is entitled to our support and protection.

On behalf of Women for Faith & Family, who has filed "friend
of the court" briefs in other similar cases in Missouri, where we
are based (Christine Busalacchi and Nancy Cruzan), I ask you to
review Terri Schiavo's case and to intercede on her behalf.

Sincerely yours in Christ,
Helen Hull Hitchcock, Director
Women for Faith & Family

MEMBERS OF CONGRESS
Here is an AP news release dated March 24, 2005. It was picked up by many
major news departments, including those of ABC, CBS, and Fox television:

**Schiavo Case Taking on Political Tone Democrats and Republi-
cans Sharpen Their Political Rhetoric over Terri Schiavo Case**
By DAVID ESPO
AP Special Correspondent
The Associated Press
WASHINGTON Mar. 24, 2005—Terri Schiavo's personal tragedy is
taking on a more political tone in Congress, where House Majority

Leader Tom DeLay likens the struggle over her fate to attacks on himself, and a Democratic critic accuses Republicans of opportunism.

"I find it shameful that Mr. DeLay and Republicans have used Ms. Schiavo as their political pawn to kowtow to their conservative base," Rep. Robert Wexler, D-Fla., said Wednesday as House GOP leaders filed court papers in an increasingly desperate attempt to keep the brain-damaged Florida woman alive.

"It's unfortunate that he thinks his situation is like Terri Schiavo's," added Rep. Rahm Emanuel of Illinois, chairman of the House Democratic campaign committee. "That's a distorted view."

For his part, DeLay cast the debate over Schiavo in religious and political terms at the same time.

"One thing that God has brought to us is Terri Schiavo to elevate the visibility of what is going on in America, that Americans would be so barbaric as to pull a feeding tube out of a person that is lucid and starve them to death," he said in remarks Friday to a conservative group and made public Wednesday.

"This is exactly the issue that is going on in America, of attacks against the conservative movement, against me and against many others," added DeLay, lately at the center of a controversy concerning his overseas travel.

DeLay's remarks were made public by Americans United for Separation of Church and State, a liberal group. Dan Allen, a spokesman for the majority leader, accused Democrats and their allies of "launching politically motivated attacks questioning the motives of those trying to save Terri Schiavo."

The developments occurred as polls continued to show the public takes a dim view of congressional moves to step into Schiavo's case. CBS reported that 82 percent of those surveyed want President Bush and Congress to stay out of the situation and that 74 percent said Congress was motivated by political considerations, not concern for Schiavo. At the same time, congressional job approval has dropped to its lowest level since 1997, according to the poll.

On April 1, 2005, CBS News reported the following story:

Party Icons Clash over Schiavo
WASHINGTON, April 1, 2005
The passing of Terri Schiavo has done nothing to quell the political firestorm ignited by her life and death.

Two party icons, GOP House Majority Leader Tom DeLay and Democratic Sen. Ted Kennedy, launched harsh verbal broadsides within hours of Schiavo's death at a Florida hospice on Thursday.

"This loss happened because our legal system did not protect the people who need protection most, and that will change," DeLay said in a prepared statement.

"The time will come for the men responsible for this to answer for their behavior," said the Texan. DeLay was a driving force behind legislation Congress passed two weeks ago that gave federal courts jurisdiction in an attempt to save Schiavo's life.

Asked later at a news conference about possible impeachment proceedings against judges in the case, DeLay said, "There's plenty of time to look into that."

Kennedy took exception.

"I'm not sure what Mr. DeLay meant when he said, 'The time will come for the men responsible for this to answer for their behavior,'" the Massachusetts Democrat said in a written statement. "But at a time when emotions are running high, Mr. DeLay needs to make clear that he is not advocating violence against anyone."

Dan Allen, DeLay's spokesman, said the majority leader was merely referring to potential future action in Congress. He said one possibility was for the committee that issued a subpoena designed to assure nourishment for the brain-damaged woman to investigate why its order had been ignored by the courts.

An article published in the *Washington Post* concerns Senate Majority Leader Bill Frist:

Frist Defends Remarks on Schiavo Case
By Charles Babington, *Washington Post* Staff Writer, Friday, June 17, 2005
Bill Frist, the Senate majority leader and a heart surgeon, acknowledged yesterday that Terri Schiavo had suffered devastating brain damage and said his assertion three months ago that she was "not somebody in persistent vegetative state" did not amount to a medical diagnosis.

Frist (R-Tenn.), appearing on three network TV shows, agreed with this week's autopsy conclusion that the Florida woman had suffered severe, irreversible brain damage. "I never, never, on the floor of the Senate, made a diagnosis, nor would I ever do that," he told NBC's "Today" show. Some Democrats and doctors criticized Frist's March 17 Senate speech in which he said he was commenting on Schiavo's highly publicized case "more as a physician than as a United States senator."

In that speech, Frist said he had reviewed videotapes of Schiavo and noted that her brother "said that she responds to her parents and to him. That is not somebody in persistent vegetative state . . . There just seems to be insufficient information to conclude that Terri Schiavo is [in a] persistent vegetative state."

"I question it based on a review of the video footage, which I spent an hour or so looking at last night in my office here in the Capitol," Frist said in the speech. He said his comments were also partly based on a conversation with one of several neurologists who had evaluated Schiavo.

Frist's speech, made two weeks before Schiavo died, came as Congress held a rare Easter weekend session to order federal courts to review Florida court decisions saying that her feeding tube could be removed. Among those criticizing Frist's actions were 31 of his Harvard Medical School classmates, who sent him a letter saying he had used his medical degree improperly.

FROM A LIBERAL INTEREST GROUP'S WEBSITE

The American Progress Action Fund
April 1, 2005

Judges in the Schiavo case have already been threatened by extremists. Florida Pinellas County Circuit Court Judge George Greer has been "under 24-hour protection by two U.S. marshals due to increased threats against his life by those unhappy with his handling of the Schiavo case," according to CNN. Last Thursday, police arrested an Illinois man they said robbed a Florida gun store as part of an attempt to "rescue Terri Schiavo." The next day, FBI officials took into custody a North Carolina man for placing a $250,000 bounty "on the head of Michael Schiavo" and another $50,000 to murder Judge Greer. And police yesterday said they had "logged several bomb threats" to the hospice where Schiavo died and "the circuit and federal courts that refused to order her feeding tube restored."

**Sliming the Innocent: How the Latest in the Schiavo Case
Has Made Jeb Bush into the Al Sharpton of the Right . . .** [14]
Newsweek
Jonathan Alter
June 23, 2005

Last Friday, Bush faxed a letter to Pinellas-Pasco County State Attorney Bernie McCabe that clearly implied that Michael Schiavo, Terri's husband, had left his wife to die in 1990. Bush wrote that Schiavo testified in a 1992 malpractice suit that he had found his wife passed out at 5 A.M. of Feb. 25, 1990. But in a later interview on "Larry King," Schiavo said he found her unconscious at 4:30 A.M. He placed the 911 call at 5:40 A.M.

"Between 40 and 70 minutes elapsed before the call was made and I am aware of no explanation for the delay," the governor wrote, as if Schiavo could be expected to remember the exact time he found her and placed the call. While claiming preposterously that he was not suggesting wrongdoing, he urged a "fresh look" at the 15-year-old case and McCabe has opened an investigation.

That's all we need now—another look at this sad personal story. Bush clearly wants the public to believe that in 1990 Michael Schiavo, who spent the next several years doing everything he could to help his stricken wife (including studying to become a nurse), actually wanted her to die right then and there. After 15 years, his timeline was inconsistent! He didn't call 911 immediately!

Bush has a daughter who, sadly, is a convicted drug abuser. When she passed out (as all drug abusers do), did he immediately call 911? Does he remember the exact time of the call? Was there a gap between the time he first saw that she might be ailing and when he took her for treatment?

The governor is buying into the most extreme rantings of fanatics—the same people who, before the autopsy proved otherwise, charged that Schiavo had been abusing his wife.

Bush is doing this for transparent political reasons. In March, he disappointed the extremists by not using state police to storm the hospice

---

14. This headline compares Governor Bush to the Reverend Al Sharpton, who in 1987 championed the claims of Tawana Brawley, a teenager who falsely claimed she was raped to avoid parental punishment because she had run away from home.

where Terri Schiavo resided and forcibly reattach her feeding tube. Actually, Bush was planning to do just that—in total violation of the law—when the head of the county police (determined to uphold the law) warned the governor's office of an armed confrontation if he did so. When Bush backed down, he was pilloried by the extreme right. . . .

FROM A "PRO-CHOICE" BLOG

The following is from *The Daily Blatt*, in response to a *Los Angeles Times* front-page story of March 27, 2005, that carried the headline "DeLay's Own Tragic Crossroads: Family of the Lawmaker in the Schiavo Case Decided in '88 to Let His Comatose Father Die":

> Oh my loaves and little fishes. DeLay is a hypocrite? Who would have thought it?
>
> I don't downgrade the tragedy of his father's death. But to have had that lesson in humility as a part of his life and to then act as he has during the Schiavo mess only points out even more strongly what an evil little fuck of a scum-sucking toad-raping needle-dicked phlegm wad Tom DeLay really is.
>
> Either that or he's been huffing bug bomb in his basement in a vain attempt to recapture his glory days as an exterminator.

Summary

Let us summarize the assertions so vigorously debated among politicians, bloggers, and interest groups, remembering that while "pro-life" positions seemed to dominate the news, the "pro-choice" position also found a voice. We're not interested in whether the public rhetoric, filtered and translated, of course, by the media's own reporting practices and frameworks, was "biased" or "liberal" or "conservative." Rather, we ask how different this rhetoric is from the methods, concepts, and language that the legal system applied to this case, and whether the legal system's methods, concepts, and language are better ways to resolve problems such as those posed by the Schiavo case. Consider the claims and counterclaims made in just this small sample of public debate over the Schiavo case:

- Terri is or is not in a persistent vegetative state; she is or is not capable of responding to loved ones and is or is not at times "lucid."
- Terri is or is not more terminally ill than an infant who has not yet learned to feed itself. We would not hesitate to prosecute for murder a parent or guardian who deliberately starved a helpless child.

- Michael and those who defend him are or are not attacking basic American values and the Republican Party and its politicians, who represent those real American values.
- Republican conservatives are or are not shamefully playing politics with the tragedy of Terri's situation, especially Senator Frist and Governor Jeb Bush, who are or are not angling for the Republican Party's nomination for the presidency in 2008.
- Judges have or have not murdered Terri and should or should not be impeached. Tom DeLay did or did not invite violence against those judges.
- The courts have or have not ignored Congress's explicit instructions. As a Roman Catholic, Terri would or would not follow the dictates of the church, which does not sanction euthanasia of this sort.
- Senator Frist has or has not used his medical degree improperly.
- Tom DeLay is or is not either a hypocritical sexual abuser of amphibians small enough to pleasure him, all the while suffering from bad breath and a persistent cold, or an inhaler of insecticides in an infantile attempt to return to his past.

The rhetoric on both sides of this debate was frequently bombastic and vicious—and often irrelevant to the fundamental issues in Terri's case. The case cannot be resolved by debating whether Tom DeLay is a bad man, Bill Frist a good doctor, or Jeb Bush a candidate for the presidency. Whatever your political sympathies, we hope you can see that this kind of discourse falls far short of generating concrete decisions about law and public policy that the community can trust and accept.

Terri's case, for all its notoriety, raises very common issues about end-of-life decision making. Doctors and hospitals and loved ones face these issues every day. It is critical that judges settle the law on such issues so that these primary decision makers—people who know far better than judges what is best in the specific cases they face—can get on with the hard work of making the best decisions they can in the circumstances.

What's Going on Here?

We return now to the distinction between thinking fast and thinking slow developed in chapter 6. There we described some of the ways in which the practice and institutions of judging are designed to curb the human tendency to think fast and jump to moralistic conclusions that one's gut instincts say are right, and to stick to those conclusions even as evidence against them mounts. Alas, the institutions and practices surrounding legislative and electoral politics seemed in the case of the Schiavo controversy to reinforce these very tendencies.

JUMPING TO CONCLUSIONS

All of us jump to conclusions hundreds of times a day. We could barely get through the day if we had to stop to verify every assumption we make. We do not check our car tires for leaks every time we drive; we do not test that our food is safe before we eat, and so on. So Helen Hull Hitchcock and Bill Frist, among others, believed they saw evidence of physical movement on some online videos of Terri Schiavo in her hospital bed. They jumped to the conclusion that Terri's twitches established that she was not in a vegetative state.[15] Although Frist's statements were criticized by his political opponents, there was no fact-finding process to evaluate them, and they became part of the rationale for passage of legislation both in the Florida state legislature and in Congress aimed at keeping her on life support.

MAGICAL THINKING

Magical thinking describes beliefs and systems of belief that have no factual foundation or, worse, are contradicted by the vast weight of evidence from scientific findings and patterns of experiences in ordinary life. No evidence suggested that someone with brain damage at the level of Schiavo could recover normal functioning except by a supernatural miracle, but in the public debate many people insisted otherwise, and pleas to just "look at the facts" fell on deaf ears.[16] Again, although magical thinking was contested in both legislative and popular debate, it was used to justify legislation enacted at both the state and federal levels.

15. To give a particularly tragic illustration of jumping to conclusions in another context, Rashid Rehman, a civil rights attorney in Pakistan, was murdered on May 7, 2014, for taking on the case of someone accused of blaspheming Islam under Pakistan's blasphemy laws. Rehman believed that every accused deserves a lawyer. His killers believed that he therefore must be hostile to Islam and murdered him, but in fact Rehman was a faithful Muslim. The defendant, a university lecturer, had not been found guilty at the time of Rehman's murder. Accusations of this sort are often brought for personal reasons to settle scores. Nicholas Kristof, "Religious Freedom in Peril," *New York Times*, July 10, 2014.

16. As we write, the American political conversation is replete with examples of magical thinking, for example, the denial by Senator James Inhofe, chair of the Senate Environment and Public Works Committee, that man-made burning of fossil fuels is causing climate change. Rebecca Leber, "Congratulations, Voters. You Just Made This Climate Denier the Most Powerful Senator on the Environment," *New Republic*, November 5, 2014.

CHANGING THE SUBJECT

One of the elementary techniques that successful politicians learn early in the political game is how to avoid answering hard questions. They do so by answering an easier but unstated question, which leaves them less politically exposed.

Thus, the question of whether Terri Schiavo's feeding tube should be removed was often sidelined while other questions, about Michael Schiavo's conduct, Senator Frist's medical opinions, Representative DeLay's personality, and Governor Bush's political ambitions took center stage.[17.]

WHEEL SPINNING

For a politician in the game of modern electoral politics, an issue or a question presents not so much an opportunity to learn an answer as an opportunity to win votes. And winning votes entails keeping votes and campaign contributions coming from the candidate's base in the electorate. As David Espo's piece for the Associated Press reported, 82 percent of those polled thought politicians should not interfere in the Schiavo case, but that fact did not curtail the barrage of political posturing and statements from those who needed to avoid offending their base, in this case the powerful set of interest groups that represent Christian conservatives. When issues help politicians advance their hopes of winning elections, politicians do their best not to resolve issues but to keep them alive and their base committed.[18]

The partisan world of electoral politics instills in candidates for office,

17. Alabama's Roy Moore provided a perfect example of changing the subject when he claimed that the order to remove the Ten Commandments from the courthouse denied public acknowledgement of God; in fact, public acknowledgements of a nonsectarian God, as in the motto "In God We Trust," are perfectly legal. He also ignored the fact that "Roy's Rock" presented a sectarian translation of the Decalogue that many Christians and Jews do not accept. For another vivid example of this phenomenon, see Ezra Klein's description of how the Republican Party changed its position regarding national health-care policy after President Obama built Obamacare on a structure first proposed by Republicans and adopted in Massachusetts with the strong support of the Republican then governor Mitt Romney. Ezra Klein, "Unpopular Mandate: Why Do Politicians Reverse Their Position?" *New Yorker*, June 25, 2012.

18. This is an ongoing, bipartisan, and familiar pattern. Democrats for years have won elections by arousing fears that Republicans will destroy the Social Security system, yet they have not exerted much energy in proposing reforms to resolve the fiscal issues in the system. Those seeking to discredit Hillary Clinton before her expected run for the presidency in 2016 kept alive for years a controversy about her responsibility while secretary of state for a fatal attack on the U.S. consulate in Benghazi, Libya, even after bipartisan investigations concluded that Clinton was not at fault. Adam Housley, "GOP Lawmakers, Benghazi Survivors Fume over House Report," *Fox News*, December 4, 2014.

and in all of us who take positions on anything, commitments to beliefs and behaviors that no amount of reasoning will undo. What scholars call "confirmation bias"—the human tendency to look for evidence that upholds one's views and to discount or ignore disconfirming evidence—is strongly reinforced by the institutions and practices of electoral and legislative politics.[19] Politicians usually line up with the interest groups and the party that helped them into office; most will not question the "party line," and so a kind of political tribalism results.[20] Electoral and legislative politics resolves disputes not primarily through the weighing of evidence, but instead by simply counting votes, first in elections, and then within legislatures. Political campaigners win in this game not by making the more compelling arguments but instead by mobilizing more political resources—campaign contributions, interest-group support, and party organization—than do their opponents. In the case of the Schiavo controversy, the incentives of the electoral and legislative game generated outrageous and divisive rhetoric rather than a settlement of differences.

The Law Frames the Schiavo Case

Perhaps the most disturbing quality of the political debate over Terri Schiavo is its utter open-endedness. Each question generated new questions, each argument new arguments. Without a set of rules to determine which questions were relevant and which irrelevant, the debate spiraled ever

19. Scholars have recently shown just how powerful confirmation bias can be in their studies of "backfire." They find that when people with strong political views are confronted with facts that go against their beliefs, they embrace those beliefs even more strongly—attempts at correction backfire. Brendan Nyhan and Jason Reifler, "When Corrections Fail: The Persistence of Political Misperceptions," *Political Behavior* 32 (2010): 303–330.

20. For many years this tendency was mitigated in the United States by the ideological and regional diversity of the two major parties, but recently the parties have become homogenous, and the Republican Party has moved considerably to the right, a phenomenon scholars label "asymmetric polarization." For a vivid report on the how these shifts have damaged the legislative process, see Thomas Mann and Norman Ornstein, *It's Even Worse Than It Looks: How the American Constitutional System Collided with the New Politics of Extremism* (New York: Basic Books, 2012). Nor is the American legal system immune to the influences of ideological polarization, which the media make most visible at the U.S. Supreme Court level. See Adam Liptak, "In Supreme Court Clerks' Careers, Signs of Polarization," *New York Times*, December 22, 2009; and Jeff Shesol, "Should Justices Keep Their Opinions to Themselves?" *New York Times*, June 21, 2011. Justice Thomas's behavior does not, according to Shesol, seem consistent with Thomas's promise at his confirmation hearings to "strip down like a runner," which we noted in chapter 2.

outward, far beyond the complex factual and moral questions in the case. Even when the debate did focus on issues relevant to the case, it lacked an agreed-upon framework for sifting through the evidence and coming to some conclusion. Terri is alert and responds to her loved ones when they visit, claim her parents. Is this true? How are we to tell? Michael claims Terri said she didn't want to live hooked up to a machine. Did she? How do we know? Certainly, a public shouting match won't tell us. Nor can shouting sort out the moral issues. For example, given that Terri was raised Catholic, what weight should the Catholic Church's position on end-of-life issues receive? How can we tell which moral claims should govern in this or any particular case?

As we hope you will see when you read Judge Greer's opinion in this case, the legal process provided a much more effective forum for resolving the issue than that provided by electoral or legislative politics. This is not because the law is "objective" or because the judges "got the right answer" in the case, but simply because, as in organized sports, there was an agreed-upon framework for resolving disputes. The legal process routinely does what other forms of political debate only occasionally accomplish. Law separates factual questions from moral issues. Law frames what does and does not count as relevant. Law places the relevant questions in a narrative sequence without which a coherent "end of the story" would not be possible. In other words, when people vigorously disagree about how a specific case should be decided, we can count on law to make decisions without falling into the socially disruptive "two against one" power politics, which creates division, distrust, and sometimes even violence.

Just as we don't need to canvass all aspects of the political debate and commentary on the Schiavo case to illustrate the open-ended (and sometimes wacky) political debate, so we do not (and could not in fewer than five hundred small-print pages) reproduce all the legal documents and decisions that this case generated. Instead, we report, with minimal editing, how Judge Greer handled the case, trusting that this example, like our examples from the electoral and legislative realms, illustrates our theory.

The legal background for Schiavo's case in court included *Cruzan v. Director, Missouri Department of Health*, a case with superficial similarities to that of Schiavo.[21] An automobile accident had rendered Ms. Cruzan in a persistent vegetative state, and her legal guardians, her parents, petitioned to have her life support systems withdrawn. As in the case of Ms. Schiavo, there was evidence that Ms. Cruzan had made informal oral statements

---

21. *Cruzan v. Director, Missouri Department of Health*, 497 U.S. 261 (1990).

that she would not want to be kept alive in a vegetative state. However, the Missouri State Supreme Court concluded that these informal statements did not amount to "clear and convincing" evidence of a patient's wish to have life support withdrawn under state law. The U.S. Supreme Court, upholding the Missouri Court, held that the state had the power under the Constitution to establish a "clear and convincing" standard to protect the rights of incompetent patients. *Cruzan* thus left to states and state courts broad authority to decide end-of-life issues.

Here is Judge Greer's initial decision in the case, entered on February 11, 2000. Note in particular the way in which Judge Greer interprets Florida law:

In Re: The Guardianship of Theresa Marie Schiavo, Incapacitated.
File No. 90–2908GD-003
Circuit Court for Pinellas County, Florida
Probate Division
February 11, 2000
ORDER

THIS CAUSE came on to be heard upon the Petition for Authorization to Discontinue Artificial Life Support, and Suggestion for Appointment of Guardian Ad Litem. The case was tried before the court sitting without jury during the week of January 24, 2000. Before the court were Michael Schiavo, Guardian of the Person of Theresa Marie Schiavo (sometimes referred to as "Petitioner"); George J. Felos, Esquire, and Constance Felos, Esquire, attorneys for Petitioner; Robert Schindler and Mary Schindler, the parents of Theresa Marie Schiavo, (sometimes referred to as "Respond[ents]"); and Pamela A.M. Campbell, Esquire, attorney for Respond[ents]. The court took testimony from eighteen witnesses, including the parties, the brother and sister of Theresa Marie Schiavo, (sometimes referred to as "Terri Schiavo"); the brother and sister-in-law of Petitioner, and the treating physician for Terri Schiavo. The court also received into evidence certain exhibits, including CAT scans of Terri Schiavo and, for comparison purposes, Dr. James Barnhill. The court has carefully reviewed its notes, the transcribed testimony of those non-parties who testified to conversations with Terri Schiavo regarding end of life declarations, the report of the Guardian Ad Litem, the video tape (Respondents' Exhibit No. 1) and the other exhibits introduced as evidence. The court has also reviewed the case law submitted by and argued on behalf of the parties. Based upon the foregoing, the court makes the following findings of fact and conclusions of law.

Terri Schiavo was reared in a normal, Roman Catholic nuclear family consisting of her parents and her brother and sister. She spent the majority of her life in New Jersey and moved to Pinellas County, Florida[,] in 1986 with her husband, Michael Schiavo, whom she married on November 10, 1984. They had dated for a total of two years, being engaged for a year prior to their marriage.

Shortly after the move to Pinellas County by Mr. and Mrs. Schiavo, her parents and sister followed. The families on and off lived together, on and off shared expenses and generally functioned well together. Mr. Schiavo had a series of jobs including manager of a McDonald's restaurant. Terri Schiavo, after a brief period immediately following the move, resumed her employment with Prudential Insurance Company.

On February 25, 1990, in the early morning hours, Terri Schiavo suffered cardiac arrest, apparently due to an imbalance of potassium in her system. Michael Schiavo awakened when he heard a thump, found her lying in the hallway and called 911. He then called her brother who was living in the same apartment complex and her mother. The paramedics came, performed CPR and took her to a hospital. She has never regained consciousness and to this day remains in a comatose state at a nursing home in Largo. Terri Schiavo is currently being nourished and hydrated via a feeding tube and by this Petition her husband seeks authority to withdraw such life support.

In 1992, Michael Schiavo filed an action against the physicians who had been treating Terri Schiavo prior to her cardiac arrest. In late 1992, the case was resolved with a settlement and jury verdict, which resulted in Mr. Schiavo receiving $300,000 as regards his loss of consortium claim and the Guardianship of Theresa Marie Schiavo receiving net funds of $700,000 as regards her damages. Those monies were actually received in February of 1993.

During the period of time following the incident of February 25, 1990 the parties worked together in an attempt to provide the best care possible for Terri Schiavo. On February 14, 1993, this amicable relationship between the parties was severed. While the testimony differs on what may or may not have been promised to whom and by whom, it is clear to this court that such severance was predicated upon money and the fact that Mr. Schiavo was unwilling to equally divide his loss of consortium award with Mr. and Mrs. Schindler.

The parties have literally not spoken since that date. Regrettably, money overshadows this entire case and creates potential of conflict of interest for both sides. The Guardian Ad Litem noted that Mr. Schiavo's conflict of interest was that if Terri Schiavo died while he is still her husband, he would inherit her estate. The record before this court discloses that should Mr. and Mrs. Schindler prevail, their stated hope is that Mr. Schiavo would divorce their daughter, get on with his life, they would be appointed guardians of Terri Schiavo and become her heirs at law. They have even encouraged him to "get on with his life." Therefore, neither side is exempt from finger pointing as to possible conflicts of interest in this case.

By all accounts, Mr. Schiavo has been very motivated in pursuing the best medical care for his wife, even taking her to California for a month or so for experimental treatment. It is undisputed that he was very aggressive with nursing home personnel to make certain that she received the finest of care. In 1994, Mr. Schiavo attempted to refuse medical treatment for an infection being experienced by his wife. His unrefuted testimony was that his decision was based upon medical advice. Mr. and Mrs. Schindler filed an action to have him removed as Guardian based upon numerous allegations, including abuse. Mr. Schiavo relented and authorized the treatment after which a Guardian Ad Litem appointed by this court found that there was no basis to have him removed. Mr. and Mrs. Schindler ultimately dismissed their petition citing financial considerations as their motivation.

The court heard testimony as to various issues; most of which having little or nothing to do with the decision the court is called upon to make. The court also heard from witnesses who ran the gambit of credibility, from those clearly biased who slanted their testimony to those such as Father Murphy[22] whom the court finds to have been

---

22. [The following is an excerpt from the testimony of Father Murphy:]

Q: Let's take a case that medical treatment, or artificial life support may be medically beneficial. If artificial life support may be medically beneficial, if the patient deemed it too psychologically or emotionally burdensome for himself or herself, could such a patient refuse artificial life support and still be in compliance with the church's teachings?
A: Yes.
Q: Father Murphy, what materials did you review in preparation for your testimony in this case?
A: The depositions of the family. The depositions of the—the deposition of the husband. I'm not sure about that. I'm not sure. I know I reviewed the family and the report of the physicians.

completely candid. The court also has concerns about the reliability of testimony which differed from prior deposition testimony. Vague and almost self serving reasons were given for the changes including reflection, reviewed in another fashion, knowledge that this was a real issue, found a calendar, and so forth, to the extent that at trial recollections were sometimes significantly different and in one case were now "vivid." The court has had the opportunity to hear the witnesses, observe their demeanor, hear inflections, note pregnant pauses, and in all manners assess credibility above and beyond the spoken or typed word. Interestingly enough, there is little discrepancy in the testimony the court must rely upon in order to arrive at its decision in this case.

The Petition under consideration was filed on May 11, 1998 and on June 11, 1998 Richard L. Pearse, Jr., Esquire, was appointed Guardian Ad Litem. On December 30, 1998, Mr. Pearse filed his Report of Guardian Ad Litem, a copy of which is in evidence as Respondents' Exhibit No. 2. An issue was made as to the impartiality of the Guardian Ad Litem. Mr. Pearse readily agreed that he has feelings and viewpoints regarding the withdrawal of feeding and hydration tubes and that he did not so advise the court prior to his appointment. It was suggested that he should not have served as Guardian Ad Litem since he possesses feelings on the subject. The court is unable to agree with that assertion since most attorneys who practice in this area of law surely do have feelings one way or the other. For the court to preclude an attorney from serving as Guardian Ad Litem simply because of feelings would deprive the court of this valuable resource. The court finds that Mr. Pearse did a good job but unfortunately he did not have an opportunity to interview all of those persons who testified at trial. However, that is not his fault. Mr. Pearse did testify that his recommendation was a "close call" and that the outcome of his report may have been changed had he found certain of this

---

Q: I want you to assume, Father Murphy, for purposes of this question that Theresa Schiavo told her husband that if she were dependent on the care of others she would not want to live like that. And also Theresa Schiavo mentioned to her husband and to her brother and sister-in-law that she would not want to be kept alive artificially.

Assuming that information to be correct, father, would the removal of Theresa Schiavo's feeding tube be consistent or inconsistent with the position of the Catholic [C]hurch?

A: After all that has transpired, I believe, yes, it would be consistent with the teaching of the Catholic [C]hurch.

other testimony heard by the court to be creditable and reliable. Consequently, the court is unable to rely upon his conclusions except for the fact that he felt Michael Schiavo alone, due to his potential conflict of interest, was not able to provide clear and convincing evidence to support the granting of his Petition.

It has been suggested that Michael Schiavo has not acted in good faith by waiting eight plus years to file the Petition which is under consideration. That assertion hardly seems worthy of comment other than to say that he should not be faulted for having done what those opposed to him want to be continued. It is also interesting to note that Mr. Schiavo continues to be the most regular visitor to his wife even though he is criticized for wanting to remove her life support. Dr. Gambone even noted that close attention to detail has resulted in her excellent physical condition and that Petitioner is very involved. Again, these are collateral issues which have little or nothing to do with the decision the court must render.

There are no written declarations by Terri Schiavo as to her intention with regard to this issue. Therefore, the court is left with oral declarations allegedly made to parties and non-parties as to her feelings on this subject. The testimony before this court reveals that she made comments or statements to five (5) persons, including her husband and her mother.

There was a lot of testimony concerning the Karen Ann Quinlin case in New Jersey [Judge Greer is referring to the 1970s case of Karen Ann Quinlan, whose family fought to remove her ventilator]. Mrs. Schindler testified that her daughter made comments during the television news reports of the father's attempts to have life support removed to the effect that they should just leave her (Karen Ann Quinlin) alone. Mrs. Schindler first testified that those comments were made when Terri was between 17–20 years of age but after being shown copies of newspaper accounts agreed that she was 11, perhaps 12 years of age at the time. A witness called by Respondents testified to similar conversations with Terri Schiavo but stated that they occurred during the summer of 1982. While that witness appeared believable at the offset, the court noted two quotes from the discussion between she and Terri Schiavo which raise serious questions about the time frame. Both quotes are in the present tense and upon cross-examination, the witness did not alter them. The first quote involved a bad joke and used the verb "is." The second quote involved the response from Terri Schiavo which used the word "are."

The court is mystified as to how these present tense verbs would have been used some six years after the death of Karen Ann Quinlin. The court further notes that this witness had quite specific memory during trial but much less memory a few weeks earlier on deposition. At trial she mentioned seeing the television movie on Karen Ann Quinlin and had no hesitancy in testifying that this was a "replay" of that movie and she watched such replay at college in Pennsylvania. She also knew precisely what song appeared on a TV program on a Friday evening when Petitioner was away at McDonald's training school. While the court certainly does not conclude that the bad joke and comment did not occur, the court is drawn to the conclusion that this discussion most likely occurred in the same time frame as the similar comments to Mrs. Schindler. This could well have occurred during this time frame since this witness and Terri Schiavo, together with their families, spent portions of summer vacation together which would have included the mid-1970s.

Michael Schiavo testified as to a few discussions he had with his wife concerning life support. The Guardian Ad Litem felt that this testimony standing alone would not rise to clear and convincing evidence of her intent. The court is not required to rule on this issue since it does have the benefit of the testimony of his brother and sister-in-law. As with the witness called by the Respondents, the court had the testimony of the brother and sister-in-law transcribed so that the court would not be hamstrung by relying upon its notes. The court has reviewed the testimony of Scott Schiavo and Joan Schiavo and finds nothing contained therein to be unreliable. The court notes that neither of these witnesses appeared to have shaded his or her testimony or even attempt to exclude unfavorable comments or points regarding those discussions. They were not impeached on cross-examination. Argument is made as to why they waited so long to step forward but their explanations are worthy of belief.

The testimony of Ms. Beverly Tyler, Executive Director of Georgia Health Discoveries, clearly establishes that the expressions made by Terri Schiavo to these witnesses are those type of expressions made in those types of situations as would be expected by people in this country in that age group at that time. They (statements) reflect underlying values of independence, quality of life, not to be a burden and so forth. "Hooked to a machine" means they do not want life artificially extended when there is not hope of improvement.

Turning to the medical issues of the case, the court finds beyond all doubt that Theresa Marie Schiavo is in a persistent vegetative state or the same is defined by Florida Statues Section 765.101 (12) per the specific testimony of Dr. James Barnhill and corroborated by Dr. Vincent Gambone. The medical evidence before this court conclusively establishes that she has no hope of ever regaining consciousness and therefore capacity, and that without the feeding tube she will die in seven to fourteen days. The unrebutted medical testimony before this court is that such death would be painless. The film offered into evidence by Respondents does nothing to change these medical opinions which are supported by the CAT scans in evidence. Mrs. Schindler has testified as [to] her perceptions regarding her daughter and the court is not unmindful that perceptions may become reality to the person having them. But the overwhelming credible evidence is that Terri Schiavo has been totally unresponsive since lapsing into the coma almost ten years ago, that her movements are reflexive and predicated on brain stem activity alone, that she suffers from severe structural brain damage and to a large extent her brain has been replaced by spinal fluid, that with the exception of one witness whom the court finds to be so biased as to lack credibility, her movements are occasional and totally consistent with the testimony of the expert medical witnesses. The testimony of Dr. Barnhill establishes that Terri Schiavo's reflex actions such as breathing and movement show merely that her brain stem and spinal cord are intact.

Argument was presented regarding the woman in New Mexico who awakened from a coma a few months ago after sixteen years. Dr. Barnhill testified that he would have to believe that patient had a different kind of condition or else it was a miracle. Since he knew nothing more than what appeared in the newspaper, any medical explanation would be "speculative." The court certainly would have expected a more complete explanation from the stipulated expert but the unrebutted evidence remains that Terri Schiavo remains in a persistent vegetative state. Dr. Barnhill earlier drew the distinction between comas which are catatonic in nature (no brain damage) and those caused by structural brain damage as in this case. Again, the court cannot speculate on the New Mexico situation as neither party has offered evidence in that regard.

The controlling legal authority in this area is a case which arose in St. Petersburg. A little over nine years ago, the Florida Supreme

Court rendered its opinion in a case in which the State of Florida was opposing the withdrawal of feeding tubes. In that case Estelle Browing had a living will and the issue was essentially whether or not an incapacitated person possessed the same right of privacy to withhold or withdraw life supporting medical treatment as did a competent person. *In re: Guardianship of Estelle M. Browning*[,] 568 So.2nd 4 (Fla. 1990). The Florida Supreme Court began with the premise that everyone has a fundamental right to the sole control of his or her person. They cited in 1914 New York decision in holding that an integral component of this right of privacy is the "right to make choices pertaining to one's health, including the right to refuse unwanted medical treatment." The court also found that all life support measures would be similarly treated and found no significant legal distinction between artificial means of life support. Citing its earlier decision of *John F. Memorial Hospital, Inc. v. Bludworth*, 452 So.2d 921 (Fla. 1984), the Court held that the constitutionally protected right to choose or reject medical treatment was not diminished by virtue of physical or mental incapacity or incompetence. Citing the lower court, the Florida Supreme Court agreed that it was "important for the surrogate decisionmaker to fully appreciate that he or she makes the decision which the patient would personally choose" and that in Florida "we have adopted a concept of 'substituted judgment[,]'"[] and "one does not exercise another's right of self-determination or fulfill that person's right of privacy by making a decision which the state, the family or public opinion would prefer."

The Florida Supreme Court set forth a three pronged test which the surrogate (in this case the Petitioner/Guardian) must pursue in exercising the patient's right of privacy.... The surrogate must satisfy the following conditions:

"1) The surrogate must be satisfied that the patient executed any document knowingly, willingly and without undue influence and that the evidence of the patient's oral declaration is reliable;

2) The surrogate must be assured that the patient does not have a reasonable probability of recovering competency so that the right could be exercised directly by the patient; and

3) The surrogate must take care to assure that any limitations or conditions expressed either orally or in the written declaration have been carefully considered and satisfied."

The Florida Supreme Court established the clear and convincing test as a requirement and further held that when "the only evidence of intent is an oral declaration, the accuracy and reliability of the declarant's oral expression of intent may be challenged."

The court is called upon to apply the law as set forth in *In re: Guardianship of Estelle M. Browning, supra,* to the facts of this case. This is the issue before the court. All of the other collateral issues such as how much was raised in the fund-raising activities, the quality of the marriage between Michael and Terri Schiavo, who owes whom between Michael Schiavo and Mr. and Mrs. Schindler, Mr. and Mrs. Schindler's access or lack of access to medical information concerning their daughter, motives regarding the estate of Terri Schiavo if deceased, and the beliefs of family and friends concerning end of life decisions are truly not relevant to the issue which the court must decide. That issue is set forth in the three pronged test established by the Florida Supreme Court in the *Browning* decision, *supra*. The court must decide whether or not there is clear and convincing evidence that Theresa Marie Schiavo made reliable oral declarations which would support what her surrogate (Petitioner/Guardian) now wishes to do. The court has previously found that the second part of that test, i.e. the patient does not have a reasonable probability of recovering competency, is without doubt satisfied by the evidence.

There are some comments or statement[s] made by Terri Schiavo which the court does not feel are germane to this decision. The court does not feel that statements made by her at the age of 11 or 12 years truly reflect upon her intention regarding the situation at hand. Additionally, the court does not feel that her statements directed toward others and situations involving others would have the same weight as comments or statements regarding herself if personally placed in those same situations. Into the former category the court places statements regarding Karen Ann Quinlin and the infant child of the friend of Joan Schiavo. The court finds that those statements are more reflective of what Terri Schiavo would do in a similar situation for someone else.

The court does find that Terri Schiavo did make statements which are creditable and reliable with regard to her intention given the situation at hand. Initially, there is no question that Terri Schiavo does not pose a burden financially to anyone and this would appear to be a safe assumption for the foreseeable future. However, the court notes that the term "burden" is not restricted solely to dollars and cents since one can also be a burden to others emotionally and physically. Statements which Terri Schiavo made which do support the relief sought by her surrogate (Petitioner/Guardian) include statements to him prompted by her grandmother being in intensive care that if she was ever a burden she would not want to live like that. Additionally, statements made to Michael Schiavo which were prompted by something on television regarding people on life support that she would not want to live like that also reflect her intention in this particular situation. Also the statements she made in the presence of Scott Schiavo at the funeral luncheon for his grandmother that "if I ever go like that just let me go. Don't leave me there. I don't want to be kept alive on a machine[,]" and to Joan Schiavo following a television movie in which a man following an accident was in a coma to the effect that she wanted it stated in her will that she would want the tubes and everything taken out if that ever happened to her[,] are likewise reflective of this intent. The court specifically finds that these statements are Terri Schiavo's oral declarations concerning her intention as to what she would want done under the present circumstances and the testimony regarding such oral declarations is reliable, is creditable and rises to the level of clear and convincing evidence to this court.

Those statements above noted contain no limitations or conditions. However, as Ms. Tyler noted when she testified as to quality of life being the primary criteria in artificial life support matters, Americans want to "try it for awhile" but they do not wish to live on it with no hope of improvement. That implicit condition has long since been satisfied in this case. Therefore, based upon the above and foregoing findings of fact and conclusions of law, it is

ORDERED AND ADJUDGED that the Petition for Authorization to Discontinue Artificial Life Support of Michael Schiavo, Guardian of the Person of Theresa Marie Schiavo, an incapacitated person, be and the same is hereby GRANTED and Petitioner/Guardian is hereby authorized to proceed with the discontinuance of said artificial life support for Theresa Marie Schiavo.

DONE AND ORDERED in Chambers at Clearwater, Pinellas Country, Florida at the hour of 11:50 o'clock 2 m this 11th day of February, AD, 2000.

George W. Greer, Circuit Judge

Judge Greer's opinion illustrates the detail with which judges need to sift conflicting evidence and testimony to determine case facts. The process does not guarantee that Judge Greer found the "true facts" of the case, only that his factual conclusions are plausible based on the evidence introduced during the trial. Do not the painstaking—indeed, often tedious and repetitive—methods of trial court fact-finding make his determination of the facts more plausible and trustworthy than the "factual" statements embedded in the politicians' debates sketched earlier in this chapter? Note also how the trial court process conforms to the elements of good games. For example, the process scrupulously treats both sides as equal participants, each of which has a chance to win depending on the evidence they bring to court. The process was transparent. The hearings were open to the public, and Judge Greer observed the witnesses' words and demeanor first hand in open court.

But what about Judge Greer's legal conclusions? The precedent under Florida law, *Estelle Browning*, permitted withdrawal of life support because Ms. Browning had a written "living will." By the process of fact freedom, then, was it legal error for Judge Greer to follow *Browning* in Schiavo's case, where there was no living will?

We have appellate courts to answer such questions. The Schindlers appealed Judge Greer's decision. On January 24, 2001, Florida's Court of Appeals for the Second District affirmed Judge Greer. Judge Altenbernd's unanimous opinion for Court of Appeals concluded:

> In the final analysis, the difficult question that faced the trial court was whether Theresa Marie Schindler Schiavo, not after a few weeks in a coma, but after ten years in a persistent vegetative state that has robbed her of most of her cerebrum and all but the most instinctive of neurological functions, with no hope of a medical cure but with sufficient money and strength of body to live indefinitely, would choose to continue the constant nursing care and the supporting tubes in hopes that a miracle would somehow recreate her missing brain tissue, or whether she would wish to permit a natural death process to take its course and for her family members and loved ones to be free to continue their lives. After due consideration, we conclude that the trial judge had clear and convincing evidence to answer this question as he did.[23]

In April 2001 the Florida Supreme Court declined to hear the case further.

23. *Schindler v. Schiavo (In Re Schiavo)*, 780 So.2d 176 (Fla. 2002), 180.

As you ponder the adequacy of the legal analysis here, do not forget the concrete conclusion in the *Cruzan* case: the Constitution permits states, through their court systems when their legislatures are silent, to determine state policy about when to withdraw life support. In that case, the Missouri courts denied the parents' request. Under the same principle, the Florida courts may determine policy on life support for the state of Florida, and the Florida courts in the Schiavo case came to a different conclusion.

Law and Politics

At last we examine the contrasts between the electoral and legislative framing of Schiavo dispute, on one side and the legal frames on the other. The courts narrow the scope of their decisions in important ways. The judges, unlike the bloggers we encountered, do not speculate about the motives of the actors, nor do they assess the wider ramifications of their decisions. Law is a kind of politics, but it is a very different form of politics from that performed by the other political actors in the Schiavo case. We define the core difference this way: The logic of electoral and legislative politics is the logic of winning public support, votes, and agreement on public policies. The logic of law is the logic of ideas, both their internal consistency with one another and their consistency with observable reality. This distinction often parallels, as the *Schiavo* case illustrates, differences between the Dionysian, emotional world of poetics and theatrics, and the often slogging and boring Apollonian, rational world of taking meticulous testimony in court, hearing arguments, and weighing them. In his attempt to reason through the Schiavo case, Judge Greer, like wise judges everywhere, observes four principles:

NO MIRACLES

Both law and democratic electoral politics are games, and to perform any game well requires mastering its particular craft. But the rules of these two games differ. A political campaigner may win votes by appealing to voters' desire for something like a religious leader who will work miracles, but Judge Greer does not rely on miracles to reach his conclusion. He avoids magical thinking, instead weighing all the evidence before him. As we noted in the *Prochnow* discussion near the beginning of this book, law simply cannot operate as law if it tries to accommodate miracles and other supernatural phenomena. After all, in the world of the supernatural, anything can happen. Judge Greer does not speculate about the supernatural but instead bases his findings on the evidence introduced at trial.

NO JUMPING TO CONCLUSIONS

Recall how both Senator Frist and Helen Hull Hitchcock, in her letter to Jeb Bush, reviewed a tiny fraction of the empirical evidence on Terri Schiavo's condition. Because they were both factually and politically partial, they jumped to the conclusion that Terri was not in a persistent vegetative state. Contrast this with Judge Greer's review of the whole history of Terri's medical diagnosis and treatment. Of course, elected politicians don't always jump to conclusions, and this book has provided many examples of unthinking judges. But for legislators, executives, and other elected politicians, deliberation is just one small part of the job; they must constantly raise money, listen to their constituents' problems, and pay attention to their coalitions and the interests they support. Judges are not called upon to do any of these things. At the center of their job is the need to convince others that they have considered all the relevant issues in a case fairly and impartially. If they appear to be jumping to conclusions, they will lose the trust not only of the parties to the case but also of their colleagues in the legal system.

SEQUENCING THE QUESTIONS

In the political world, political actors with a jumble of competing claims and interests jockey for power. Their job—and when politicians do their job well, it's an art—requires them to maximize their chances of winning votes, both votes in their legislatures and votes in elections. Smart politicians know that sometimes they should obfuscate, change the subject, hurl mud, and so on, to achieve their objectives. But lawyers and judges know that they must sequence questions so they can be answered one at a time and "checked off." Law has elaborate mechanisms for sequencing questions. On many occasions, this forced sequencing can seem bothersome; the parties to a case can become bogged down in procedural issues and lose sight of the "substance" of a dispute. The process is undeniably costly, so costly as to give wealthier litigants such an advantage as to force the less wealthy out of the game altogether.[24] But the sequencing of questions in litigation is a virtue because it provides an agreed-upon structure for resolving controversy. The first question in the Schiavo case was who should speak for Terri as her guardian, either her husband or her parents. Normally spouses have priority over parents in guardianship matters. (In-

24. As Mark Galanter contends in his classic article, the organized, who tend to be the "haves," enjoy huge advantages over the unorganized, the "have-nots," in the legal game. See Galanter, "Why the Haves Come Out Ahead: Speculation on the Limits of Legal Change," *Law and Society Review* 9 (1974): 95–160.

deed, the now-dated rite of the father "giving away" his daughter to the groom at the altar symbolizes this preference for spouses.) The Schindlers did not object to Michael's initial appointment as guardian, and they subsequently failed to show that he was abusing his responsibilities as their daughter's guardian. Once the Court checked off the question of guardianship, it could turn its attention to the evidence of Terri's wishes, and from there to the question of whether Florida law would count the evidence of Terri's wishes as clear and convincing.

ANSWERING QUESTIONS THOROUGHLY

Perhaps the greatest virtue of the legal process is that it creates a self-contained framework that permits judges, and on some occasions juries, to answer questions thoroughly. The decider can consider only evidence and testimony admitted and debated before him or her, but within that frame the decider is expected to consider and weigh all the evidence and testimony. Competitors in the electoral world routinely ignore evidence that goes against their views; electoral politics is often a matter of "spinning" the facts and reframing issues in ways that support one's side. The precise structures of trials and appellate hearings, by contrast, encourage decision makers to go beyond "spin" and painstakingly consider all the facts in the case. In Terri's case, for example, recall how thoroughly Judge Greer needed to weigh the relevance of the timing of a television program on the *Quinlan* case in determining the clarity of Terri's wishes.

We by no means think these four features exhaust the meaningful distinctions between law and other forms of politics, nor do we believe that the differences necessarily favor the legal over the electoral game. While, for example, the narrowing quality of law, its ability to restrict the range of the questions in dispute, is often a virtue,[25] it can in some circumstances be a vice: legal resolutions of public policy questions can produce narrow, black-and-white answers when nuance and compromise are called for.[26] Hence, there's a flip side to all the virtues displayed in the

25. See Robert Burns, *A Theory of the Trial* (Princeton, NJ: Princeton University Press, 1999). Perhaps the most dramatic example of what the legal frame excluded in the Schiavo case—excluded because the Schindlers never made anything of the point—is that some time in the later 1990s, Michael, without divorcing Terri, began living with another woman. They had one child and had conceived another when Terri died.

26. Mary Ann Glendon argues that the abortion debate in the United States has remained intense precisely because of the intervention of courts, which she argued polarized the struggle and so made compromise more difficult. Glendon, *Abortion and*

Schiavo case, and we certainly don't believe that law offers the best framework for resolving all controversies. Unbridled "juristocracy" would be just as pernicious as unbridled electoral democracy.[27] Still, the features we've described suffice to explain our choice of the epigraphs to this appendix. Where the competition for votes in electoral politics can sharpen differences, law, done well, can resolve them, and in so doing, it can ensure community peace. Law, then, is not about getting the right answer. It is about finding an answer that is good enough to settle the matter in a way people trust and can accept.

Did Judge Greer decide "correctly"? Who knows? Another judge in Terri's case might have written equally persuasively that Terri's prior and somewhat casual statements did not amount to a credible expression of her wishes. Another judge could have put more weight on the need to defer to "the voice of the people" as articulated by the Florida legislature in Terri's Law; after all, if Florida legislators guessed wrong about public opinion, they might pay a price for that on Election Day. We can't say that Florida courts decided the one and only correct way in the Schiavo case, but we don't need to. The question in legal politics, as in electoral politics, is never whether the deciders got "the" right answer, but instead, whether, like umpires in games, these deciders practiced their craft well in ways that allowed people to get on with their games and their lives.

Conclusion: There Is Reason in Law

An impressive art-deco installation displays a godlike figure looking down benevolently over one of the entrances to 30 Rockefeller Center in Midtown Manhattan. Its inscription reads "Wisdom and knowledge shall be the stability of thy times." Our analysis may seem to strip law of the romance and excitement that make courtroom dramas a perennial favorite on stage and screen. If law is merely a set of utilitarian practices that make it easier for people to get on with whatever they want to get on with, the profession of law may seem rather pedestrian. But the stakes in law's game—wisdom, knowledge, and stability—are very high. Behind the utilitarian practices of law lies perhaps the most important political and social dynamic imagin-

Divorce in Western Law (Cambridge, MA: Harvard University Press, 1987). On the effects of judicializing political struggles, see Gordon Silverstein, *Law's Allure: How Law Shapes, Constrains, Saves and Kills Politics* (New York: Cambridge University Press, 2009).

27. Ran Hirschl, *Towards Juristocracy: The Origins and Consequences of the New Constitutionalism* (Cambridge, MA: Harvard University Press, 2007).

able, a dynamic that ought to generate our deepest commitment. Thomas Friedman described this dynamic in his book *The World Is Flat*:

> We trust when we park our car downtown in the morning that the car next to it is not going to blow up; we trust when we go to Disney World that the man in the Mickey Mouse outfit is not wearing a bomb-laden vest underneath; we trust when we get on the shuttle flight from Boston to New York that the foreign student seated next to us isn't going to blow up his tennis shoes. Without trust there is no open society. . . . Trust is essential for a flat world, where you have supply chains involving ten, a hundred, or a thousand people, most of whom have never met face-to-face.[28]

This is the dynamic of trust. Human groups, from married couples to traders across the globe, do not thrive unless people trust that the actions of others—and particularly the actions of strangers—are not out to hurt them.

As Friedman's quote implies, trust is not a warm fuzzy feeling about other people. It is a practical calculation that people make about the threat that other people do or do not pose. The less a person perceives other people as threatening, the more they will trade and share with them. Our concluding lesson from the Schiavo case is not merely that the courts resolved the dispute, but that they did so in a way that facilitated social cooperation. The courts produced a conclusion that allowed the Schindlers and Michael Schiavo as well as many other Floridians facing similar end-of-life issues to make confident decisions about what they may and may not do, and so to move on.

This appendix thus loops back to one of the themes at the outset of the book, the critically important concept of triadic dispute resolution. Just as games cannot function without rules and referees to make those rules stick, so societies cannot function civilly without some independent and impartial institution—a system of elections that people trust in electoral politics, and an independent judiciary or something like it in legal politics.

As several of the epigraphs to this appendix hinted, it is simply not possible to govern wisely and peacefully by resorting to fundamentalism of any form, political, ideological, religious, or moral. This is so, in a practical sense, because people disagree, and they must be mollified, so compromise to reach political outcomes is usually the wisest course. Litigation is

28. Thomas Friedman, *The World Is Flat: A Brief History of the Twentieth Century* (New York: Farrar, Straus & Giroux, 2005), 557–558.

inherently a zero-sum game. Judges often work hard to get parties to settle before trial, or when that fails to settle after the trial to avoid the expense and delay of an appeal. But when attempts at settlement fail, litigation typically is "all or nothing." In such cases legislative politics, which usually encourages compromise among parties, can provide a superior resolution of differences. But when politics fails to generate compromises, falling back on some fundamental belief like "My truth is the only truth" heightens and prolongs conflict. That path can lead to two-against-one authoritarian rule. And this uncompromising world in turn can provoke, we have seen, first humiliation and then violence. This is precisely what we saw when fundamentalists reacted to the prospective removal of Terri Schiavo's feeding tube, in one case with veiled threats of violence and in another with the outright threats that required U.S. marshals to guard Judge Greer because his life had been threatened, much like the case of Rashid Rehman in Pakistan (see note 15), the lawyer who was killed for agreeing to defend an alleged blasphemer.

This book has shown how in a common law system judges inevitably make public policy. In Terri Schiavo's case the courts made policy for Floridians about end-of-life decisions. We hope we have suggested a framework within which judges can make plausible and coherent public policy. We have fleshed out in this appendix the path that judges can follow to do their jobs impartially and independently, and we have no doubt that, given the right incentives, ordinary people are capable of the impartiality that all good games require of their referees. People *can* in the right circumstances "go outside their own will for judgment," as Robert Cover wrote. People *can* practice the integrity of "leaning over backwards" to consider all sides of an issue. We trust jurors to do so. The people who become judges— Judge Andreen in chapter 3 and Judge Greer here come to mind—can do so too, just as those who become sports referees and umpires routinely practice their craft wisely and impartially.

This book has noted some instances of cases in which the legal reasoning on which U.S. Supreme Court opinions rest has been met with public controversy, just as did past Supreme Court decisions that called for desegregating public schools or creating a woman's "right to choose" in the early stages of a pregnancy. In electoral political debates these older decisions were labeled "liberal," either positively or negatively. How are we citizens to judge the adequacy of these decisions? How are we to judge whether more seemingly conservative but equally controversial recent Court decisions under Chief Justices Rehnquist and Roberts are any different, any better or worse? If we assess these cases solely in terms of our liberal or conservative political opinions, why prefer judicial results over legislative ones? Why bother with "reason in law" at all?[29]

We hope this book helps answer these questions, but in doing so it raises other questions for readers to ponder and debate: If professional sports referees such as Major League Baseball umpires can be trained to do their jobs with excellence and rewarded in proportion to the quality of their work, can judges be selected, trained, and rewarded in roughly the same way? Do current features of judicial training and selection—electing judges at one end of the spectrum while giving lifetime tenure for others who survive the appointment gauntlet at the other—put in judicial robes people with the skills and motivation to practice the craft of judging with excellence that this appendix has described?[30]

An effective legislator or governor reasons in politics about many things—the need to represent one's constituents, to build up one's party, to attract votes for favored policies, to raise money, and to win reelection. As the Schiavo case illustrates, judges who *reason in law* calculate about different things in a different way. Law's way of reasoning, done well, demonstrates the capacity of humans to act impartially, and so sustains the social trust that undergirds peaceful and secure communities.

29. See in this regard Jeff Shesol, "Should Justices Keep Their Opinions to Themselves?" Shesol raises, among other things, Justice Breyer's concern that the justices run the risk of becoming "junior varsity politicians" who do not merit the final word their constitutional authority gives them.

30. Herbert Kritzer's book on judicial elections provides a good starting point for answering this question, see Kritzer, *Justices on the Ballot*.

INDEX OF CASES

Boldface page numbers indicate pages that contain a significant excerpt from an opinion in the case. All other page numbers denote in-text case references. This index excludes cases of minor significance—for example, cases cited only within other quoted cases and secondary citations, particularly in the footnotes.

INDEX

Made in the USA
Las Vegas, NV
23 December 2023

83475169R00180